Ultimate Risk

The Inside Story of the
Lloyd's Catastrophe

Ultimate Risk

The Inside Story of the Lloyd's Catastrophe

By Adam Raphael

Four Walls Eight Windows, New York

Published in the United States by:
Four Walls Eight Windows
39 West 14th Street, room 503
New York, N.Y., 10011

First printing September 1995.

Originally published in Great Britain by Bantam Press, a division of Transworld
Publishers Ltd.

Library of Congress Cataloging-in-Publication Data:
Ultimate Risk: The Inside Story of the Lloyd's Catastrophe/by Adam Raphael.
     p.   cm.
  Includes bibliographical references and index.
  ISBN: 1-56858-056-8
  1. Lloyd's (Firm) 2. Insurance companies—England—London —
Management. I. Title.
HG8039.R37   1995
368'.012'0604212—dc20   95-11797
                                                   CIP

10 9 8 7 6 5 4 3 2 1

Text design by Acme Art, Inc.
Printed in the United States

Contents

Glossary

Active underwriter: The person employed by a managing agent with authority to accept risks on behalf of a syndicate.

Agent: There are two types of agent at Lloyd's. Members' agents are responsible for looking after the Names' personal affairs; managing agents are responsible for the control and management of syndicates.

All Risks: Insurance of property against loss or damage from every cause apart from war, which is normally excluded.

Assured: A person whose life or property is protected by insurance.

Binding Authority: A type of contract by which an underwriter authorizes an agent (usually a broker) to issue policies and accept risks on the underwriter's behalf.

Box: The open desk where an underwriter conducts his business on the floor of the market.

Broker: A middleman who, for a commission, places (buys) insurance with an underwriter on behalf of a client.

Cedant: An insurer who lays off risks by reinsurance.

CERCLA: Comprehensive Environmental Response, Compensation and Liability Act passed by Congress in 1980.

Claims made: A policy wording under which a claim is valid only if made during the period of the policy, in contrast with an occurrence form which provides cover of losses occurring during the policy period regardless of when the claim is actually made.

Double counting: The scale of Lloyd's losses was exaggerated because errors and omissions and stop loss policies had been placed within the market. Claims led to double counting of losses.

Deductible/Excess: The agreed part of any claim which is to be borne by the insured.

E&O: short for errors and omissions, which provides cover for professional liability such as the negligence of a broker or members' agent.

Excess of Loss (XL): An insurance policy which provides protection above an agreed limit.

IBNR: incurred but not reported losses. The reserve set aside for claims which the underwriter expects but which have not yet been formally reported.

Insurance: A contract whereby an individual or company, in return for a premium paid to an insurer, can protect itself against a specified event.

K&R: kidnap and ransom insurance, a speciality of some Lloyd's syndicates.

Line: The proportion of a risk which an underwriter agrees to insure.

Long-tail: A type of business where claims may arise long after the period of the cover has expired (e.g. for asbestosis and pollution).

LMX: London Excess of Loss market.

Managing agent/agency: An agent/company which manages a group of syndicates and appoints the underwriters.

Marine: The insurance of ship's hull, cargoes and freight, as well as sea-going platforms such as oil-rigs.

Members' agent/agency: An agent/company which acts directly on behalf of Names, helps select syndicates, and liaises with managing agents.

Name: An underwriting member of Lloyd's.

Non-marine: A general term which describes all insurances other than marine, aviation and motor. A non-marine syndicate may write a wide variety of business, from fire to professional liability.

Policy: Legal evidence of an agreement to insure.

Premium: A sum of money paid by the purchaser of insurance to the insurer.

Quota-share reinsurance: A type of reinsurance in which the reinsurer will accept a fixed proportion of every risk from the original underwriter in return for the same percentage of the premium.

Reinsurance: Insurance by which an underwriter will lay off part of his risk to another syndicate or company.

Retrocession: The insurance of a reinsurer—a type of policy in which reinsurers lay off all or part of their risk to another reinsurer, known as a retrocessionaire.

Reinsurance to close (RITC): When closing a syndicate year of account, an underwriter will pay a reinsurance premium to the following year of account which then accepts all known and unknown liabilities for the previous closed year and prior years.

Roll-overs: A tax avoidance method, widely used in the 1970s by underwriters, of parking profits offshore via a financial mechanism which masqueraded as a reinsurance policy. If there were no claims the premiums, together with any interest owed, were rolled over to the following year.

The Room: The shorthand description used by all at Lloyd's to describe the underwriting floor where trading takes place.

Slip: The paper prepared by the broker outlining a risk, which the underwriter accepts by marking the percentage share he will accept with his initials.

Stop loss insurance: A form of reinsurance by which a Name can protect himself to a limited extent against serious loss.

Time-barred: A civil action for tort has to be brought within a six-year period otherwise it is regarded as time-barred. An exemption can be sought under the Latent Damages Act if the damage becomes obvious only years later.

Time and Distance: A form of insurance collectible on future dates to fit the projected cash requirements of a syndicate. Such policies are widely used by underwriters as a means of discounting their reserves against future claims.

Uberrima Fides (Utmost Good Faith): Both parties to a contract of insurance have a duty to reveal all facts that may have a bearing on the policy.

Introduction

Utmost Good Faith?

"The more he talked of his honour, the faster
we counted the spoons."
Ralph Waldo Emerson

In three centuries of trading, Lloyd's built up a reputation for integrity
and fair dealing. From its earliest days as a coffee house on Tower Street,
the world's most famous insurance market was based on a foundation of
trust.

Its motto, *Fidentia*—"Confidence," and its trading standard, *Uberrima
Fides*—"Utmost good faith," signalled Lloyd's pride in the way its business
was conducted. Other insurers might cut corners, might dispute policies,
might fail to pay up; Lloyd's was different. The security of a Lloyd's policy,
with its emblem of an anchor, was epitomized by the decision of its most
distinguished underwriter Cuthbert Heath, who, when San Francisco was
devastated by an earthquake in 1906, cabled his agent: "Pay all our policy-
holders in full irrespective of the terms of their policies."

At the beginning of the twentieth century, more than half the world's
marine premiums flowed through London. To be rated A1 at Lloyd's was the
goal of any aspiring shipowner. Those invited to put up capital to support
this prestigious market, whether they were aristocrats, landowners, wealthy
businessmen or merely aspiring members of the middle class, felt they were
joining a privileged club. To be a Name at Lloyd's, as an investor in the

market is known, was a matter of pride. It was not generally the route to a fortune, but in most years the market made money.

Suddenly, in the 1980s, everything turned sour. The vast expansion of the market in the past two decades hid serious conflicts of interest and declining standards of underwriting, and also a terrible legacy from latent asbestos and pollution risks. Instead of profits, Lloyd's faced ruinous losses which threatened to bankrupt thousands of its Names who had joined on the basis of unlimited liability and now discovered what this meant. When times were good, the occasional chicanery and the odd underwriting disaster went unnoticed. But as the losses grew larger and larger, "Utmost good faith" seemed to have disappeared in the cauldron of a perverted market riddled with insider dealing.

Some underwriters cheated their Names by diverting funds to their own benefit, others defrauded them by funnelling the best risks into baby syndicates from which they, their friends and their families stood to benefit. Even a chairman of Lloyd's was found guilty of discreditable conduct after failing to ensure that interest on syndicate funds was properly credited to the benefit of his Names.[1] "Many members of the Lloyd's community in senior positions were not even vaguely aware of the legal obligations on agents to act at all times in the best interests of their principals and not to make secret profits at their principals' expense," noted the report of an official inquiry chaired by Sir Patrick Neill in 1987.[2] "Lloyd's recent history," wrote a leading members' agent, James Sinclair, managing director of Willis Faber & Dumas, "is an outrageous disgrace with greed, bad management, incompetence and catastrophes bringing the market to its knees. Lloyd's has been bewitched, battered and bewildered to such an extent that its capacity to survive is in real doubt."[3]

In what follows, I have tried to explain, and to trace the seeds of, by far the most serious crisis Lloyd's has ever faced. Its scale is not yet widely understood. It threatens the market's very survival. Insurance companies have gone into liquidation since time immemorial, swamped by claims they could not pay, but Lloyd's, in its three centuries of trading, had always seemed impregnable. No longer. The idea that it might default on claims appears unthinkable, but the setting up of a new limited liability company to handle all claims prior to 1986 is a sign that the new Lloyd's is determined not to be swamped by the problems of the past. The losses from old year pollution and asbestos claims are, at present, unquantified and unquantifiable, but the possibility cannot be ruled out that they will precipitate the greatest insurance smash in history.

The Yale School of Organization and Management predicts that there will be nearly 200,000 asbestos-related deaths over the next quarter of a century, at a cost to asbestos manufacturers and their insurers of $50 billion. That sum is almost ten times the combined net asset value of the asbestos producers, and is roughly equal to the total assets of the US liability insurance industry. The figures on pollution claims are worse. The US actuarial company Tillinghast predicts the cost of cleaning up corporate America under the Superfund legislation could be as high as $1,000 billion, more than the combined resources of casualty insurers worldwide. If only a fraction of these claims are upheld by the courts, widespread liquidations are inevitable.

If such a smash occurs, it will not be only Lloyd's which will be affected, for London is merely the epicentre of the whirlwind of asbestos and pollution claims facing the world's insurance industry. The consequences for policy-holders would be serious: not just higher premiums, but billions of pounds of valid claims remaining unpaid. The abyss of default is not far off. In five years including the current year, Lloyd's will have lost more than £8 billion—the equivalent of 4p on the standard rate of income tax—wiping out the profits of the past two decades. As its chief executive, Peter Middleton, has noted: "No British institution has ever taken the losses that Lloyd's has and survived."[4]

Many questions are posed by this extraordinary disintegration. How could a market built over so many years on a reputation for fair dealing allow itself to be destroyed by the greed of a few? Why was the excess of loss market allowed to spiral wildly out of control? Why were the dangers of latent disease and pollution liabilities not anticipated and reserved against? Why should some of the most skilled underwriters in the world have allowed themselves to be undermined by the folly and negligence of a handful of incompetents? Why did Lloyd's allow the recruitment of thousands of Names with inadequate resources to stake the little they owned in high-risk syndicates? Lastly, what future is there for a market which depends on trust when trust has been destroyed? Financial institutions are about confidence; once that has gone, nothing remains. To be fair, not all Lloyd's problems are of its own making, yet neither asbestos nor pollution nor the quixotic decisions of the American courts nor an extraordinary run of natural catastrophes can explain the extent of the crisis it now faces. Insurance is concerned with assessing, quantifying and, above all, spreading risk; Lloyd's has failed in these most basic tasks.

As much of what has gone wrong is a result of undisclosed conflicts of interest, I should make clear at the outset that my perspective is that of a Name who joined Lloyd's more than a decade ago and, along with many others, is now facing serious losses. I am chairman of one of the syndicate action groups conducting multi-million-pound legal actions against their Lloyd's agents. I have also been on the steering committee of the Lloyd's Names Associations' Working Party, the central liaison body representing some thirty syndicates and more than 15,000 Names engaged in litigation.

It may well be asked what led me and thousands of others, some of them shrewd businessmen, to risk their fortunes by placing them in the hands of strangers, a few of whom proved unworthy of trust. Was it naivete or merely greed? That too is part of the story. What follows is thus not disinterested nor is it always dispassionate, but I have tried to be fair in seeking to understand and explain what has gone wrong. I owe thanks to all those in the market who have helped me in that task and given generously of their time. I hope they will forgive me if I do not name them; some, no doubt, would prefer to remain anonymous.

Finally, my readers will have to excuse a lack of political correctness. There are many women Names at Lloyd's, and many women work in senior positions for managing agents and members' agents and for the corporation of Lloyd's, but I have used the masculine throughout in order to make the text less cumbersome.

Adam Raphael
London, Spring 1995

1

The Lutine Bell Tolls

"Life has become a burden because you're never at peace,
you're never at rest, you can't relax, you get ill. I'm practically
physically sick when the postman calls because I don't
know what he's going to bring."
Denys Axelberg, former British Airways pilot

How pleasant it is to gaze out to sea,
When the waves are lashed by the tempest,
And watch from the safety of land,
The desperate struggle of others.
Lucretius (94-55BC)

It was April Fool's Day 1993. For Diana Weston, the wife of a fifty-one-year-old solicitor and Lloyd's Name, there were to be no jokes. Early that morning, she found the body of her husband Harold hanging from a noose tied to a banister in their North London home. In recent weeks, as he became more and more depressed by his Lloyd's losses, he had taken pills each night to help him sleep. Harold Weston had told his wife that he could see no end to his financial problems, which he feared would result in his professional disgrace. But he had promised several times that he would not take his own life. "They asked for more and more money, that's when he started to sleep badly," Diana Weston told the coroner. "He was told he might go bankrupt and would not be able to practise as a solicitor."[1] Mrs. Weston, while trying to recover from the trauma of her husband's death, has had to meet his continuing Lloyd's losses stemming from his membership of nine syndicates. Not even death ends a Name's unlimited liability for the results of his underwriting.

Two years before Harold Weston killed himself, the chairman of Lloyd's gave an interview to *The Times*. A plump Old Etonian, who appeared, as the interviewer put it, to survive on a diet of port and spotted dick, David Coleridge was in a defiant mood as he prepared to announce the market's first losses in two decades:"We have the misfortune to blush very publicly. We had 30,000 members. Many of them will have lost money and they make a lot of fuss. The insurance industry worldwide is having a very tough time. Most of the people who are bitching and whining are doing it because they don't like losing. I understand that. It's human nature to only want to win. No one has been swindled and it has nothing to do with unlimited liability. It's simply pure losses."[2]

At the annual meeting a few weeks later, in June 1991, the chairman, who had made £10 million from his own participation in the market, sounded a more contrite note. Gone was the talk of "bitching and whining" as he stood in front of the prized Lutine bell, traditionally rung when news of an overdue ship was received, seeking to explain to Names why they had lost £510 million, the first loss in twenty years. For nearly four hours Coleridge, a great-great-great-great nephew of the poet Samuel Taylor Coleridge, did his best to defuse the bitterness of his audience:"At a time of losses when Names are suffering distress—with which I and the council really do sympathize deeply—it is entirely natural that people ask 'What is going on?' and 'What are you doing about it?'" Lloyd's, he pointed out, was the victim of a worldwide recession. Insurance companies in both the United States and the United Kingdom, not only Lloyd's, were recording huge losses. The problems of long-tail pollution and asbestos claims were common to all insurers. The future of the market was bright, concluded the chairman:"Our adaptability is one of our greatest assets. It is this quality that will ensure we surmount this difficult period as we have surmounted many before, and that together we prosper in the decades to come."

It was a masterly performance. Only at the end did the strain show."Tears were streaming down his face as I gave a vote of thanks," recalls Robert Hiscox, then chairman of Lloyd's Underwriting Agents' Association.[3] As the Names filed away from Richard Rogers' high-tech building on

Lime Street, few if any of them appreciated the scale of the crisis that lay ahead. A complacency born of three centuries of successful trading was about to be stripped bare; an inbred commercial culture was to be cruelly exposed; thousands of its investors were to be ruined. Lloyd's was about to lose more money than at any time in its history.

A few years earlier a revealing exchange had taken place between a previous chairman of the market, Peter Miller, and a worried Name who had expressed his concern over the rapid increase in the market's capacity. In less than half a decade, the number of members had grown by a third, and the amount of premium underwritten had grown by nearly 40 percent, noted Raymond Nottage, a member of the committee of the Association of Lloyd's Members. Why, he asked, had capacity been allowed to let rip at a time when the market was having great difficulty in finding good business?"It seems to some of us that this really does not comply with commercial logic or good business practice and we find it perplexing."

For his pains Nottage was slapped down."There is a commercial imperative today for Lloyd's to expand its capacity to take advantage of the turn in business," was the firm riposte of Peter Miller, who emphasized that market forces must be allowed to work freely. The chairman's reproof to the 1984 annual meeting was endorsed by John Robson, a leading under-writing agent. Such comments from outside Names were symptomatic of a current malaise:"It is what I would call the unit trust allergy. It started with a call for a standard underwriting agency agreement, strident calls for an annual meeting of syndicate members, the syndicate members' right to appoint the auditors, removal of the one agent/one class rule, and now the concept of a syndicate rights issue every time a syndicate wishes to increase its capacity."

Warming to his theme, the members' agent went on with more than a hint of contempt:"Mr. Nottage, sir, underwriting membership of Lloyd's is not about averages. It is a highly personal investment into a very competitive market-place. We may call ourselves collectively underwriting agents or indeed underwriters, but we all, thank God, continue to do things quite differently from one another. If what you, Mr. Nottage, and others like you, are seeking is an average return with a standard account and a standard report with a standard agreement, then please resign, because what you should be investing your money in is an insurance unit trust, not a Lloyd's syndicate." This rebuttal was greeted with a great round of applause from the assembled audience of mostly professional Names."That evident expression of the membership feeling," said the chairman,"is, of course, helpful and will be taken into due consideration by the council."[4]

The complacent, *laissez-faire* conviction that individual underwriters knew best and must be allowed to pursue underwriting profits in any way they saw fit, was to contribute to Lloyd's downfall. The extraordinary losses of the five years 1988-92, a large part of which were concentrated in a handful of syndicates, wiped out the declared profits of the previous two decades. The shock was all the greater because, since Hurricane Betsy's devastation of the US East Coast in the mid-1960s, Lloyd's had recorded a series of unbroken profits for twenty-one years, totalling £3.9 billion (£8.5 billion in today's money). All this, and eventually much more, was to be swallowed up. A loss of £510 million in 1988 was followed by losses of £2.1 billion in 1989, £2.3 billion in 1990, and £2.1 billion in 1991; a further loss of more than £1 billion is predicted for the 1992 account year. The known losses, moreover, make no allowance for the hundreds of syndicates with open years which have been unable to close their accounts because of potential future liabilities from claims which are at present unquantifiable. This has led one former broker, David Springbett, to claim that the true losses in these loss making years will eventually exceed £12 billion, equivalent to £500,000.[5]

JOY OR SORROW

There is no English word for the German *"schadenfreude,"* the joy that comes from watching other people's misfortunes, but there is little doubt that the crisis at Lloyd's has afforded pleasure to many. The editor of the *Daily Telegraph*, Max Hastings, summed up a common view when he congratulated himself on having not been foolish enough to join:"Whenever life has looked a little glum in the last year or two, I have been able to console myself with the reflection that I am not a member of Lloyd's," he wrote in the *Spectator*."Once upon a time smug, fat men sidled up to one on shoots and smirked horribly: 'Just got the Lloyd's cheque. Very nice number—pays for the wife to go to Portugal with her boyfriend, settles the school fees and takes care of the cartridges. You really ought to think about it.' Now, of course, a frightful inverted snobbery has taken over, whereby everyone boasts about the size of his losses."[6]

The gloating over those who were seen to have gambled on unlimited liability and to have lost everything was encouraged by the myth that only the rich and famous had been stung. The roll-call of Names certainly includes the well-born. There are two royals: Princesses Michael and Alexandra of Kent, a brace of dukes: Norfolk and Atholl, a dozen earls and twenty or so viscounts, countesses, marquesses and marchionesses, and upwards of thirty peers and peeresses. Other Names are also well known: the publisher Lord Weidenfeld, the hotelier Rocco Forte, tennis players Mark Cox, Buster Mottram and Virginia Wade, the champion driver the late James Hunt, the boxer Henry Cooper, the golfer Tony Jacklin, the actress Susan Hampshire, and some sixty Conservative MPs including several cabinet ministers and a former prime minister, Edward Heath. Yet the majority of Names are neither rich nor famous. It makes no sense to risk unlimited liability if one is seriously rich, for the rich have no need of a few thousand pounds of additional income. Those who were to be worst hit were mostly of middling wealth; they were certainly not poor, but nor were they particularly rich.

In the mid-1970s, a mini-Name had to show only £37,500 in assets to begin underwriting. A third of that amount had to be deposited at Lloyd's, often via a bank guarantee secured on the value of a house. Membership of the society was therefore within the reach of a wide range of ordinary members of the public, from the owner of a corner shop to a middle-aged widow existing on a small pension. More than half of the 29,000 members underwriting in 1986 had declared assets of under £150,000.[7] Many Names who joined in the 1970s and 1980s had retired or were near retirement, and were looking for additional income. Others saw membership of Lloyd's as a means of paying school fees. Pilots, lawyers, accountants, farmers, writers, doctors and small businessmen were attracted by the prospect of making their savings work twice. The appeal of Lloyd's for such investors was that, in addition to the profits from underwriting, a return could be expected from the cash or shares used for the Lloyd's deposit. With some Lloyd's members' agents actively touting for new members, often lubricating the process with commission payments, few could resist an invitation to join what seemed to be an honourable and historic profit-making enterprise.

One such recruit was Betty Atkins. In 1979 she celebrated twenty-five years of working as a secretary for a small firm of insurance brokers, the Rowbotham Group. As a reward for her faithful service the chairman, Dick Rowbotham, invited her and a fellow secretary, Sylvia Hatton, to become members of Lloyd's. He said the firm would provide a bank guarantee and pay for a stop loss policy. Delighted by this generous reward for their long service, both women accepted gladly. They were put on three syndicates: a

£20,000 line on Outhwaite 317, and £15,000 split between Marchant's motor syndicate 254 and McKay Forbes aviation syndicate 463.

Their hopes of a retirement nest egg were soon dashed as notifications of large losses on the Outhwaite syndicate began to thud through their letter boxes. Betty Atkins contacted Dick Rowbotham, now retired as chairman, the firm having been taken over by C.I. de Rougemont & Co, only to find that he appeared to have completely forgotten her existence. She then contacted one of her former executives, now working for C.I. de Rougemont, who told her that she had nothing to worry about and that he"would go to the ends of the earth" for her.

Nothing came of these reassurances so, with her losses growing menacingly high, Betty Atkins wrote to the new chairman of Rowbotham's, Robin Baxter, on 1 June 1988. Three weeks later he replied:"I was very concerned to hear of the predicament in which you now find yourself in relation to your membership of Lloyd's. I have made enquiries as to the circumstances in which the Company assisted your membership, but I am afraid that there is nothing to suggest any sort of commitment to indemnify you against losses incurred as a result of that membership. Indeed, it would be highly unusual if any such arrangement did exist. Regrettably, whilst I have every sympathy with you on a personal level, I am unable to make any sort of commitment so far as the companies are concerned."

Sickened by this response, Betty Atkins wrote to the then chairman of Lloyd's, Murray Lawrence, who told her that there was no documentary evidence to back her claims that her losses would be met, and that in the meantime she must do nothing"to prejudice the reputation of Lloyd's." With losses approaching £100,000 each, far more than their total assets, both Betty Atkins and Sylvia Hatton were forced to apply to Lloyd's hardship committee. Their position was made worse by the refusal of their stop loss underwriter to honour their policies on the grounds that the wording was defective."I can make no plea on my behalf, I was extremely naive and foolish to believe my former employer's word was his bond," Betty Atkins wrote in her application to the hardship committee."At that time I did believe in the principle of utmost good faith and I must now suffer the consequences of my trust. . . I can only hope that Lloyd's will accept the realization of the house, any money which can be raised from its contents, my savings, my late Mother's estate (about £2,500), my pension contributions etc. to satisfy the debt for I cannot see, even if the present debt could be cleared, how I could ever keep up with the future calls and Lloyd's Central Fund interest charges." At the time of writing, Betty Atkins does not know what her future holds. The Outhwaite syndicate is still open and the losses continue to mount. If the future is uncertain, the past has been a ghastly trauma for this proud woman. The last four years have changed her life but, as she says, that "in no way describes the turmoil, fear and worry" that have dogged every waking hour.

Another innocent snared by Lloyd's was Bridget Milling Smith, the twenty-six-year-old widow of a Royal Marine officer killed on active service in Oman. On her return to England in 1979 with her two small children, she was advised by David Bentata of Charterhouse Japhet to join Lloyd's."I don't want you to think I was a wimp, but I had been married since I was twenty-one, and I didn't know anything about how to manage my financial affairs," she said later. Her financial adviser listened to her worries about how she would be able to bring up and educate her children on her own."Join Lloyd's, I know just the right man," he advised his client, who had a small cottage but no job and no income apart from dividends from her capital of £70,000 in shares."Don't worry your pretty little head," said Brian Bell of Osborne Bell, the Lloyd's agent to whom she was introduced.

A decade later, Mrs. Milling Smith finds herself in the nightmarish situation of facing never-ending calls from several open year syndicates with huge asbestos and pollution liabilities. She has given up counting how much she owes, but it must be more than £200,000."It doesn't make any difference to me any more," she says bleakly. She has had to appeal to the Lloyd's hardship committee which has allowed her to stay in her house for the time being. An added complication is that she has since remarried and had a third child, who suffers from cerebral palsy. She is determined that the house, which has been specially adapted for him, should not be sold. Looking back, she blames her naivete: "I didn't know anyone in the City and I relied on David Bentata and Brian Bell. I suppose that was my biggest mistake. I thought that Charterhouse Japhet was a huge organization and they would not put me into anything that could go wrong. I did say at the time, please remember that I don't have an awful lot. They never even suggested that I should have a stop loss policy. If I'd known then what I know now, I wouldn't have dreamt of going anywhere near Lloyd's." When David Bentata was asked why he had encouraged someone of such modest means to join Lloyd's, he replied:"I have a lot of sympathy for Mrs. Milling Smith and I have a lot of sympathy for myself. I have lost much more money than she has. I am about to lose my house. You have to take the rough with the smooth in life."[8]

Though public and professional sympathy may be in short supply, the human tragedies that lie behind the Lloyd's crisis are undeniable. On 13

February 1993 Richard Burgoyne, a former broker, was found by his wife, Sarah, lying on the family sofa with his head blown apart; his gun case was open. The couple had two young sons aged eight and eleven. His widow wept as she told the Eastbourne coroner's court that the family feared they might have to sell their house because of his underwriting losses. Her husband had been most concerned about the future, she said."He felt he had been unfairly treated and often complained that the estimates of the losses he might face were never accurate. He was very depressed, and unable to trust the information he was given."[9]

Three months earlier, Margaret Jones, a former eye specialist and a local magistrate, drank a large amount of whisky and swallowed barbiturates before ending her life by connecting the exhaust of her car to its interior with a vacuum cleaner. She owed Lloyd's £200,000. Her husband Francis, a retired shipbroker, who found her body near their home at Lunnon, West Glamorgan, had tried to reassure her that the family would be able to cope, whatever happened. But he recalled:"It was no use. She was frantic over what was happening." The Swansea and Gower coroner recorded an open verdict at the inquest.

It was not only outside Names who were victims. Roy Bromley, a leading underwriter, shot himself through the heart with his Holland and Holland gun, following heavy losses at the excess of loss syndicate 475 which he ran. A former war-time lieutenant-colonel who founded R.J. Bromley underwriting agencies after a distinguished career in the company market, he had been dismissed in May 1991 when concern arose over the scale of catastrophe risks he was underwriting. For two years Bromley worked from his home in Dorset Square, Marylebone, hoping to retrieve the position, but as the full scale of his syndicate's underwriting losses from Hurricane Hugo and other catastrophes became apparent, he sank into depression."Lloyd's was his life," said one associate."He'd found it very difficult to come to terms with the realization that the syndicate was going to make very significant losses and it is only recently that he did so." His son Nicholas, a civil servant, told the coroner that his father had felt a great deal of responsibility towards the Names he had represented, whom he felt he had let down."He was calm on the surface but underneath it there was a degree of panic and fear. In the end, it seems, he just could not bear it any more."[10]

The shock waves of the crisis at Lloyd's are far from spent. A torrent of litigation has been launched by thousands of angry Names against their agents. Lives have been ruined, fortunes wrecked, careers ended, houses sold, marriages sundered. As most of those affected shy away from publicity, the consequences are rarely obvious, but the plight of individuals caught up in the death throes of an ancient institution is very real. Lloyd's will probably survive, albeit in a very different form. But the price in human misery and ruined lives will be a heavy one, paid by those who had least and knew least. That too is in line with the market's traditions. "For the last three hundred successful years," noted the chairman of the Association of Lloyd's Members, Mark Farrer, in 1992, "the formula of Lloyd's has been that those who worked in the market looked after themselves first and left the surplus for Names through good years and bad years and through great events and periods of little significance."[11] With that sobering philosophy in mind, it is time to take a brief look at the history of Lloyd's, from coffee house to catastrophe.

2

Coffee House to
Catastrophe

"The future is but the past entered by another door."
Pinero

Go to the heart of the city, walk down Leadenhall Street and onto Lime
Street, and you are faced by one of the most unusual buildings in London.
Richard Rogers' gleaming tangle of glass and steel pipes, a mid-1980s
creation, looks more like the launch site for a space rocket than the centre of
an insurance market.

Step inside, and you will see frock-coated waiters resplendent in blue
uniforms straight out of the eighteenth-century coffee house, contrasting
with soberly suited brokers swarming up and down the escalators. There is
a distinct hum in the air, drowned every now and then by the sound of a
loudspeaker calling a broker to the rostrum. Dotted around the Room, as
Lloyd's calls its market place, behind unassuming wooden boxes
honeycombed with files and reference books, sit the queen bees of the
market, the underwriters. A broker brings a policy; a quick stamp, a scribble
of an initial with a percentage amount of the line underwritten on a slip of
paper, and the deal is done.

This commercial beehive of insurance is a tribute to the new technology, with computer screens instantly recalling and recording details of
complex risks. But do not be fooled by the high-tech image; the past and its

traditions are never far away at Lloyd's. In the middle of the underwriting room stands the Lutine bell, recovered from a thirty-two gun French frigate which was surrendered to the British fleet by the royalists to prevent her falling into republican hands. She was eventually lost in a storm during the Napoleonic Wars, flying the White Ensign. Her bell, recovered from the depths, was traditionally rung to alert underwriters to news of an overdue ship, once for bad news, twice for good. These days it is sounded only on ceremonial occasions; losses of ships are still recorded with a quill pen in a ceremonial loss book. Upstairs, on the eleventh floor, is the magnificent eighteenth-century committee room designed by Robert Adam for Bowood House in Wiltshire, the home of the Marquess of Lansdowne.

The strands of past and present are hard to disentangle. A society of individuals, Lloyd's has over the years, albeit with reluctance, accepted the imperative of collective discipline. "What is Lloyd's?" a puzzled visitor once asked one of the market's most famous servants, Walter Farrant. "Individually, Madam," came the reply, "we are underwriters; collectively we are Lloyd's." That answer encapsulates the paradoxical nature of a market place in which underwriters compete fiercely against one another while at the same time trading under a single reputation. There are other tensions. Though Lloyd's is, like all markets, at least in part a conspiracy of insiders against outsiders, it prides itself on fair dealing. A place where money talks to money and great fortunes have been made and lost, it likes to pretend that service rather than profit is its main motive. The proud trading standard of Lloyd's is *Uberrima Fides*, a term taken from contract law, though "utmost good faith" has been noticeably lacking in recent years. It would be cynical, however, to regard these pretensions as mere Victorian humbug. To understand the peculiar inbred culture of this most competitive of market places, it is necessary to retrace its history.

The earliest mention of the man who was to give his name to the world's most famous insurance market came in an advertisement which appeared in the *London Gazette* of February 1688: "Stolen the 30th Instant from Edward Bransby in Darby, five watches . . . Supposed to be taken by a middle sized man having black curled Hair, Pockholes in his Face, wearing an old brown Riding Coat, and a black Bever hat: Whoever gives notice of them at Mr. Edward Loyd's Coffee House on Tower Street . . . shall have a Guinea Reward."

Not much is known about Edward Lloyd, a member of the Framework Knitters' company, but he was clearly a capable businessman with a shrewd eye to new developments. Three decades earlier, in 1652, the first coffee house in London had been opened by an Italian manservant, Pasqua Rosee, in St Michael's Alley, Cornhill. Rosee, born in Ragusa, was not shy of boasting about the merits of his brew: "It so incloseth the orifice of the stomach, and fortifies the heat within, that it is very good to help digestion, it is therefore of great use to be taken about three or four o'clock in the afternoon as well as in the morning. It much quickens the spirits and makes the heart lightsome; it is good against sore eyes and the better if you can hold your head over it and taken in the steam that way. It suppresseth the fumes exceedingly and therefore it is good against the headache and will very much stop any deflexion of rheums, that distill from the head upon the stomach, and so prevent and help consumptions and the cough of the lungs. It is excellent to prevent and cure the dropsy, gout and scurvy. It is known by experience to be better than any other drying drink for people in years or children that have any running tumours upon them, as the King's Evil etc. It is a most excellent remedy against the spleen, hypochondriac winds and the like . . . it is neither laxative nor restringent."

The huge success of the new coffee houses in the late seventeenth century owed less to the medical merits of the brew than to their convenience as business and social meeting places. They had a number of advantages over taverns, being soberer, cleaner and more orderly. With coffee at a penny a cup, and newspapers, pen, ink and paper thrown in free, not to mention gossip, they became very popular. By the time Edward Lloyd opened his establishment around 1680, there were said to be no fewer than 300 coffee houses, many of which attracted a specialist clientele. Poets were to be found at Button's in Covent Garden, doctors at Child's in St Paul's churchyard near the Royal College of Surgeons, journalists at the Grecian in Fleet Street, and merchants and bill brokers at Hain's in Birchin Lane. Edward Lloyd chose his site with care. Close by Tower Wharf and the Customs House, it was well placed to capture the trade of ship captains and shipowners trading overseas. Their information and contacts in turn attracted a following of merchants who dabbled in marine insurance, a trade which was already well established in London.

"Whereas it hathe bene tyme out of mynde an usage amongste Merchantes," goes the preamble to the famous Insurance Act of 1601, "both of this Realme and of forraine Nacyons, when they make any greate adventure (speciallie into remote partes) to give some consideracon of Money to other psons (which comonlie are in noe small number) to have from them

assurance made of their Goodes Merchandizes Ships and Things adventured
. . . whiche course of dealinge is comonly termed a Policie of Assurance; by
meanes of whiche Policies of Assurance it comethe to passe, upon the losse
or perishinge of any Shippe there followethe not the undoinge of any Man,
but the losse lightethe rather easilie upon many, than heavilie upon fewe."

That last phrase, "the losse lightethe rather easilie upon many, than
heavilie upon fewe," neatly sums up the philosophy behind a trade which
can be traced back to the Phoenicians. The market in the late seventeenth
century was conducted by insurers, who underwrote the risks, and brokers,
who were called office keepers, broking being regarded as disreputable. It
was an informal relationship, and the trade was wide open to abuse. Merchants tended to dabble in insurance as a side-line to their main business and
regarded it as a speculation. The diarist Pepys recorded how he had been
sorely tempted to write a policy on a ship which was thought to be overdue
but which he, being an admiralty clerk, knew to be safe in port. Instead of
using his information to enrich himself, "I went like an asse to Alderman
Bakewell and told him of it. Now what an opportunity had I to have
concealed this and seemed to have made an insurance and got £100 with the
least trouble and danger in the world. This troubles me to think that I should
be so oversoon." Pepys's scruples were not consistent, for within days he
was gleefully noting a juicy bribe on insuring some Admiralty shipments
"whereby something may be saved to him and got to me." The little
something turned out to be £320, a handsome sum in those days.

There were many opportunities for turning an honest or a dishonest
penny in marine insurance, for London was then the heart of world shipping.
"It may be said without vanity," wrote a contemporary, "that no River in the
World can show a braver sight of Ships than are commonly to be seen like a
floating forest from Blackwall to London Bridge." It was during this boom
in marine trade that Edward Lloyd saw his opportunity. His coffee house
specialized in shipping, but he was not a man to turn down any sort of
business, as witnessed by this advertisement which appeared on 2 January
1693:

"A negro maid aged about 16 years, named Bess, having on a stript stuff
waistcoat and peticoat, is much peck't with the Small Pox, and hathe lost a
piece of her left ear, speaks English well, ran away from her Master Captain
Benjamin Quelch, on Tuesday, the 8th of December. A Guinea for anybody
delivering her to Mr. Edward Lloyd."

Lloyd knew that the attractions of his coffee house depended on its reputation as a source of reliable information. In 1696 he brought out the first copy of *Lloyd's News*, printed on a single sheet containing snippets of shipping news padded with other odd pieces of general information. "All Gentlemen, Merchants, or others," proclaimed an announcement that year, "who are desirous to have this News in a whole Sheet Paper, for to write their private Concerns in, or other Intelligence for the Countrey, may be supply's with them done upon very good Paper for a Penny a Sheet, at Lloyd's Coffee-House in Lombard Street."

Even by the standards of the time *Lloyd's News* was not a good paper, and it survived for only five months. But it paved the way for a paper which still exists—*Lloyd's List*, an authoritative daily journal of shipping intelligence. An early and notable scoop was the first news of Admiral Vernon's capture of Portobello in the War of Jenkins' Ear. This was conveyed post-haste to Walpole, the prime minister, who handsomely tipped the bearer of the good tidings. It was the practice of the day for news to be read out to the market from a rostrum, a precursor of the modern-day caller who summons brokers to the telephone. Steele records the practice "upon the first coming in of the news, to order a youth, who officiates as the Kidney of the coffee-house, to get into the pulpit, and read every paper with a loud and distinct voice, while the whole audience are sipping their respective liquors."

THE EARLY YEARS

That Lloyd's survived these casual seventeenth-century origins and developed into one of the world's most influential insurance markets owes much to chance. Its earliest years were precarious, dominated by a rivalry between the independent merchants, who were the customers of the coffee house, and more established companies which sought to restrict the insurance trade to themselves. This decade-long struggle, which took place against the speculative background of the South Sea Bubble, ended with the defeat of the merchants and the establishment of the Royal Exchange and the London Assurance Companies. Yet ironically the Bubble Act of 1721, which gave the companies an exclusive royal charter, far from crushing the merchant underwriters, enabled them to prosper. The two groups soon realized their mutual interest and cooperated in keeping competitors at bay. The companies were under-capitalized, and suffered badly from the bursting of the Bubble.

They soon turned their attention to what they saw as the safer trade of fire insurance, leaving the bulk of marine insurance to the merchants.

The founder of Lloyd's did not live to see these developments. On 17 February 1713, the *Flying Post* announced: "London. On Sunday last Died Mr. Loyd the Coffee-man in Lombard Street." The years that followed Lloyd's death saw his coffee house pass through many hands, by no means all as capable as his. It continued to attract the custom of sober shipping merchants and also loucher characters who regarded insurance as just another form of gambling. One favourite bet was to hazard a guess on the life expectancy of some individual who was known to be sick, a practice which did nothing for the morale of the patient. "This inhuman sport affected the minds of men depressed by long sickness," wrote a contemporary, "for when such persons, casting an eye over a newspaper for amusement, saw that their lives had been insured at 90 per cent, they despaired of all hopes; and thus their dissolution was hastened."

The outbreak of gambling led a group of the more respectable underwriters to break away in 1769 and set up a new Lloyd's coffee house on Pope's Head Alley, off Lombard Street, under the mastership of Thomas Fielding, a waiter from the old establishment. It soon saw off its rival, and within two years the underwriters were pressing for larger premises. This led to what has been described as "the most important document in the history of Lloyd's." A group of seventy-nine merchants and brokers decided to pay £100 each in order to set up a formal organization: "We the Underwriters do agree to pay our Several Subscriptions into the Bank of England in the Names of a Committee to be chosen by Ballot for the Building A New Lloyd's Coffee House." The declaration marked the beginning of a new era, in which the coffee house was transformed into a formal market place run by a committee.

At this decisive point in its history, Lloyd's was fortunate in finding an outstanding leader. John Julius Angerstein was the son of a German merchant family which had emigrated to St Petersburg, where he was born in 1735. When barely fourteen years old, he was sent to London as an apprentice in the counting house of a leading merchant who specialized in the Russian trade. On coming of age, he switched to marine insurance and rapidly established himself as one of its leaders; his policies were so respected that they became known in the market simply as "Julians." Angerstein also acted as a broker, placing one of the largest ever insurances, a cargo of gold and other valuables worth £656,800, as it was transported from Vera Cruz to

London on the frigate *Diana*. Few are said to have matched his reputation for honour and fair dealing. The portrait of the "father of Lloyd's," which hangs in the old library, shows a shrewd, commanding man with more than a touch of disdain for his inferiors. When, many years later, he was asked by a parliamentary committee about the probity of the many adventurers who thronged the underwriting rooms, Angerstein replied scornfully: "I cannot speak to it—I do not know their names."

Leading underwriters enjoyed then, as now, a grand style of life. The following contemporary account is of a dinner given by Angerstein: "We dined at 6oClock. The dinner consisted of two courses, viz: a fine Turbot at the top, a Sirloin of Beef at the bottom and vermicelli Soup in the middle, with small dishes making a figure of 9 dishes. The remove roast ducks at the top & a very fine roast Poulet at the bottom, macaroni, tartlets &c, &c. afterwards Parmesan and other cheese and Caviere with toast. Champagne & Madeira were served during dinner. . . I observed that Mr. Angerstein drank very little wine after dinner. While the conversation went on, he for some time slept. After He awoke He eat an orange with sugar. He appears to consider his Health but looks very full & well. His dress was a Blue coat, striped pointed waistcoat—drab cloth breeches, mixed coloured worsted stockings, buckles in His shoes, very plain but respectable."

Angerstein was one of the select group of underwriters who had joined the break-away from Tower Street, though he was not a member of the founding committee. Despite this, it appears to have been on his initiative that Lloyd's found a permanent home. The temporary premises in Pope's Head Alley were crowded, hot and unsanitary. When Angerstein heard that two large rooms formerly occupied by the British Herring Fishery in the Royal Exchange had become vacant, he moved swiftly. The minutes of the Gresham committee of the Mercers' company for 3 November 1773 records: "Mr. Angerstine from the gentlemen who attend New Lloyd's Coffeehouse Attended to be informed if there was any large room to be lett over the Exchange. The Committee ordered the Clerk with the Surveyor to let Mr. Angurstine view the two Rooms late in lease to the British fishery." Four months later, Lloyd's coffee house moved to its new premises, which had been acquired on a twenty-one-year lease at a rent of £160 per annum. Sedan chairs were banned from the underwriting rooms, but even so within a few years they had become uncomfortably crowded. It is one of the recurring features of the market's history that the buildings never quite keep pace with the expansion of business.

The period immediately after the move to the Royal Exchange coincided with the Seven Years War, which brought lucrative shipping risks. Large fortunes were being made in the market. But in August 1780 came a blow which shook Lloyd's to its foundations. The Spanish and French fleets patrolling 300 miles off Cape Saint Vincent came upon a combined British merchant convoy heading for the West and East Indies. The escorting frigates fled, and of sixty-three merchant ships carrying valuable cargoes, fifty-five were captured. It was the heaviest single reverse for British commerce since the loss of the Smyrna fleet in 1693, when underwriters were said to have left the Royal Exchange "with the faces of men under sentence of death." The latest disaster was enough, according to John Walter, the founder of *The Times*, to bankrupt half the underwriters, including himself. As he later wrote: "I was twelve years an underwriter in Lloyd's coffee house and subscribed my name to six millions of property; but was weighed down in common with about half those who were engaged in the protection of property, by the host of foes this nation had to combat in the American War."

Walter may have been exaggerating the problems to excuse his own default, but there is no doubt that the loss of the fleet in 1780 was one of the blackest days in the history of Lloyd's. What is perhaps surprising is not that some underwriters defaulted, but that failures were not a more frequent occurrence. "We see not a few Instances," wrote a veteran underwriter, John Weskett, "even of Tradesmen, Shopkeepers, etc., lured by the golden, but delusive bait of Premiums, especially in time of War, drawn like Gudgeons into the Vortex of this perilous Abyss, Insurance." Weskett was a sour old pill but a good observer of the scene. "Litigation is become so rife," he complained, "there is a Necessity, however strange it may appear, for the almost daily Attendance, which may be observed, especially in Term Time, of no less than 4 or 5 Attornies at Lloyd's Coffee House! What a Degradation is this of mercantile character and Abilities, even in a single Branch of Commerce!"

The years following Lloyd's move to the Royal Exchange saw a huge increase in the number of underwriters—from seventy-nine in 1771 to 2,150 in 1814. A time of war is often a time for large profits. The library at Lloyd's has a risk book dating from 1807. In one year a single underwriter acting on his own account took in premiums of more than £54,000 and paid out claims of just under £23,000, leaving a handsome balance even after working expenses and return of some of the premiums. Such golden profits were an irresistible magnet to every sort of adventurer. Many were men of straw, eager for whatever crumbs the established brokers and underwriters cared to throw them. There were also hundreds of hangers-on and gatecrashers who were not finally ejected from the underwriting room until a resolution was passed on 2 April 1800, restricting membership to those approved by the committee and who had paid a subscription of £15.

With the passage of this motion, Lloyd's finally came of age. It was now a properly organized market. Before the year was out, more than 800 subscriptions had been received, and the numbers quickly grew. A decade later, a parliamentary committee was told that there were between 1,400 and 1,500 members of whom about two-thirds were regular or occasional underwriters. Formal organization was spurred in 1804 when the secretary of state for the War Department, Earl Camden, declined with a notable snub "to enter into epistolary intercourse with the waiters of Lloyd's Coffee House." This led the committee to appoint an official secretary. In the minutes of 14 August 1804 it is "Order'd that all Letters &c on the Business of the Committee, be signed by John Bennett Jnr as Secretary."

A TRIAL OF STRENGTH

The next stage was a written constitution. In 1810, a parliamentary select committee had been set up to look into the privileges enjoyed by Lloyd's and the two chartered insurance companies, Royal Exchange and London Assurance. The hearings turned into a trial of strength between the market and those jealous of its success. The charges against Lloyd's have a familiar ring: insurance was expensive, claims were delayed, sometimes unpaid and too often litigated. According to one witness: "In Lloyd's Coffee-house there are, I believe, very few instances upon a large policy that there are not one or two bankrupts upon it before we can effect a settlement." The witnesses for the defence were persuasive, however, and though the eventual report of the select committee was hostile, Lloyd's reputation emerged from the hearings largely unscathed.

Before that, Lloyd's had gone through a bitter internal row. This arose from heavy claims during the Napoleonic Wars when a large number of Swedish, Prussian and other ships were seized in the Baltic. Unknown to the underwriters, the secretary of Lloyd's, John Bennett, had been warned by the Admiralty about the growing risk, but though he had told the committee, the correspondence was not published. Smarting from their losses of more than £1 million, and claiming that they had been misled, the underwriters turned on the committee and passed a vote of censure. Though this rebuke was subsequently cancelled, it led to the setting up of a special group of twenty-one members to consider what reforms were needed. Thus came about the Trust Deed of 1811, Lloyd's first formal constitution establishing the authority of the committee, by which the society was governed for the next sixty years.

Its internal crisis over, the influence of Lloyd's grew fast, thanks to burgeoning war-time profits. Underwriters were in a position to charge high premiums to nervous shipowners. An analysis of one underwriter's book for 1808 showed rates as high as 40 percent on the Baltic routes, reflecting the advance of Napoleon. After the United States declared war in 1812, rates on the crossing to the West Indies soared for a brief period to 19 percent, then fell to a more normal 3.5 percent in 1816. The often forgotten truth of insurance is that bad news is usually followed by large profits. Certainly Lloyd's flourished, and so did its self-importance. "In short Lloyd's coffee house is now an empire within itself," wrote an observer of the time, "an empire which, in point of commercial sway, variety of powers, and almost incalculable resources, gives laws to the trading part of the universe." The market had at its disposal substantial corporate funds with which it proceeded to help finance a lifeboat service for the British and Irish coasts, and launched a patriotic fund to help "animate the efforts of our Defenders by Sea and Land" during the Napoleonic Wars.

The battle of Waterloo marked the high point. With the coming of peace the market fell into such a depression that one commentator accusing the committee of mismanagement wrote of the spectacle of distressed underwriters "seen daily begging on the stairs of the House." A few years later, a benevolent fund was set up to provide relief to "worthy unfortunate members of Lloyd's, their widows or children." In the next thirty years, the number of underwriters fell by half to fewer than 1,000 as profits declined from a high of 8 percent to barely 1 percent of annual premiums. A broker, Thomas Reid, asked by a parliamentary select committee how he could justify his excessive remuneration, cried: "The labour, the agitation of mind, the perpetual vexation, is not to be described. I would rather begin the world again and pursue any other line. It is painful to a degree; we can hardly ever satisfy our principal."

During this prolonged recession Lloyd's was hit by a severe blow. The worst conflagration in the City of London since the Great Fire of 1666 broke out on the evening of Wednesday 10 January 1838, destroying the market's headquarters and many of its records. The event was treated as a national disaster. "It affords," said the *Morning Herald*, "but a melancholy subject for reflection that the commencement of the new reign has been distinguished by a rebellion in Canada and the burning down of the Royal Exchange in London. Persons whose minds are at all tinctured with superstition will look upon these calamities of fire and blood as omens of evil augury."

The committee of Lloyd's were more interested in profits than auguries, and under its new and energetic chairman, George Richard Robinson, soon found new offices, first in the Jerusalem Coffee House and later, when those proved too small, in the London Tavern off Bishopsgate. Six years later the market was able to return to the rebuilt Royal Exchange, an event marked by a majestic banquet attended by Queen Victoria, the Prince Consort, the Duke of Wellington, Sir Robert Peel and William Ewart Gladstone. It was by all accounts a memorable feast, worthy of the new importance of Lloyd's, and was celebrated with a "magnificent baron of beef weighing upward of 20 stone" washed down by tankards of "remarkably fine sherry."

The opening of the new underwriting rooms, lauded as the last word in luxury—"the elegant soap dishes, the spotless napkins, the china basins, the ivory-tipped cocks for the supply of hot and cold water"—was accompanied by a tightening of membership. Four different categories were devised by the committee. The first two: underwriting members, who alone could sign policies, and annual subscribers, who were not entitled to underwrite but acted as brokers, bringing business to the Room, were the core. The £25 entrance fee for the underwriting members, plus a four guineas annual subscription fee paid by both groups, allowed them the exclusive use of the underwriting rooms. The two additional categories: Merchants' Room subscribers and Captains' Room subscribers, were aimed at increasing the flow of business into the market. Their smaller annual subscriptions of two guineas and one guinea permitted them the use of the Captains' Room and the Merchants' Room, continuing the social tradition of the old Lloyd's coffee house.

The new membership list and its enforcement led to the disappearance of the flock of hangers-on and impecunious chancers which had haunted the old Exchange. From this point Lloyd's was a coherent market rather than an anarchic, if engaging, group of individuals. In December 1851, the committee passed a bye-law providing that any member or annual subscriber who became bankrupt should be expelled. This was no idle threat, for three years later nine members and sixteen annual subscribers were struck off. The committee, however, still regarded its powers as strictly limited. In 1855 a Liverpool merchant, the creditor of a defaulting underwriter called Gibson, wrote to the committee urging it to accept responsibility for its member's outstanding claims. The committee replied that they had no powers to interfere—they were "simply a committee for managing the affairs and the establishment of Lloyd's." This hands-off attitude could not be sustained. Within twelve months the committee was anxiously considering whether security should be required from all new underwriters. The first such bond for £5,000 was posted in April 1856 by the relatives of Henry John Philip Dumas; it was the start of the distinguished underwriting career of the founder of one of Lloyd's most prominent families. A year later, the principle of a guarantee was modified when the father of a young underwriter called Sharp wrote to the committee saying he was averse to guarantees but was happy to provide a deposit. The £5,000 he deposited for his son was to become the standard figure for a marine underwriter for more than a century.

GROWTH AND CHANGE

A recurring theme in the history of Lloyd's is that reform comes in this most conservative of institutions only after overwhelming pressure. Underwriters are skilled at predicting the odds of a catastrophe, but they are much less good at anticipating events concerning their own affairs. As the definitive early history of the market by Wright and Fayle notes: "The history of Lloyd's is a history of continuous growth and change; but no step forward was ever made until its necessity had been proved by some crisis."

Such a crisis occurred in March 1870. The steamer *Venezuelan*, six days out of Barbados on its way to Liverpool, lost her rudder and stern post. By luck she was sighted by another ship which took off the passengers and some of the crew. Once in New York, the purser wired the owners, the West India and Pacific Steamship Company. Its managing director was a wealthy Liverpool shipowner, A.B. Forwood, who was also an underwriting member of Lloyd's. The news of the accident to the *Venezuelan* was at first received calmly by the market, reassured by the company's view that it was unlikely to be serious. But the underwriters' attitude changed when the *Liverpool Courier* reprinted a sensational article from the *New York Herald* headlined: "Mid-ocean Horror." The rate in the market speculating on a total loss shot up to 50 percent. But that same day Forwood had received a letter from the captain saying that things were not at all serious; the bulkhead was tight, the propellor sound, and a safe arrival could be anticipated provided the weather held. On the basis of this inside information, which the market only learnt twenty-four hours later, Forwood wired his London agent to underwrite £1,000, thus ensuring for himself a virtually risk-free profit of £500. This piece of sharp practice so infuriated the committee that it set up an inquiry which, without even bothering to interview Forwood, found him guilty and recommended that he should be expelled. On being told that it had exceeded its powers, the committee compounded its error by passing a retroactive bye-law. When Forwood sought an injunction from the Lord Chancellor restraining the committee from such arbitrary action, Lloyd's was forced into a humiliating retreat.

The exposure of the limits of its authority forced the committee to consider the defects in its constitution. The result was a bill which turned the Society of Lloyd's into a corporation with proper disciplinary powers over its membership. The act of 1871 was an important milestone, transforming the market into a legal entity, a basic structure which was to endure for more than a century. The act laid down what offences a member could be expelled for, such as bankruptcy and fraud. It also provided for expulsion on account of "discreditable conduct," but only on the finding of two arbitrators and with the assent of a four-fifths majority at a general meeting. The lessons of the Forwood case had clearly been learned. But the most important part of the 1871 act was its insistence that only an underwriting member could sign a Lloyd's policy. The Lloyd's anchor was henceforth to be a guarantee, a symbol of security stamped on every policy.

The years following the new act saw a rapid increase in the number of Lloyd's agents who represented the interests of underwriters at ports throughout the world. Supplying information on cargoes and shipping movements, the agents also acted as a crucial link in surveying damage, passing on instructions, and approving claims. The system had begun informally, with individual underwriters having their own agents in the major ports, but gradually it had become more centralized under Lloyd's able first secretary, John Bennett. By 1880 there were more than 1,000 agencies and sub-agencies, a reflection of Lloyd's worldwide influence.

The agents were an invaluable link with the shipping world but occasionally there was trouble. In 1824, a Lloyd's agent in Kinsale on the south coast of Ireland wrote from the local gaol appealing for help from the committee. He had, he explained, offered assistance to an American vessel in distress which turned out to be carrying an illicit cargo of tobacco. In faithful discharge of his duties, the agent joined the master in a bond guaranteeing the value of the cargo, whereupon the ungrateful master absconded. The cargo had been seized and he, a respected Lloyd's agent, had been arrested and thrown in prison. What did the committee advise? For his pains the agent received a letter expressing sympathy but advising him to resign. He responded that this was unnecessary, as he expected to be released shortly and would then resume his duties. By return of post the heartless committee sacked him.

Lloyd's supremacy in shipping intelligence due to the agency system was bolstered by the development of signal stations around the British coast. The first was built at Deal in 1869 and rapidly proved its usefulness. A ship would arrive off the coast from some Far East port, laden perhaps with spices, and would await instructions from its owners, relayed via the newfangled invention of the telegraph to the signal station, which used semaphores and Morse code to communicate with the ship. "Report me to Lloyd's," was the famous signal used by incoming ships around the world. The information on shipping movements was useful to underwriters and invaluable to shipowners, because it enabled them to direct their cargoes to whichever port was offering the highest price at the time.

The network of Lloyd's signal stations spread around the world, a development fostered by a commanding new secretary of the market. In 1874 the committee had appointed an army officer, Colonel Sir Henry Hozier, to its top administrative post. The father of Clementine, Winston Churchill's wife, Hozier was an archetypal Victorian. Forceful, vain, ambitious and autocratic, he rapidly established his authority, putting proposals for the reform of the market to the committee within a week of his arrival. He introduced an innovative system for paying cargo claims at foreign ports, which put an end to much delay and many administrative hassles. But the development of which he was proudest was securing for Lloyd's access to exclusive shipping information through the rapidly expanding network of signal stations. For the next three decades he toured the world buying key sites, from the Straits of Magellan to Belle Isle at the approach to the St Lawrence River. By 1884, when Lloyd's had seventeen signal stations at home and six abroad, Hozier was claiming that 90 percent of shipping bound for Britain was contacted by Lloyd's before arrival in port. "After the close of the Napoleonic Wars," he boasted, "the position that Lloyd's held with regard to maritime intelligence appears to have sunk; but within the last quarter of a century Lloyd's has again risen, and at the moment holds practically the monopoly of the collection and distribution of shipping intelligence throughout the world."

Marconi's invention of wireless telegraphy in the late 1890s threatened this monopoly of intelligence. With characteristic energy, Hozier teamed up with the famous magician Maskelyne to conduct experiments with the recent invention. Two years after the first English patent had been filed in 1866, Lloyd's began transmitting signals between Ballycastle and Rathlin Island, a distance of seven miles. Marconi was sufficiently impressed to enter into an agreement for Lloyd's to handle ship-to-shore messages on behalf of the new company. But the deal ended in a row five years later, when Marconi claimed that the service Lloyd's was providing was inadequate. This was a bitter disappointment to Hozier, who was so enraged by a statement made to the House of Commons by the postmaster general, Sydney Buxton, questioning some of his figures, that he challenged him to a duel. The duel did not take place, but the dispute led to the end of Hozier's career. An energetic newcomer to the committee, Sidney Boulton, later a distinguished chairman of Lloyd's, began to ask pointed questions about the cost of the signal stations. Hozier, under attack for his extravagant lifestyle, resigned in 1906 but was made an honorary member. A year later he died in Panama while surveying a site for a new station. Of the worldwide chain established under his secretaryship, the only one that survives is operated by the Royal Navy at Gibraltar. But ships entering the Mediterranean still flash the signal: "Report me to Lloyd's."

Lloyd's monopoly of shipping intelligence was not to everyone's liking. In 1871 the Salvage Association, which represented the interests of the marine companies, sought to gain control of the Lloyd's agency system and signal stations. The failure of the take-over prompted a virulent attack on Lloyd's by a Liverpool merchant, J.T. Danson. His message to underwriters, published at length in the *Shipping Gazette*, was blunt: "You are living on the past, you are effete, your premium income compared with the companies is almost trivial, but you still behave as though the monopoly of 1720 had never been abolished. Lloyd's," he predicted, "will either shrink to the dimensions of a mere trade club, or will complete its existence as a miserable sham."

AN OUTSTANDING UNDERWRITER

That the market met neither of those fates is due in no small part to one of its outstanding underwriters. Cuthbert Eden Heath was the son of a distinguished admiral. Afflicted with severe deafness which prevented him from following his father's profession, he became an underwriter. He was elected in 1880 at the age of twenty-one, with the help of a £7,000 loan from his father, and rapidly showed a streak of originality. The vast majority of underwriting at Lloyd's was still concentrated on marine business as it had been a century earlier. But Heath, an imposing figure who carried his hearing aid everywhere in a black box, calculated that there were better opportunities in non-marine risks, which underwriters had previously avoided. His breakthrough came to him from his father who was a director of the Hand in Hand Fire Office, one of the oldest non-tariff fire insurers. He mentioned to his son that the company was having difficulty in finding reinsurance for its conventional book of fire risks. The son responded that he could see no reason why his syndicate should not take on the business. The open-minded "Why not?" approach to insurance was to become the symbol by which Cuthbert Heath built an enormously prosperous career, one that was to change the course of the whole market.

Heath was a genuinely innovative underwriter. His developing book of fire risks was extended when he began to offer cover for damage caused by fire and the consequent loss of profits. The established companies threw up their hands in horror and predicted ruin for the young underwriter, but eventually they were obliged to follow suit. Another new form of cover came when Heath was approached by a Lloyd's broker who, half in jest, asked whether he would cover him against burglary as well as fire for an insurance policy he wanted to place on some of his own furniture. The response was "Why not?" and so the first ever household burglary policy was written in 1887. The new cover, written at rates ranging between two shillings and six pence to five shillings for each £100, was hugely popular at a time when Victorian London was in a panic about crime. The *Pall Mall Gazette* reported the development in glowing terms, and several brokers began advertising that they could effect insurance at Lloyd's against theft and robbery with or without violence.

Cuthbert Heath was not content with this advance. When a relative lost a piece of jewellery that she had insured against theft and found to her disappointment that she was not covered, this set off a new train of thought. Why, if you could insure valuables against theft, could you not also insure them against loss? Heath pondered the problem at his box and came up with a rate of ten shillings per £100. It was a tribute to his shrewdness that this initial rate stood for the next half-century. The cover against loss was the origin of "all-risks" policies, a form of insurance which was to prove increasingly popular and which today brings in millions of pounds in premium every year. The new loss policy led directly to another form of trade cover. The bookkeeper of a diamond merchant in Hatton Garden, worried by the risks run by his employer as he carried his stock around the street, sought cover from Heath who agreed to insure the gems both inside and outside the office. The policy was called a jeweller's "block policy," a term still in use today wherever diamonds or other gems are insured.

Other innovations sprang from Heath's restless mind—workmen's compensation, bankers' insurance and trade indemnity. But most of all, Lloyd's is indebted to him for the insurance links which he forged with the United States. Right at the start of his underwriting career, Heath began reinsuring transatlantic fire risks; he also pioneered earthquake and hurricane insurance. The rate for regions considered to be at risk was £1 per £100 for wooden houses, and fifteen shillings for steel and concrete buildings.

The moment of truth came on 6 April 1906 with a natural disaster that will never be forgotten. Shortly after dawn, the geological fissure in California known as the San Andreas fault shifted, causing devastation in San Francisco. Seven hundred people died, a quarter of a million were made homeless, 30,000 houses were ruined—virtually a whole city had been destroyed. Many insurance companies failed, others disputed their liability on the grounds that their policies covered fire but not earthquake damage. Lloyd's took a different course. Cuthbert Heath's famous telegram to his San Francisco agent: "Pay all our policy-holders in full irrespective of the terms of their policies," became a watchword for fair dealing. It cost Lloyd's underwriters an estimated $100 million ($1.5 billion in today's money), but the goodwill it created was worth many times that huge sum.

After the San Francisco earthquake, Heath was approached by the Hartford Company which sought to insure against a comparable future catastrophe. It wanted protection against a single huge loss, not a complicated policy covering all its business. Heath's answer to this challenge was the then novel concept of an excess of loss insurance in which the policy would respond when the loss exceeded a pre-determined level. It was a far-sighted innovation, the beginning of the modern complex reinsurance market in which large risks such as hurricanes and North Sea oil platforms can be spread in layers across the market. Today over a third of Lloyd's business derives from the United States, most of it in reinsurance. The development of American liability business fuelled a rapid expansion in the market. In 1870 Lloyd's had only 400 underwriting members; by 1913 the number had risen to 621; fourteen years later it had doubled to 1,285. Lloyd's reputation across the Atlantic was so high that several states had to pass laws preventing imitators from purloining the name. In New York before the outbreak of the First World War, there were thirty-seven companies illegally using the name "Lloyd's" in their title.

It is impossible to exaggerate Heath's influence on the development of the market, for he not only wrote a huge book of non-marine business on his own account but also led large numbers of risks to which other underwriters were only too happy to put their names. Lloyd's has always been a market where a few skilled underwriters give the lead to the far more numerous sheep. This pre-eminence was the passport to vast wealth. At Heath's country house in Surrey the staff included no fewer than fifty maids, but neither their wages nor the large sums he gave to charity made much of a dent in his income. He was once heard to remark that however much he gave away, it seemed to make no difference. "His name is honoured today," wrote a contemporary, "not because he started non-marine underwriting at Lloyd's but because he revolutionized, both at Lloyd's and elsewhere, the business of non-marine insurance and enormously widened the service it offered to the commercial world."

Another development pioneered by Heath was a growth in syndicate size. Before 1860 most underwriters wrote for themselves and occasionally for one or two close friends. By the end of the century it was noted that some underwriters were writing on behalf of "half a score" Names, which was thought to be a dangerous phenomenon. Yet without this growth in syndicate numbers, Lloyd's would have been unable to take on the growing competition from the company sector. Today the largest syndicates have more than several thousand Names, in order to minimize administrative expenses and cope with larger and larger risks.

THE EROSION OF TRUST

Growth often brings problems. At the beginning of the twentieth century, the market was operated largely on trust. The Burnand smash showed this was not enough. Burnand was an underwriter who had run a profitable marine syndicate since his election in 1885. Unknown to the four other members of his syndicate, he was heavily in debt, due to his involvement in a travel agency of which he was a director. Instead of cutting his losses, he milked the syndicate's premiums and saddled his fellow members with liabilities of more than £100,000 secured under policies backed by their names. The final blow came when King Edward VII's coronation was postponed in 1902—Burnand's travel company had speculated heavily on seats for the event. Three of the Names found themselves bankrupted by their underwriter's folly; the fourth was impoverished.

This scandal spurred the committee into recognition of the need for reform. At first there was a good deal of resistance in the market, but on 17 July 1908 *The Times* published a powerful leader urging Lloyd's to institute an audit of all underwriters in order to maintain confidence. The article was probably inspired by members of the committee who were exasperated by the delay. Finally, Cuthbert Heath pre-empted further consideration by drawing up an agreement to be signed by all underwriters under which they agreed to hand in to the committee of Lloyd's an annual statement, signed by an approved accountant, that they had sufficient assets to wind up their underwriting accounts. That took the wind out of the sails of the opponents. A further important step to improve the security of a Lloyd's policy was the insistence that in future all premiums were to be paid into a premium trust fund. The committee was fortunate that it had showed it could keep its own house in order. A year later, in 1909, Parliament passed legislation to regulate fire and accident insurance which called for deposits of £2,000 from individual underwriters and £20,000 from companies. Lloyd's successfully claimed exemption—in essence it managed to convince Parliament that it should be allowed to regulate itself, a position it has maintained, albeit with some difficulty, to the present day.

No system of control, however rigorous, is proof against fraud. That lesson was learned just over a decade later, shortly after the end of the First World War, in a case which proved a landmark. Stanley Harrison was a second-rate underwriter who wrote a mixed account of marine, non-marine and motor risks. The latter account proved his downfall. The post-war growth of the car trade, financed by hire purchase, created a demand for credit insurance. Harrison thought he had spotted a nice little earner guaranteeing finance houses against defaults by their customers. In theory the business was relatively safe; there was, after all, the physical asset of the car which could be seized if the debtor defaulted. But Harrison, who had a knack for attracting rogues, failed to distinguish between credit insurance of vehicles which had actually been sold and those which were alleged to be awaiting sale in the hands of dealers. The grandiloquently titled Industrial Guarantee

Corporation, an aggressive finance house with a capital of under £2,000 but with a turnover running into millions, was the first to latch on to this trusting source of credit. The final blow was dealt by a Swedish con-man called Holsteinson who invented a large number of vehicles as a means of extracting large sums of money from hire purchase companies which were reinsured in turn by Harrison. When the Swede disappeared early in 1923 leaving a trail of fictitious invoices behind him, Harrison's syndicate found itself short of £17,000. If he had come clean at this point, probably the worst that would have happened is that he would have been barred from underwriting. But Harrison was unwilling to do this. Unknown to members of his syndicate and to the committee, he was up to his neck in fraud. He had kept the credit insurance business secret by the old trick of having two sets of books. For a few months he managed to keep the creditors at bay by increasingly desperate and expensive manoeuvres, borrowing money on bills guaranteed by his syndicate. But in the first week of October a cheque bounced, and he was required by the committee to face a full audit.

The Harrison scandal is remembered to this day in the market, not so much for the sorry details as for the response of the committee. Barely a week after the smash, the chairman of Lloyd's, Arthur Sturge, called a general meeting of underwriters. He told them bluntly that the amount owing might be as much as £300,000, and while he could not compel them to make good this debt, if they did not "the name of Lloyd's will be seriously injured and will never recover in our lifetime." With such a challenge, the outcome was never in doubt, though there was argument about how the burden should be apportioned. In the end, every underwriting member agreed to share the losses in proportion to his syndicate's income. The largest syndicate had to pay £10,269 (about £230,000 in today's money); the smallest subscription from a veteran underwriter was eight pence. The settlement of Harrison's debts is an important milestone, because it was the first time that the market publicly acknowledged its collective responsibility for the actions of its members. The good name of Lloyd's and the security of its policies was not just a matter of pride; it was a crucial trading asset which had to be preserved whatever the cost. To buyers of insurance, the message was equally clear. A Lloyd's policy carried a guarantee of payment well beyond that which any commercial company was able to offer. For behind every individual underwriter at Lloyd's stood the good name and assets of the whole market.

The Harrison smash was not the only scandal which troubled Lloyd's in the first half of the twentieth century. As the number of members increased and the market expanded, there were others. The Wilcox fraud in the early 1950s, in which a crooked underwriter conspired with an equally crooked accountant, and the Roylance affair a few years later, in which a former chairman of Lloyd's retired leaving his Names in desperate straits, were reminders that Lloyd's reputation crucially depended on the character of its underwriters. But what is remarkable in a market driven by money, where opportunity for dishonesty is rampant, is not the surfacing of the odd fraud and the odd failure, but how infrequent they were.

THE CRISIS OF THE 1980s

In its first three centuries of trading, up to 1980, Lloyd's reputation for probity and profitability was rarely assailed. From time to time a few underwriters were unable to meet their liabilities, but this was rare. For instance, between 1870 and 1891, not the best of periods for the market, there were only six Names whose deposits had to be seized to pay their debts. One underwriter lost £200,000 (equivalent to £10 million today) and was reported to have had to sell 20,000 acres of Sussex to pay his losses. "The big difference was that they paid up and shut up," says the current deputy chairman, Robert Hiscox. At most times, however, underwriting was generally profitable. Lloyd's has sometimes made large fortunes for those who work in the market. The high point was during the Napoleonic Wars, when underwriters were making huge profits; the books of one underwriter in 1807 show that he was making at least £30,000 a year (roughly equivalent to £600,000 today) after expenses. Even in peacetime, one sober observer of the market put the average net profits at "not less than 8 percent" of premium income. In the twentieth century, until the present time, the only known recorded years of loss were three years in the mid-1960s, following Hurricane Betsy, when the market lost £52 million (£540 million in today's money). Lloyd's own figures for the years between 1952 and 1979 showed that the profits on underwriting reached 11 percent in 1953 and fell to a low point of minus 8 percent in 1965, before rising again to 7.5 percent in 1979.

All of this raises the question which this book seeks to address: What has gone wrong? After three centuries of profitable trading, Lloyd's is facing the most serious crisis in its history, a crisis of confidence not just about profitability but, more seriously, about its integrity. The history outlined in this chapter is one of gradual recognition that the fortunes of those who work in the market depend on their collective reputation for fair dealing. From the first hesitant rules limiting membership to paid-up subscribers at the end of the eighteenth century, to the tough audit restrictions in the early twentieth century, the market has adapted to every threat to its good name. The challenge it now faces is how to restore the confidence of those who provide its capital. The huge expansion in the market from the end of the Second World War, when there were fewer than 2,000 members, to more than 32,000 in the mid-1980s has inevitably led to profound changes. As the history by Wright and Fayle concluded nearly seventy years ago: "The vital question for the Lloyd's of the future is the character of its members, and no magnificence in its building will atone in even a small degree for deterioration in moral calibre or in business efficiency."

3

The Market

"A mob of upper-class bookies with a mild talent for PR"
New Statesman *editorial*

"It's a wonderful price," grunted the underwriter as he glanced down at the policy slip. The young broker standing at syndicate 702's "box"—an open desk piled high with computers—smiled at the sarcasm. He knew he had a difficult task in persuading Reg Brown, 702's underwriter, to renew a policy for a client who had just put in a big claim. A much respected local weekly newspaper found itself facing a £50,000 libel action after a local solicitor took exception to what appeared at first sight to be a mild and inoffensive story reporting that his offices were being picketed. The paper's lawyers first took an insouciant view, saying it was a storm in a teacup and wasn't a matter for damages. A month later, after counsel had been consulted, the paper's solicitor said he thought it might be advisable to offer a £10,000 settlement which, with expenses, would cost the insurers £22,000. The legal advice to settle did not go down well with Reg Brown. After shuffling through the papers for a few minutes, he looked up and said firmly: "I am not accepting that. We'll fight." The broker looked apprehensive, but smiled when the underwriter picked up his pen, banged down the syndicate's stamp, and wrote 100 percent of the renewed risk for £1,250, almost double the original premium.

Until recently few people outside Lloyd's, even those working in the City, knew much about how it operated. Apart from brief mentions in a few specialist financial papers, little was written about the market, and the few items that did appear were more often than not ill-informed. Lloyd's did nothing to dispel this public ignorance, which was sustained by a highly developed culture of secrecy. "The practice of underwriting at Lloyd's was for many years shrouded in an aura of mystique," admitted Stephen Burnhope, a former Merrett underwriter, now with Speckley Villiers Burnhope. "It was to a large extent a state of affairs perpetuated by the practitioners, guarding the secrets of their craft as zealously as any member of the Magic Circle protects that mysterious interaction of white bunny rabbits and top hats."[1]

Market rows and misdemeanours were hushed up, reports to the committee were suppressed, syndicate results were not published. As a result, many of the market's professionals—the working Names—had only a partial view of what was happening, while external Names—the outside investors who provided the bulk of the capital—remained for the most part in total ignorance. The worst agents did almost nothing to keep their Names informed; the best did quite a lot. But as syndicate results were confidential, Names had little basis for comparing the skill and competence of individual underwriters. Once a year they attended a social lunch with the members, agent who handled their underwriting affairs, at which it was unusual for anything of interest to be discussed, apart from the runners in the Derby. When the annual cheque arrived, as it usually did each July, they pocketed it gratefully, with little understanding of the risks to which their fortune had been exposed.

Before a Name could begin underwriting, he had to appear before a Rota committee composed of three or four members of Lloyd's council, who solemnly asked him if he appreciated the risk of unlimited liability that he was undertaking. Lloyd's insiders tend to place great weight on this brief encounter but in reality the Rota was nothing more than an empty ceremony. There was no questioning of either the candidate's understanding or the members' agent's suitability, let alone whether the syndicates chosen for the Name were properly balanced. Those who joined Lloyd's in the mid-1980s and were concentrated on disastrous long-tail and spiral syndicates received not a flicker of a warning.

"Before 1982, it was simple," the Society of Names was later to comment sardonically. "Little had changed this century. The power was held tightly by those atop the pyramid. No eunuchs they. Select, key insider City professionals invented the rules and umpired the game. They practised *noblesse oblige*. The relationship was not dissimilar to that of the way the masters of smart Midland hunts treat the rest of the field; favoured gentlefolk are spoken to but the bulk are lucky to be there and allowed to ride to pay the bills: to be seen but never heard except in a grunted good morning. Vulgar complainants are sent home to go ratting if they so choose."

The condescending relationship, it should be noted, was a two-way street. A Name once wrote to his members' agent: "Well done, thou true and faithful servant." One leading managing agent recalls being told by a Name that he proposed to go up to London to visit his tailor, his dentist and his underwriter: "He obviously regarded all three as varieties of tradesmen and was strongly of the view that he, as a landowner, should no more expect to discover how underwriters underwrote than to discover how a tailor cut a suit."

The scandals of the early 1980s, combined with the publication of individual syndicate results, began to blow away these traditional veils of secrecy, much to the displeasure of many in the market. "We never had any trouble before the press began to report our affairs," one disgruntled veteran underwriter remarked. When John Rew, one of the founders of the independent research group Chatset, wrote to Robert Hiscox, then a leading managing agent, in the summer of 1981 seeking information, he received this reply: "I have no sympathy for Names who regularly get lousy returns from their syndicates," wrote Hiscox, now deputy chairman of Lloyd's. "They should be able to realize this fact without your list and should be adult enough to change agents if they are being permanently abused." As Eli Wallach said to Steve McQueen: "If God had not meant them to be sheared he would not have made them sheep." And as Robert Hiscox says regularly to everyone: "We must not legislate for the lowest common denominator."[2]

That comment, which now graces the downstairs lavatory of Rew's Dorset house in a suitable frame, reflects an era when many Names were treated as cannon fodder. This cavalier approach to Lloyd's capital base, combined with the mistaken belief that the sins of a few incompetent or reckless underwriters would not affect the market as a whole, led directly to the catastrophic losses of the 1980s. It has been a sobering decade, but despite the avalanche of media publicity there is still much ignorance about how the market actually operates. What follows is an attempt to explain in layman's language.

BROKERS AND UNDERWRITERS

The kingpin at Lloyd's is the active underwriter who scrutinizes risks, fixes rates, and writes insurance policies on behalf of a syndicate of investors who are called Names. From the early days of Lloyd's until the twentieth century, underwriters wrote risks for themselves and no more than a handful of friends or relations. Syndicates remained very small until the Second World War, but the postwar years saw a gradual expansion in numbers. This accelerated in the 1970s, so that the largest now have several thousand investors. Syndicates are controlled and operated by a managing agent, which employs the underwriter. The largest syndicate, Charman 488, named as is the custom after its underwriter, is an old-established marine syndicate with 7,000 Names and a capacity of £209 million. Most tend to be much smaller, averaging about 500 members and a capacity of £20 million.[3]

Though there has been a vast expansion of numbers, the pattern of trading at Lloyd's has hardly changed for three centuries. The broker, who acts as a middleman on behalf of those seeking insurance, approaches an underwriter at his box, which is nothing more than an open desk with a bench along either side. He presents him with a piece of paper, known as a slip, setting out the terms of a risk. If the risk is large, say an oil rig, the underwriter will write only a very small percentage. As in all markets there are leaders and followers. The lead underwriter will set the rate and will usually write the largest share of the risk, and following underwriters will take a smaller fraction.

During the day I spent with Reg Brown at syndicate 702's box, there was a constant stream of brokers bringing a wide variety of risks, ranging from insuring charities against "exotic liabilities" to the professional indemnity insurance of a large construction company. After a few sharp questions to the broker, Brown would bang down the syndicate's stamp, write the percentage of line (the amount of the risk) he was prepared to underwrite, and sign his initials with a flourish. "Our style of underwriting," he explained, "is to write lots and lots of small business." Brown, the chairman of Lloyd's Non-Marine Association in 1993, was philosophical about the difficulties facing the market. "Until this year we have made a profit, and are pretty sick that this June we will not. But we have done very well up till now." On the larger problems of Lloyd's, he was less sanguine: "We have made a huge mistake with our capital base. We've bankrupted three to four thousand Names, and there is not much that can be done. But you've got to be positive in this business otherwise you would blow your brains out like poor Roy Bromley [a non-marine underwriter who committed suicide in January 1993]."

The management of underwriting syndicates is conducted by a managing agency, which operates syndicates across different areas of the market, such as marine, motor and aviation. At its height in the mid-1980s, the market had more than 140 managing agencies, controlling more than 400 different syndicates with a combined capacity of £11 billion. The managing agency charges Names an annual fee of between £150 and £300 for participation in a syndicate, and also a commission, ranging from 10 to 20 percent, on any profits made from the underwriting. Traditionally syndicates, each headed by an active underwriter, specialized in one of four different areas: marine, mainly writing traditional shipping policies; non-marine, covering a wide field of liability and industrial risks; and the aviation and motor markets. But as the market has expanded, these old boundaries have begun to break down, and today a marine syndicate will often write a large book of non-marine and even aviation risks.

The skill of a good underwriter, who conducts the syndicate's business, is difficult to define. He needs to be confident in his own judgment and to have a wary knowledge of the frailties and wickedness of the world as well as the ability to know whom to trust; above all he has to have the sixth sense to be able to spot a dangerous risk. A nattily suited broker from Fenchurch, a large broking firm, approached syndicate 702's box with a line slip for an indemnity policy underwriting a financial company operating offshore. "These fellows," said the broker encouragingly, "have had only two small incidents [potential claims]." Reg Brown would have none of it. "Only two," he responded tartly. "They're all crooks running tax avoidance companies out of Jersey." The proposal was rejected smartly: "Nice try." The young broker walked away shaking his head sadly. The relationship between broker and underwriter is a complex one, but it is essentially based on trust. The underwriter needs to keep the flow of business coming, he cannot afford to be totally negative about even the hairiest of risks. "We believe here that the good risk always pays too much and the bad risk always pays too little and that many risks are uninsurable," said one leading underwriter. Others subscribe to the old market saw: "There's no such thing as a bad risk, only a bad rate." The relationship between underwriter and broker has a degree of give and take. A broker who brings a large amount of business to an underwriter will expect a fair hearing on even the most unattractive of clients.

Equally, an underwriter who has had a bad run will look for a degree of flexibility from the broker to help soften his future losses.

Business is brought to Lloyd's via a worldwide network of insurance intermediaries, but only the 200 or so brokers accredited to Lloyd's are allowed to deal directly with underwriters. Most of the world's largest brokers own a Lloyd's broking company; in 1990 the ten largest brokers accounted for more than half of all insurance policies placed at Lloyd's. It is the broker's responsibility to prepare the slip documenting the precise nature of the risk, which is then shown to the underwriter. A typical policy will be placed with about twenty underwriters who will each write a small percentage of the risk. Once the slip has been placed, the broker will issue a cover note and collect the premium from the policy-holder; this he will forward to the underwriter after deducting his agreed commission.

THE NAMES

If the underwriter is king, Lloyd's cannot function without the Names who provide the risk capital. At the peak of the market in the late 1980s there were more than 32,000 Names, each writing on average £400,000. There are two kinds of Name: working Names, the professionals who work in the market as underwriters, brokers and agents, who constitute just under a fifth, and—the majority—external Names who are, in effect, passive investors. Most are British, but no fewer than eighty-five countries are represented at Lloyd's. There are sizeable numbers of Names in the United States, Australia, Ireland, Canada, South Africa and New Zealand. There are even Names in such unlikely capitalist havens as North Yemen, China and Tonga.

Lloyd's is unlike any other investment; those who put their capital at risk in the market may regard themselves as investors, but technically they are sole traders. Each Name trades on his own account, with unlimited personal liability. That means he is responsible only for his own share of losses or profits, not for those of any other member of the syndicate. But if he does incur losses on his share of the syndicate, he is liable, as Lloyd's likes to boast, "down to his last shirt button." That is quite unlike, for example, an investor in an insurance company, whose potential loss is limited to the value of the shares he has purchased. The Name's gamble of unlimited liability is all the greater because he has no control whatsoever over the underwriter and the sort of business he is prepared to write. In an attempt to spread their risk, Names normally join several different syndicates specializing in different areas of the market. In 1991, the average Name wrote £25,000 on each of seventeen syndicates, a much wider distribution than had been usual in the past.[4]

To become a Name, the investor does not have to hand over capital, he merely has to show that he possesses it. In the 1970s the amount required was £100,000; today the minimum is £250,000. But this undertaking is rather less onerous than it sounds. Though houses are not allowable, Lloyd's will accept a bank guarantee based on the value of a Name's house. A proportion of this "shown" capital, normally about a third, has to be deposited with Lloyd's for safe keeping in the form of shares or other easily liquid form of assets. But again a bank guarantee is accepted. In this way thousands of individuals who could hardly be described as rich were attracted into the market in the past two decades.

Names are placed on syndicates by members' agents, who are responsible for supervising the Names' affairs, and who act as the link between the Name and the underwriter. There are various kinds of members' agents. Some are independent, some are owned by brokers, and some are run in tandem by managing agents. The selection of a competent, trustworthy members' agent is the most important decision that a Name has to make on joining Lloyd's. It is the members' agent who has complete charge of a Name's underwriting and will guide him as to which syndicates he should be on and which managing agents are competent. As a market report pointed out, the relationship of total trust between a Name and those who underwrite on his behalf is "probably unique as a form of capitalist association."[5]

Until very recently, the information available to a prospective Name trying to make an informed choice of agent was woefully inadequate. But that was remedied by a rule passed in 1988 which requires all members' agents to publish annual information about their results. A competent agent can make the difference between amassing or losing a fortune. A study published by the Association of Lloyd's Members revealed that the best performing agent would have provided an annual average return of 12.1 percent over five years from 1986-90. For a Name writing an annual premium of £400,000, that would have meant a very high return of nearly £250,000 over five years. The worst agent, on the other hand, would have bankrupted most of its Names with losses of more than £1 million over the same five-year period.[6]

Names are able to safeguard themselves to a limited extent against large losses by reinsuring with another Lloyd's syndicate or an insurer outside

Lloyd's. A typical stop loss policy costing £3,500 will cover annual losses in excess of a deductible 10 percent of a Name's overall premium limit up to a maximum loss of perhaps £100,000. Thus if a Name is writing £350,000, he would be covered for any losses above £35,000 up to a policy limit of £135,000. In normal years that would be a sufficient safeguard, but it was not in the disastrous years of 1988 to 1990. Unfortunately these were the years which saw a big expansion in the market. Postwar Lloyd's had fewer than 2,500 Names. By the time of Hurricane Betsy in 1965, there were 6,000. A decade later, as a result of the relaxation in entry requirements, the number of Names had tripled, and at the peak in 1988 it had nearly doubled again to just over 32,000.

Who were these Names? The pre-war Lloyd's was composed largely of the market families, their friends and close relations—the Bowrings, Fabers, Greens, Pulbrooks, de Rougemonts and d'Ambrumenils. There was a good representation of landed wealth such as the Duke of Marlborough, the Marquis of Salisbury, the Cadogans, who owned much of Chelsea, and the Portmans, who owned much of Marylebone. The great banking families, the Rothschilds, Barings, Tennants and Couttses were also much in evidence. There was also a lot of old money—Cazenoves, Sebag-Montefiores, William-Powletts, Asquiths, Waley-Cohens, Bonham-Carters. The list of Lloyd's Names was not unlike a social register of the wealthy.

The recruits of the 1970s were a rather different breed. Women and foreigners began to join, and soon comprised nearly a quarter of all Names. A galaxy of sports stars, Virginia Wade, Tony Jacklin, Henry Cooper, Lester Piggott, Buster Mottram, James Hunt, urged on by their sporting management companies, were persuaded to join; so were impecunious royalty, advised by their accountants: Princess Michael of Kent, Princess Alexandra of Kent and her husband, Angus Ogilvy. Conservative politicians such as Edward Heath, Jeffrey Archer and Michael Howard, and tycoons such as Rocco Forte and Robert Maxwell also joined. In their wake came many aspiring members of the middle class—lawyers, accountants and businessmen—even the odd journalist. The range of wealth of the new Names was enormous, from the seriously rich to the long-serving Lloyd's secretary earning £15,000 a year who was sponsored by a grateful employer.

It was not just the lure of profits that attracted so many new investors to Lloyd's. A key advantage of being a Name is that it allows you to make whatever wealth you have work twice over. The Name is able to make a return not only on his underwriting at Lloyd's, but also on any funds or shares he has deposited in support of his underwriting. In good times, the gearing provided by this partly paid capital on which Lloyd's operates can bring Names high returns. Between 1960 and 1988, the average annual return was £29,000. But in bad times Names can be called on to put up large amounts of cash at short notice to meet underwriting losses. There are, however, tax advantages. As underwriting losses can be offset against taxable income, a Name has the comfort of knowing that if his syndicates do lose money the losses will be cushioned by the Inland Revenue to the extent of his highest rate of tax. In the 1970s, when the top rate of tax reached 98 percent, Lloyd's was very attractive to high income earners, who were able to treat it as a risk-free punt. The widespread practice of bond-washing, stripping the capital gains out of gilts, which was not outlawed until the mid-1980s, allowed syndicate managers to make capital gains for their syndicates which were taxed at only 30 percent. The trick was turned by buying government securities ex-dividend and selling them cum-dividend—thus deferring income in favour of capital gains. Lastly, the tax payable on a syndicate's profits is not assessed for three years because of the Lloyd's system of three-year accounting. Taken together these tax advantages were considerable. Ironically, one of Lloyd's problems in an era of low personal taxation is that today the tax breaks are worth much less than they were in the heyday of egalitarian Socialist governments.

ANNUAL VENTURE

One other distinctive feature of the Lloyd's market makes it unique in the world of insurance. In addition to Names having unlimited liability, the syndicates whose risks they share have an unusual accounting structure. Though they appear to trade continuously under the same underwriter, they are in fact "annual ventures;" at the end of each year of account they are wound up, but their results are only calculated three years in arrears. The practice derives from the historic system of "voyage accounting" used by medieval merchants, under which the assets and liabilities of a voyage were not determined until the ship had returned safely to the home port. At Lloyd's, because of the need to preserve equity between Names on different syndicate years, the precise calculation of profit or loss is made at the end of thirty-six months, when the results should, in theory, be clearer. Even then the process is very uncertain. An underwriter with exposure to "long-tail" liabilities such as pollution or asbestos may not know his true profit or loss position for decades. The accounting device used to bridge this uncertainty is known as a reinsurance to close (RITC), an unlimited reinsurance policy placed by the prior year syndicate with its successor year. The RITC has to be large enough to meet not only known claims but also claims which have been incurred but not yet reported. The calculation is crucial. If the RITC is too large, the Names on the prior year of account will have paid too much. If it is too small, the Names on the successor year syndicate could face huge liabilities without adequate reserves.

This problem is at the heart of the crisis now facing Lloyd's. When an underwriter is unable to determine a fair reinsurance to close because the future liabilities are too uncertain, he is forced to leave the syndicate's year open. During the 1980s, the number of open years has grown rapidly as syndicates have found themselves facing huge and unquantifiable claims for pollution and latent diseases in the United States. The problems this poses for Names are serious, for they have no idea what their eventual liabilities will be. Names on open years are unable to resign from Lloyd's until they are closed. Even death does not release the Name, because the liabilities of an open syndicate will be charged against his estate.

Until recently, the governance of Lloyd's was a cosy arrangement in the hands of a sixteen-member committee composed largely of leading underwriters with a sprinkling of brokers and members' agents thrown in. The conflicts of interest that this encouraged, allied to the committee's view that its regulatory powers were inadequate, led to the appointment of a working party under Sir Henry Fisher. This concluded that Lloyd's needed a new governing body on which the interests of external Names would be represented. The new council, which started work in 1983, balanced the sixteen professionals with six external Names and three nominated outsiders approved by the governor of the Bank of England.[7]

Six years later, the process was taken one step further by the report of another distinguished outsider, Sir Patrick Neill, who was asked to consider whether Names at Lloyd's were sufficiently protected, despite not being covered by the Financial Services Act. His report came to the same conclusion as Fisher: that the market's conflicts of interest were too direct, and the influence of the inside professionals had to be diminished. He therefore recommended that the council should be bolstered by a further four nominated members who would take the place of four professionals, thus ensuring that the insiders would be in a minority on the council.[8] The latest change came in 1992 as a result of the Rowland Task Force. It recommended that the duties of the council should be split between a board responsible for the business of the market, on which there would be a preponderance of professionals, and a regulatory council, composed mainly of outsiders, which would be responsible for regulating the market.

In this necessarily brief summary, one characteristic needs to be stressed. Lloyd's is a place where individualism flourishes and where suspicion of authority runs deep. It has an inbred culture all of its own. The famous response of the nineteenth-century caller Walter Farrant to the question: "What is Lloyd's?"—"Individually, Madam, we are underwriters; collectively we are Lloyd's" sums up the paradoxical character of an institution which, despite its international reputation, has found it difficult to adjust its trading practices to the vastly changed market place of the late twentieth century.

4

Hurricane Betsy

"People of the same trade seldom meet together even for
merriment or diversion but the conversation ends in a
conspiracy against the public."
Adam Smith, Wealth of Nations

The origins of the crisis at Lloyd's go back at least a generation. In the early
hours of 4 September 1965, Hurricane Betsy spiralled out of the Caribbean
and, taking an unusual course, twisted towards Cape Hatteras before crossing
Florida into the Gulf of Mexico. By the time it had blown itself out this
phenomenally intense storm, with winds of 135 miles per hour, had claimed
hundreds of lives. It had also smashed dozens of offshore oil and drilling
barges, many of which had been insured through oil companies' package
policies on the London market. The impact of this and other disasters—a
North Sea oil platform, Sea Gem, also foundered in heavy storms—was
severe. Lloyd's lost £38 million in 1965, the equivalent of 13 percent of net
premiums, the worst result since the end of the Second World War. For the
average Name, it meant having to write a cheque for £6,000 and a further
£3,000 the following year, about £70,000 in today's money. The number of
Lloyd's Names had grown steadily for three decades, from 1,832 in 1938 to

just over 6,000 in 1966, but in the four succeeding years the numbers joining halved and resignations doubled. For the first time in a century membership of Lloyd's fell.[1]

This decrease in capacity alarmed the committee of Lloyd's, which feared the market would be unable to meet a growing wave of competition from continental and American insurers. It invited Lord Cromer, a former governor of the Bank of England, to chair an inquiry to examine whether the existing capital structure was adequate to meet the needs of the market. Cromer, head of the Baring banking family, was not a man to be corralled; his committee contained powerful figures such as Sir Alexander Johnston, Sir Alexander Cairncross and Ralph Hiscox, and they proceeded to interpret their brief widely.

His report, completed a year later in December 1969, and sent in confidence to the professionals in the market but not to external Names, made a number of trenchant criticisms. It pointed out that new capacity was unlikely to be attracted to the market unless the risk-reward ratio was made more favourable to those who provided the capital. It identified excessive charges by managing agents, the companies which controlled syndicates, as being of particular concern. The managing agent, it noted, not only drew a fixed fee of up to £300 from each Name, but in addition took as much as 25 percent of any profit in commission. For an agent managing a small 200-member syndicate writing risks of £7 million a year with a profit margin of, say, 5 five percent, this provided rich pickings of more than £100,000 a year. While Names were debited with profit commission, their agents made no return of either commission or fees if there were losses. All the risks were one way—the Names stood to lose everything down to their last shirt button, their agents nothing at all. "Some Names consider that their agents treat them rather cavalierly," remarked Cromer with characteristic understatement. He went on to point out that the fattening up and consequent sale of managing agencies to brokers in order to secure large capital gains was not a basis for sound development of the market, noting the "conflict of interest which cannot be ignored" in such a relationship. Brokers, the report said, should be acting solely on behalf of the assured and should be in a hands-off, if not adversarial, relationship with the underwriter. If a broker owned and con- trolled a managing agency, impartiality was impossible.

A number of recommendations were made to tackle these defects. The report said that profit commission should be cut to "substantially less than 20 percent," and urged that managing agents should adopt a deficit clause to compensate Names where there were losses. As for the broker-underwriter relationship, brokers were urged "to reduce their involvement in underwriting in the long-term interest of their broking businesses." The report also drew attention to the urgent need for Names to put more funds into reserves in order to provide a cushion against future losses. The lack of a catastrophe fund left Names badly exposed. The Inland Revenue allowed Names to put only £7,000 a year from profits into a special reserve, an amount which had been increased just once in twenty years.

If these warnings had been heeded, Lloyd's would have been in a healthier condition to deal with later blows of fate. It was not to be. The Cromer report was kept under lock and key, and not sent even to the Names whose interests it was designed to protect. When Alan Smallbone, a former broker, asked his members' agent if he could see it as he had given evidence to the committee, he was told it was not available. He then wrote to the chairman of Lloyd's, who repeated the official line that the report was not for publication. When he remonstrated in person with a deputy chairman, pointing out that it was a settled point of English law that "no agent may conceal from his principal matters of interest to him," he was told that he was being impudent. Many of Cromer's recommendations were distinctly unfavourable to the big brokers and wealthy underwriters who dominated Lloyd's, so perhaps one should not be surprised that they decided that suppression was the wisest course. It was not a period of openness; moreover there was little understanding of the duty of care that an agent owes to his principal. Conflicts of interest were so endemic in the market that they were simply ignored.

In the long term the suppression of the Cromer report was very damaging, for it postponed much-needed reforms for a generation. Names continued to bear all the risk of losses, and they began to be milked of more and more of the profits which rightfully belonged to them. In the 1970s there was a rapid expansion of the role of members' agencies, which looked after the Names' personal affairs at Lloyd's, leaving managing agents to specialize in the management of syndicates. Both types of agent, however, took profit commission from the Names and, as intermediate levels of the market flourished, the Names' share of the profits diminished. In 1988, for example, the market made an overall loss of more than £500 million, but £124 million was paid to managing and members' agents in profit commission.

The conflict of interest between Names with unlimited liability and managing agencies with limited liability was identified by Cromer as a serious threat to the market's long-term future. The relationship between the Name and the agent, the report pointed out, was probably unique as a form of capitalist association: "The Name does not invest in Lloyd's, as does a shareholder in a company, but he does put his capital at risk in the anticipation of profit being earned thereon by the skill of the underwriter. Against these considerations, the Name is liable to the last penny of his possessions to meet underwriting losses. . . He is therefore accepting an unlimited liability without any control over the conduct of the business and can only withdraw from participation (profitable or unprofitable) after a protracted period."

The extraordinary degree of trust on which the market operated, Cromer noted, had lessons for both the Names and the professionals at Lloyd's: "We do not believe that a market will continue in existence indefinitely in a form wherein certain components of that market enjoy substantial and even growing earnings whilst simultaneously other equally essential components of the same market have been left to carry heavy losses. . . If a *sauve qui peut* attitude were to be pursued on the argument that the Names knew the risks they were running when they became members of Lloyd's, and anyhow there have been many years of profitable underwriting, the market would, in our opinion, in time disintegrate as capital was withdrawn . . . We feel that it would be a mistake to disregard the degree of bitterness felt by some outside Names called recently to draw heavily on their personal capital to meet underwriting losses whilst seemingly the earning power of underwriting agents and brokers was less affected by such losses."

The report pointed out that inevitably recent losses had caused Names to lose faith: "We think it would be a mistake to assume that this more critical attitude is a passing phase. Many Names are waiting to see what comes out of the present review of the organization of Lloyd's. Many have also made substantial losses which only a long series of profitable years will wipe out. In present conditions Names are likely to look for something akin to the relationship which would exist if they were shareholders in a company and expect at least the same degree of accountability and consideration as is generally extended today to the shareholder."

REFORM AND EXPANSION

At the time these warnings were ignored, but they came back to haunt Lloyd's a generation later. Ironically, the impact was the greater because in one important respect the report *was* implemented. The pressing need for new capacity led Cromer to recommend that the means requirements for membership should be reduced from £75,000 to £50,000. The amount which the Name had to deposit with Lloyd's was also reduced. Previously a deposit of £35,000 had allowed an external Name to underwrite £180,000 worth of risks—the amount of premium he could accept in any one year. In future the same deposit would underwrite £350,000, almost twice as much. Even laxer provisions were proposed for working Names. They did not have to meet a means test and, after depositing £3,000, could underwrite five times that amount. Lastly, a new class of "mini-Names" was allowed, who had to show wealth of only £37,500.

The consequence of these reforms was a sharp increase in membership which gathered pace throughout the 1970s as the market started to return steady profits. At the time of the completion of the Cromer report, there were just over 6,000 Names. Six years later the numbers had crept up to 7,700. By 1980 they had trebled to nearly 19,000, and at the end of the 1980s the membership peaked at 32,433.[2]

The new Names were very different from the old-style member of the 1950s with his 10,000 acres in Scotland, a couple of grouse moors, and a baronial home. In 1950, the wealth requirement of £75,000 was equivalent to almost £1 million in today's money. The £50,000 means test set by Cromer, even when increased a decade later to £100,000, was barely the price of a modest London flat whose value could be used to secure a bank guarantee in order to satisfy the requirement. Lloyd's had become affordable not just to the affluent middle classes but also to the aspiring owner of a corner shop. For thousands of potential members of the society, it proved to be a fatal temptation. George Aldrich, a retired pharmacist from Evesham, who scraped together the necessary £100,000 by means of a mortgage on his house and an insurance policy, was one of those who succumbed. He joined the Lime Street members' agency and was placed on a series of syndicates heavily exposed to asbestos, pollution, and catastrophe risks. A decade later, confronted by losses of more than £2 million, he has been forced to sell his house and faces a retirement of penury. "I was not given the information I should have been given," he says bitterly. "I feel we were cannon fodder."[3]

The explosive growth in Lloyd's membership in the 1970s and 1980s was the root of future troubles. It led to considerable over-capacity, and set off a cycle of rate-cutting that was to pave the way for the horrendous losses of the late 1980s. "With the benefit of hindsight, we made the most awful and crucial misjudgment," admits Michael Wade, former chairman of the leading stop loss broker, Holman Wade, now head of a company raising corporate capital for Lloyd's.[4] The large number of new Names also led to a profound change in the character and style of Lloyd's. In a small market it was possible to sustain the relationship of trust which was Lloyd's essential lubricant. Most people knew each other; they had gone to the same schools, married each others' cousins; the inter-relationships often went back generations. This self-enforcing discipline was bound to erode as the market expanded five-fold. Some of the new professionals were not prepared to play by the old rules, and Lloyd's soon found to its cost that it had no power to make them do so.

THE *SAVONITA* AFFAIR

One of the first signs that the old order was breaking down was a bitter market dispute between two brokers. In early December 1974, a fire broke out on the SS *Savonita* which had sailed from Savona, near Genoa, for the United States, with a cargo of more than 2,500 Fiat and Alfa Romeo sports cars on board. The *Savonita* turned back to its home port, where 301 of the most seriously damaged cars were offloaded and declared by marine surveyors to be "a constructive total loss." The damaged cars were then sold on an "as is, where is" basis to a Fiat main dealer in Naples, Signor Antonio Dotoli, at the knockdown price of 81 million lire, about 15 percent of their retail value. The Società Italiana Assicurazini Trasporti (SIAT), the main insurer, which had laid off part of the risk in the London market through the small broking firm of Pearson Webb Springbett (PWS), now sought to collect more than $700,000 on its reinsurance policy. It was a routine claim which in the normal course of business would have been paid without a murmur. "All these cars," confirmed SIAT, "appeared immediately and were indeed discharged also because their prosecution [sic] to the USA would not have been practical and economical." But this time there was a hitch. The chairman of PWS, Malcolm Pearson, who had married into the Agnelli family which controlled SIAT, had heard whispers that the *Savonita* claim was fraudulent. His suspicions increased when he was handed a message when visiting the Fiat office in Turin: *"301 vetture rimaste a Savona perchè molto danneggiate. Che fine hanno fatto? A chi sono state vendute? Rottamete? No. Sono state messe all' ASTA?"* ["The 301 cars left behind at Savona because they were damaged. How did they end up? Who were they sold to? Written off? No. Were they put up for sale at auction?"]

Malcolm Pearson inquired further and discovered that most of the "written off" cars, sold at near market prices by Signor Dotoli, were happily running round Italy. An Italian colleague of Pearson's bought one of the cars, which was in mint condition. He was asked to pay with two cheques, one made to Dotoli's firm for 560,000 lire ($560) which represented the official price for VAT purposes, and the other for two million lire, made out to another company. Armed with this information, Pearson advised the lead underwriter at Lloyd's, Roy Hill, not to pay the claim. The underwriters mounted their own investigation, sending out a loss adjuster, Bob Bishop, a former Fraud Squad detective. His investigation, which took many months, found enough evidence to persuade John Mathew QC, whom Pearson had consulted, that there were "positive indications of fraud" sufficient to render the claim invalid. Indeed counsel went further and said that Pearson would be acting improperly if he sought to persuade underwriters to pay such a claim knowing it to be fraudulent. The Bishop report pinpointed some disturbing aspects of this very rum Italian affair. The Naples car dealer, Signor Dotoli, admitted he had not tendered for the 301 "damaged" cars, but had "agreed" the price of 81 million lire. Three other tenders were submitted in what was meant to be an open bidding process. But one bid was made without the cars having been inspected and the other two "rival" bids were typed on the same typewriter. Eventually Dotoli's "agreed" bid equalled the highest of the three other bidders and he was awarded the contract.

At this point, Pearson went to see Sir Havelock Hudson, the chairman of Lloyd's, who advised him, not altogether helpfully, to "play with a straight bat." Soon afterwards SIAT, growing impatient with PWS, decided to pursue its claim through another much bigger Lloyd's broker, Willis Faber. A memorandum written to the leading underwriter Roy Hill by Willis Faber's deputy chairman, John Prentice, pointed out: "Very substantial issues are at stake in this claim. Willis Faber alone received last year from SIAT approaching £5 million of premium for the London market. If this claim is resisted or compromised, a great deal of this business must be put in jeopardy." Eventually the underwriters succumbed to the pressure and settled SIAT's claim, paying out nearly 100 percent. It was a typical market compromise. Lloyd's often took the view, even on claims which it suspected to be fraudulent, that it was better to reach a commercial settlement than risk disputing the claims. Proving fraud is no easy matter, and evidence sufficient to convince a court that a claim is bogus is rarely obtainable. Where the client was powerful and brought a great deal of business to the market, commercial pressures invariably carried the day.

Shortly after this, I was telephoned out of the blue by Malcolm Pearson who said I had been recommended to him as an independent-minded reporter. Was I interested in a tale of skulduggery and fraud? I pointed out that as political editor of the *Observer* I knew nothing about either insurance or Lloyd's, but he said that was no bar, and offered to show me his file of correspondence on *Savonita*. Pearson was by now playing for high stakes, but he clearly felt he had nothing more to lose. His resistance to the *Savonita* claim had lost him an important account, had strained his relations with the Agnelli family, and had cast a cloud over his broking career. Armed with his information, I went to see the new chairman of Lloyd's, Ian Findlay, and the chairman of Willis Faber, Ronald Taylor. Both were defensive and, though courteous, made it clear that they believed there was no public interest in this "minor market dispute." Ian Findlay said that the committee of Lloyd's had no right and no business to intervene in the day-to-day settlement of claims. It was a traditional restatement of the committee's *laissez-faire* attitude. Jonathan Aitken MP, who had been at Eton with Pearson, received much the same treatment when he raised the issue in Parliament. "The only thing necessary for the triumph of evil is for good men to do nothing," he pointed out. "In this case the underwriters could, and I believe should, have been protected from such pressures. Let us not forget in this *Savonita* affair small people did get hurt. A small insurance broker lost a lot of business; some small underwriters were pressured into paying out a lot of money to replace motor cars which are being driven around Italy in good condition; and a lot of small investors also may have had their savings whittled away by the alleged fraud."

The consequent publicity forced Lloyd's to appoint a full-scale inquiry composed of four members of the committee headed by a professional arbitrator, Clifford Clark. Their report, published after six months, did nothing to still the controversy. The findings were strongly critical of Pearson, who was said to have behaved "irrationally" by failing to act in the interests of his client. The report said that he should have either withdrawn from acting for SIAT or else pursued its claim with underwriters: "The Board deeply regrets that a client should be effectively deserted by his Lloyd's broker without explanation." If that might be thought a harsh judgment on a protracted dispute (it had lasted over three years), the summary dismissal of the advice given to Pearson by his counsel struck outsiders as odd. John Mathew QC had advised: "Mr. Pearson must have nothing whatsoever to do with the collecting of this claim, whatever may be the commercial consequences to his company, because by doing so he lays himself and his company open to charges of fraud." The inquiry, however, brushed aside this opinion as largely irrelevant to the broker's duty to its client: "It is noteworthy that the opinion is primarily concerned with the question of Pearson's legal and personal responsibilities as chairman of PWS rather than with PWS's responsibility as brokers."[5]

If the findings were controversial, the manner in which they were released to the public invited further debate. The committee, advised by the veteran libel solicitor Peter Carter-Ruck, made the report available to newspapers only on condition that they sign an indemnity acknowledging that "neither the board of inquiry nor the committee of Lloyd's will accept responsibility for the accuracy or otherwise of the report." There was universal condemnation of this procedure, apparently agreed because the committee had so little confidence in the inquiry's findings that they feared they might be sued for libel. Worse, Lloyd's appeared to be hopelessly complacent and out of touch. "The way in which Lloyd's of London has handled the *Savonita* affair," said the *Sunday Telegraph*, "has dealt its reputation the worst blow in living memory. Not to put too fine a point on it, Lloyd's has succeeded in making itself appear both incompetent and somewhat cowardly." There appears to be no satisfactory explanation of why Lloyd's exposed itself to this virulent criticism. Reports issued by professional disciplinary inquiries are likely to be protected by qualified privilege; the possibility of a libel action was therefore remote. Yet again, the market's professionals appeared to be living in another world. Looking back on the affair after a decade Malcolm Pearson, now Lord Pearson of Rannoch, said: "I think it demonstrates just what an incredibly closed shop Lloyd's was. It was completely out of touch with ordinary standards of fair play." A distinguished former underwriter, now a members' agent, while not disagreeing that Lloyd's mishandled the *Savonita* affair, believes that the inquiry was right to criticize Pearson's conduct: "He created a whirl of damaging publicity, using his friends in the press and in Parliament to damage Lloyd's and the London market, whereas an adequate level of professional competence would have solved the problem."[6]

There was an interesting sequel to *Savonita*. In 1981, the Italian Guardia di Finanzia pressed charges of conspiracy and fraud against seventeen of those involved, including the General Manager of SIAT, Giorgio Mitolo, his assistant, Enzo Rosina, the Naples Fiat dealer, Antonio Dotoli, and one of the marine surveyors, Captain Pietro Ferrigno. Three years later the charges were dismissed by the examining magistrate, Dr Paola Trovati, in Turin. Ironically, one of the bits of evidence that convinced the magistrate that there was no case was Lloyd's decision to pay the claim in full.

THE SASSE AFFAIR

The perception that Lloyd's was getting into deeper, uncharted waters was reinforced by the Sasse affair which soon afterwards confirmed Cromer's warning that external Names would no longer tolerate being treated as milch cows for bad underwriting. For the first time in Lloyd's history, a number of Names refused to pay their losses on the grounds that they could not be held liable for losses as a result of fraud. A fundamental rule of the market is that all business has to be conducted in the Room at Lloyd's by those who are authorized to do business in the market. But, as with all rules, there are exceptions. One of these exceptions, a binding authority known as a binder, which allowed American fire and other property risks to be underwritten on behalf of the Sasse syndicate by a third-party American broker, landed the 110 Names on syndicate 762 with huge losses.

At the centre of this debacle was F.H. Sasse, known as "Tim," whose promising results had attracted to his syndicate a group of distinguished Names ranging from Major the Hon. Sir Francis Legh, equerry to Queen Elizabeth, the Queen Mother, to the chairman of the Combined English Stores Group, Murray Gordon. Sasse was a fashionable underwriter, particularly among those who shared his love of horseracing. But his business methods were unconventional. Instead of taking small lines on risks led by other underwriters, he preferred to give binding authorities to brokers authorized to underwrite on his behalf. In effect he was lending his pen and the good name of a Lloyd's policy to a third party. This hands-off style produced large amounts of premium for little effort, but it also meant that the fortunes of the syndicate were in the hands of whoever produced the business.

The perils of such a course became apparent when John Newman, a broker from Brentnall Beard, secured Sasse's assent to underwrite a binder given to an expatriate Englishman, Dennis Harrison, working in Florida for Transworld Underwriters. The business that Harrison produced came mainly from a convicted insurance swindler, John Goepfert, who proceeded to stuff syndicate 762 with every dubious fire and theft risk on the East Coast. Within months, claims began to pour in. The premiums, however, did not. They had been systematically skimmed by Goepfert and his dubious associates.

Within two years the 110 Names on syndicate 762 were asked for larger and larger sums to meet the mounting losses. When one of the Names, Paddy Davies, who ran an international trading company, was advised that he faced losses of more than £250,000, he went to see the chairman of Lloyd's to appeal for help. He was told courteously that nothing could be done: "Bad luck, old boy. Wrong syndicate, bad luck."[7] It was typical of the laid-back attitude of the Lloyd's committee. Davies and his fellow Names consulted lawyers. They were advised that they had a good case to pursue, both against Lloyd's for failing in its duty to safeguard their interests, and against Sasse for negligent underwriting. The legal threats, combined with the Names' refusal to pay their losses, shook the old guard at Lloyd's. The first reaction of the committee was to issue writs against the Names, demanding the money they owed, but that only produced counter-writs and much unfavourable publicity. Only after months of expensive legal manoeuvring was a settlement thrashed out. The Names put up just over £6 million, an average loss of £80,000, but nearly treble that—more than £16 million—was met by Lloyd's as the price of the Names' dropping their legal actions.

For all concerned it had been an expensive affair. Both Tim Sasse and John Newman were banned for life by Lloyd's from conducting any further business. Perhaps the chief casualty was faith in the old customs and ways of controlling the market. The affair had disclosed an appalling lack of professionalism which only optimists believed was confined to one rogue syndicate. No less important, it showed that Names were no longer prepared to pay up whatever the circumstances. The Sasse affair proved that it paid to litigate. The bonds of trust were loosening, while Lloyd's ability to enforce its own rules was more and more in doubt.

CHRISTOPHER MORAN

The case that made this point beyond argument was that of Christopher Moran. A young man in a hurry, he had achieved spectacular success after leaving school at sixteen with a distinction in O-level maths, to work for an aviation broker, Price Forbes. In ten years he built up his own broking company which went public with profits of more than £1 million a year. The owner of a Scottish estate, three Rolls-Royces and a Lagonda, as well as Crosby Hall, a London medieval manor with the best riverside views in the city, Moran now has all the trappings of wealth and respectability. But he has never believed in observing custom and practice, let alone rules. As a

result he was in constant trouble. At one point he complained cheekily that
the chairman of Lloyd's was preventing him from parking his Rolls-Royce
outside the main entrance. In 1980 he lost a libel action against the *Daily
Telegraph*, which had criticized a complicated network of reinsurance transactions in which he had been involved. Eighteen months later he and a
leading underwriter, Derek Walker, were acquitted at the Old Bailey of
insurance fraud. Moran's problems were not over. A Lloyd's arbitration
panel headed by a former chairman, Paul Dixey, found that he had exposed
a syndicate controlled by his managing agency company "to unnecessary
and unacceptable financial risk" through arranging reinsurances for the
syndicate disproportionate to its income. It also found that he had taken an
improper profit commission from the syndicate, and had concealed from the
syndicate's auditors the amount of reinsurances that had been bought. For
these offences, the panel recommended that he should be expelled for
discreditable conduct together with the underwriter of syndicate 566, Reid
Wilson. This sanction could be applied only under the archaic Lloyd's Act
of 1871 which required a four-fifths majority at a general meeting after a
finding of guilt by two arbitrators, one appointed by the committee and one
by the defendant. Eventually Lloyd's went through all these procedures, and
on 27 October 1982 Moran, protesting loudly, became the first man in the
history of the market to be thrown out under these rules. The vote, after nearly
four hours of debate, was 1,708 in favour of expulsion to 113 against. The
motion to expel the underwriter Reid Wilson failed to gain the necessary
two-thirds majority. Moran, who was subsequently fined $2 million by the
US Securities and Exchange Commission for insider trading, was defiant
after his expulsion: "I have a very big and prosperous company," he said.
"All my business is done outside Lloyd's. It just means that I am no longer
a member of the club, but I am not worried about it." Lloyd's however *was*
worried. Whatever prior doubt there may have been, the Moran case proved
that it was no longer practicable to run a modern international market with
regulations fashioned in the nineteenth century.

   In 1979 Lloyd's asked Sir Henry Fisher, a former High Court judge
who had become warden of Wolfson College, Oxford, to head an inquiry into
self-regulation of the market. Sir Henry was assisted by a carefully selected
group. There were two underwriters, Gordon Hutton and Bruce Gray, representing the marine and non-marine markets, an underwriting agent and
former member of the Lloyd's committee, Thomas Langton, a broker,
Norman Frizzell, and two distinguished outsiders: David Watt, director of

the Royal Institute of International Affairs, and a merchant banker, Robin Broadley of Barings.[8]

The committee's terms of reference made it clear that Fisher, unlike Cromer, was expected to stay within a tight brief. It was not to be an open-ended inquiry into the practices of the market, let alone an examination of whether self-regulation was the right course for Lloyd's. That was taken for granted. "I cannot really believe," said the chairman, Ian Findlay, "the time has come when Lloyd's, as a society of underwriters and as an insurance market, needs a governing body equipped with, and ready to use, ever more draconian powers in the maintenance of law and order." He warned that if it ever came to the point "where the people at Lloyd's had to be dragooned, policed and watched at every turn; if it really came to the point where one expected good faith, honesty and decency to be the exception rather than the rule, then one might well wonder whether it was worth carrying on at all." The Fisher report, published in May 1980, was short on analysis and legalistic in tone, simply stating: "We have no doubt that Lloyd's would be best served by a properly conducted system of self-regulation."

Fisher's principal recommendation was that a new Lloyd's Act should replace the old committee with a more broadly based council, charged with regulating the market. The sixteen working members of the new council would be in a majority, but would be balanced by eight external Names elected by postal ballot and three lay members whose nomination would be approved by the governor of the Bank of England. The defects of the 1871 Act would be remedied by giving the new council sweeping powers of inquiry and discipline over the actions of brokers, agents and underwriters. Day to day executive control of the market would be exercised by a committee of the sixteen working members of the council elected by their peers. All this went uncontested, but one reform proposed by Fisher caused controversy. This was that brokers should be required to divest themselves of their ownership of managing agencies. Cromer had already pointed out that duality of ownership—nearly three-quarters of the syndicates were broker controlled—led to "conflicts of interest which cannot be ignored." His recommendation that brokers should "reduce their involvement in underwriting" had been brushed aside. The Fisher committee, though divided, echoed Cromer's view that the potential conflict of interest in this relationship was unacceptable: "We have discussed this problem at length and the majority of us have reached the conclusion that divestment should be enforced and the formation of such links prohibited for the future."

Fisher's arguments on divestment carried the day when the new Lloyd's Act was debated by Parliament in 1981-82. Brokers were required to divest themselves of their interests in managing agencies. But other areas of reform were left untouched. The Fisher report was sharp on potential conflicts of interest which affected policy-holders; it was less forceful on those which affected Names. Significantly, the report failed to tackle the issue of whether managing agents, who controlled syndicates, should be allowed also to own members' agencies. This dual ownership was bound to create problems. If members' agents were not independent but controlled by managing agents, there was an obvious attraction for them to put Names only on syndicates which they themselves owned, irrespective of their performance. The Fisher report was also weak on the need to provide more information to Names about syndicate results and the degree of accountability that Names should expect from managing and members' agents. Lastly, it said nothing about the practice of agents creaming off substantial profit commissions from individual Names, even in cases where they had an overall loss on their underwriting.

Lloyd's first chief executive, Ian Hay Davison, argued a decade later that Fisher had shot the wrong horse. Instead of requiring *divestment* by brokers of managing agencies, where the conflict of interest was more potential than actual, Fisher should have required the *divorce* of managing agents from members' agencies. The House of Commons committee, chaired by Michael Meacher, Labour MP for Oldham West, initially declared itself in favour of divorce but, under pressure from Lloyd's, gave way. If such a reform had been implemented, many Names placed by members' agents on very high-risk and other unsuitable syndicates which were owned by an associated managing agency might have been saved considerable grief. At the time Lloyd's had other worries. No sooner had Parliament legislated the Fisher reforms than Names discovered that the market was engulfed in an even worse scandal.

5

The Roulette Wheel
Spins Faster

"It's human nature to get greedier and greedier and greedier."
Ian Posgate, for a time Lloyd's star underwriter

"I am totally ashamed of what some members of the society
got up to in the early 1980s."
David Coleridge, chairman of Lloyd's

The 1970s were years of high returns at Lloyd's but also high taxation. The best performing syndicates regularly returned profits of 20 percent and more. Underwriters were riding high, but were nervous of the future. In particular they wanted to protect themselves and their Names against both catastrophes and the depredations of the Inland Revenue. But reinsurance, the means by which a syndicate lays off its exposure to risk just as a bookmaker lays off heavy bets on the favourite, was expensive. A series of devastating hurricanes: Carol in 1954, Betsy in 1965, and Camille in 1969, had caused serious losses. Reinsurers, with fingers so recently burnt, were unwilling to be accommodating.

The problem was made worse by the approach taken by the Inland Revenue towards syndicates which appeared to be diminishing their taxable profits by excessive reserving. The ingenious, if somewhat artificial, solution that underwriters came up with was to invest their surplus profits in offshore funding policies, popularly known as "roll-overs." Though these masqueraded as a form of reinsurance, in reality they involved no risk. The reinsurer paid out claims only to the extent of the original investment in the funding policy. If there were no claims the premium, together with any interest owing, was rolled over to the following year. Thus in good times the value of such policies grew fast, the purpose being to provide a nest egg in case of bad times.

The advantage of roll-overs as a tax-free additional reserve was so great that most of the largest Lloyd's syndicates—encouraged by eminent firms of accountants—embraced them with enthusiasm. By the late 1970s, their combined value was estimated at more than £100 million. Nearly all the members of the committee of Lloyd's were involved in these practices and so, unsuspectingly, were the vast majority of Names. In an era of tough exchange control regulations, when Labour chancellors of the exchequer were intent on taxing the rich until the pips squeaked, the attractions of warehousing profits against a future rainy day in a secure offshore fund were undeniable. Why pay out profits to Names which were then taxed at 98p on every pound?

The borderline between tax avoidance, which is legal, and tax evasion, which is not, is narrow. Most, if not all, roll-overs crossed the divide, which is why the Inland Revenue was kept in the dark. Nor were the Names any the wiser. Underwriters, mindful of the advantages of secrecy, felt no obligation to include any mention of their offshore funds in their syndicates' accounts. That was convenient, for in some cases the premiums were diverted to reinsurance companies owned and controlled by the underwriter, despite the conflict of interest involved in such arrangements. The fact that part of the premiums occasionally ended up in the underwriter's own pocket or that of his mistress was predictable, given the secrecy surrounding these illicit deals. As for the auditors, they either did not know, or did not want to know, about the illegality of such arrangements. Lloyd's first chief executive, Ian Hay Davison, former managing partner of Arthur Andersen, was to note later: "Accountants were at the heart of the misconduct at Lloyd's." Underwriters and brokers, he pointed out, may have taken the money, but in each case an accountant planned the arrangements and failed to warn of their illegality.[1] When the Inland Revenue finally caught up with what was happening in the early 1980s, it forced Lloyd's to pay £43 million in settlement of this massive tax scam. No accountant was ever brought to book, because the profession's disciplinary body decided, when it finally got round to the issue a decade later, that too much time had elapsed to permit a fair hearing.

A taint of illegality soon leads to worse. The buccaneering climate of the market in the 1970s tempted a few of its more enterprising members onto wilder shores. From breaking exchange control regulations and evading tax, it was a relatively short step to criminal schemes designed to cream off the rewards of this financial enterprise. After all who was to know? The Names were happy so long as profits continued, the Inland Revenue was none the wiser, and the auditors were careful not to ask too many questions. A variety of skims thus ensued, ranging from direct plundering of premiums to the marginally less flagrant diversion of interest owed to the Names.

THE AMERICANS MOVE IN

The first sign of how crooked parts of Lloyd's had become came at the beginning of 1982 when the giant American broker, Alexander & Alexander, acquired the Howden Group, a fast growing Lloyd's broker. At the time it seemed a bargain at $300 million. American brokers traditionally had close ties with Lloyd's, but had been restricted to holdings of less than 20 percent. That rule proved unsustainable in the modern era of international broking. In 1980 Marsh & McLennan, one of the American giants, took over the Bowring Group, setting a pattern for future transatlantic acquisitions. Then Marsh's great rival, Alexander & Alexander, started looking. Its eyes fell on Howden, which had grown phenomenally in the 1970s at an annual compound rate of 40 percent with profits to match. Howden's chairman was Ken Grob, a hard-driving entrepreneur with dual British-Swiss nationality, who had started life as a junior insurance clerk.

Grob and his fellow directors had a reputation for being big spenders as well as big earners. Visitors to the company's office in Billiter Street, known as the "hanging gardens of Howden" because of the profusion of greenery, were lavishly entertained. Silver goblets filled to the brim with Dom Perignon champagne, and buckets of the finest Russian caviar were the style. Elegant dinner parties were held in Grob's palatial Nash house in Regent's Park. Every summer he threw a party for 500 delegates to the annual Monte Carlo reinsurance conference. It was held at the Villa Olivula, his pink Palladian-style mansion overlooking Cap Ferrat, guarded by a fearsome pack of Doberman Pinschers. Back in England, there were racehorses, boxes at

Ascot and Covent Garden, a collection of Impressionist paintings, a couple of yachts, and a fleet of Ferraris and Rolls-Royces. It was life in the fastest of fast lanes for a twentieth-century merchant prince. "Our invitations were regarded as an honour," the "Grobfather" liked to recall.[2]

Ken Grob ran the Howden Group with three close partners, Ronald Comery, Jack Carpenter and Allan Page. A fourth colleague was Ian Posgate, Howden's star underwriter, whose syndicates brought large amounts of reinsurance business to the broker. Dubbed "Goldfinger" in tribute to the spectacular profits he earned for his Names, Posgate was an extraordinary character. A ruthless, driven competitor, he was so successful that at his peak he was writing for a quarter of the entire market. Names fought to be on his syndicates—they were so profitable. Posgate was much sharper than his rivals and, to their fury, let them know it. His methods were, he claimed, simple: "I never knew much about analysing insurance risks. I just made a book. If claims came in, the premiums went up. No claims, the premiums went down. I was allowed to be a bookmaker on a huge scale, autocratic, absolutely outrageous."

Despite his brilliance as an underwriter, Posgate was incapable of keeping to any set of rules. The *Spectator*, which dubbed him Goldfinger, described him memorably: "The cut of his three-piece, double-breasted suit suggests a backwoods Conservative MP of the old school. The indiscreet, rascally charm of his conversation is redolent of a rather naughty character from an early Simon Raven novel—the sort you can't help but like." Posgate's zest for more and more premium—he often wrote huge lines of 50 percent or more—led him to undercut rates and take on risks far in excess of permitted premium limits, a serious breach of market regulations.

The committee of Lloyd's became so exasperated that after one particularly flagrant episode in the early 1970s, when he borrowed from his Names' premium funds to finance a personal house purchase, they made it a condition that he could continue to work in the market only if his work was supervised. An official notice posted in the Room on 27 November 1970, made his fall public: "As from 1st January 1971, in accordance with the directions of the Committee of Lloyd's, Mr. Ian Richard Posgate will cease to act as an Underwriting Agent at Lloyd's and will cease to be a shareholder in or Director of any Company or a Partner in any Firm acting as an Underwriting Agent at Lloyd's. Mr. Posgate has been severely censured by the Committee for the way in which he has conducted the affairs of Syndicate 126/129. Mr. Posgate has given an undertaking not to underwrite for more than one Managing Agent, who would be approved by the Committee of Lloyd's. Negotiations are proceeding which may enable a Managing Agent approved by the Committee to commence a new Syndicate as from the 1st January 1971 with Mr. Posgate as the Active Underwriter."

The managing agent appointed to supervise Posgate was Ken Grob, in retrospect hardly the soundest choice. At the time the flamboyant underwriter and the star Howden broker formed a dazzling team, which appeared to have an ability to conjure up larger and larger profits. Their performance bewitched Alexander & Alexander. Its chairman, Jack Bogardus, had first courted another Lloyd's broker, Sedgwick, but when merger talks broke down he turned his attention to Howden. Grob describes what happened: "I was on holiday in the South of France when Bogardus phoned me and said: 'Would you like to start talking again?' and I said: 'Of course, we always like to talk.'" Posgate later described the progress of this courtship to the Department of Trade inspectors: "He was played like a salmon on the Tay . . . Mr. Grob is immoral and a crook. Mr. Bogardus I think is a provincial and did not know what he was doing. It was a natural fit between the two of them."

Not even Yankee provincials, however, like being taken to the cleaners. Following the acquisition, a fair value audit was carried out by the accountants Deloitte's. During this process a young partner, Tony Shearer, noticed that several large reinsurances had been placed by a Howden subsidiary, Sphere Drake, with Southern International Re (SIR) based in Panama. When a routine check made by Deloitte's affiliate company in Panama revealed that SIR was a property company unauthorized to conduct reinsurance, alarm bells rang. Deloitte's soon discovered that more than $55 million was missing from Howden, having been diverted from its insurance syndicates via a series of reinsurances to companies controlled by Grob and his colleagues.

A large part of these diverted funds was used to dress up the accounts— Howden was a public quoted company. Its profits had peaked at £21.36 million in 1977, but had slumped the following year, causing consternation in the City. Other millions were used to provide "black box" bonus payments to Howden employees as a form of golden handcuffs. Nor did the Gang of Four neglect their own interests. Nearly $9 million was diverted to Liechtenstein trust funds, known as anstalts, controlled by Grob and his associates, with dummy names to deter inquirers. Grob's was called "Bloomers," Comery's "Blissful," Page's "Karoli," Carpenter's "Skyair" and Posgate's "Hereford."

The secret trust funds were used principally to funnel payments for the purchase of a Swiss private bank, the Banque du Rhône et de la Tamise (BRT). Originally owned by Howden, it was purchased in 1981 by an anonymous "syndicate of Swiss investors." Unknown to the Howden board, this was Grob and his fellow members of the Gang of Four. Quite why Grob wanted to own a bank has never been explained, though Posgate did once mutter respectfully, when asked: "A Swiss bank is a Swiss bank." Apart from the bank, there were other spoils to be divided. Grob and Posgate loved works of art. Between 1978 and 1982, the Panamanian companies controlled by the Gang of Four bought eleven paintings and a Henry Moore sculpture with syndicate funds. One of the more valuable pictures was Pissarro's "Route du forde de l'hermitage," worth $100,000, which, Posgate claimed, was sent unsolicited to his country house, Badgemore Grange near Henley. At his London home there were three more fine paintings "on loan": a Picasso, a Monet and a Fantin-Latour.

The Department of Trade inspectors were later to take a jaundiced view of these works of art, saying that Posgate saw them as a reward for using Howden as a broker for nearly three-quarters of his syndicate's reinsurance business. Grob, who clearly liked to keep a hold on his star underwriter, stored a document in his safe for later use. It was a scribbled note from Posgate indicating that he hoped Grob would reward him for placing his reinsurances with a Howden broker: "Ken, I have just given a firm order for 100 percent of my three bottom layers to Alan Williams [a Howden broker]. I think the brokerage is about £450,000 . . . Can I have a picture?" The word "picture" was later crossed out and replaced by "car." As Posgate already had a large company car, the assumption must be that he had his eye on a particularly luxurious model.[3]

For a brief period it seemed that the lid might be kept on the scandal. Alexander & Alexander were no more anxious to reveal to their shareholders that they had been massively cheated than the Gang of Four were to have the authorities know what they had been up to. On 14 August, three months after Deloitte's discovery of a black hole in the accounts, the two sides reached a confidential agreement under which Grob and his associates were to hand over the ownership of the Banque du Rhône, worth nearly $14 million, pictures valued at more than $2 million, the Villa Olivula, worth $3 million, and various amounts of cash and other illegally acquired booty, in return for a guarantee that no legal action would be taken against them. Within days this agreement began to fray. The $29 million in assets that the Gang of Four agreed to hand over proved to be well short of what was needed to meet the black hole of missing funds, estimated to be at least $55 million. There followed frantic negotiations between lawyers on both sides on a possible interim agreement.

The Gang of Four's bid to avoid publicity finally foundered on the objections of Roderick Hills, the chairman of Alexander & Alexander's audit committee. A former chairman of the US Securities and Exchange Commission, Hills insisted that disclosure would have to be made. On 1 September, a statement made public by the SEC tersely stated the case against Grob and his fellow directors: "Howden had entered into some reinsurance transactions with companies which were owned and controlled on an undisclosed basis by four persons who have now ceased to be officers or directors of Howden." That bomb was followed by an even more explosive SEC document published on 20 September: "The suit against the four former officers and Mr. Posgate alleges that, through a series of Liechtenstein trusts and Panamanian corporations, the four former officers and directors named above own Southern International Re Company SA (SIR), a Panamanian company not licensed to engage in the reinsurance business and that they owned Southern Reinsurance AG (SRAG), a Liechtenstein corporation engaged in the insurance business. Also, the four individuals along with Mr. Posgate owned interests in New Southern RE Company SA (NSR), a Panamanian corporation. Beginning as early as 1975, funds totalling approximately $55 million including payments purporting to be insurance and reinsurance premiums from Howden insurance companies and quota share premiums from Howden-managed insurance underwriting syndicates of which Mr. Posgate was the underwriter, were paid to SRAG and SIR, with SIR paying approximately $7 million to NSR. The monies taken in by these entities were used in part for the personal benefit of the four individuals and Mr. Posgate. The benefits included works of art received by Mr. Posgate."[4]

This damning public statement, headlined by newspapers around the world, left the authorities no choice. The Department of Trade announced an inquiry, Lloyd's suspended Grob and his fellow directors, and the Fraud Squad moved in. "I am totally innocent. I have been stabbed in the back. It's the dirtiest fight I have ever been in," said Posgate. Grob was more discreet. He moved out of the Villa Olivula and disappeared into the French countryside. Later he sought to explain the innocence of his actions to the Department of Trade inspectors: "We decided that we would do what we always did when we had a problem, that is to say, use the reinsurance route. We had been solving our own and other people's problems for years with reinsurance." The next three years were spent in prolonged investigations, as bit by bit the highly complex dealings of Howden and its former directors were unravelled.

In the summer of 1985, a Lloyd's disciplinary committee announced that Grob, Comery and Carpenter had been expelled from the market. Charges against Allan Page, the financial director, were adjourned indefinitely because of his ill-health. Posgate, the great survivor, was recommended for expulsion, but after an appeal his sentence was reduced to six months' suspension. The main findings against Grob and his co-directors was that they had conspired to buy the Banque du Rhône using money which did not belong to them. They had also dishonestly capitalized Southern International Re (SIR) with misappropriated funds, and falsified the Alexander Howden Group's accounts. The disciplinary committee did not find that Posgate's part in this conspiracy had been proved, but it did find that he had failed to disclose his interest in the Banque du Rhône and that he had realized that his 10 percent interest in the bank as well as a Pissarro painting had been given to him to influence his underwriting judgment. He was therefore found guilty of discreditable conduct.

After another four years of investigation by the Director of Public Prosecutions, Posgate and Grob were brought to justice at Southwark Crown Court. By the time of the trial they were alone in the dock. Ronald Comery had died in a car crash, Allan Page was too ill to attend, and Howden's deputy chairman, Jack Carpenter, had also succumbed to ill health. After a trial lasting fifteen weeks the jury, who were apparently lost in the complexity of the case, returned not guilty verdicts on all the charges. Posgate was cleared of conspiring to steal millions of pounds from his Names, and Grob was acquitted of sixteen charges of theft. Posgate said he felt "vindicated," while Grob praised the virtues and fairmindedness of the British court. It was a stunning reverse for the Serious Fraud Office.[5] The legal authorities, however, had the last word. When the Department of Trade inspectors finally issued their report on the Howden affair in 1990, they had this to say about the Gang of Four: "When a number of intelligent and ingenious individuals in the most senior positions, but bereft of commercial morality and intent on personal gain, set out together to rob and deceive, it is extremely difficult to ensure that they will be deterred or exposed before too much damage is caused."

Looking back on the affair, Ian Posgate has few regrets. Though clearly frustrated at being exiled from the market, he says he has little to apologize for: "In business I believe in dog-eat-dog, the survival of the fittest, not protection of the weakest. . . The powers that be said that good business should subsidize bad across the market. But I wanted 100 percent good business and I cut rates to get it."[6] The run-off of his syndicates 126/129 has, however, led to spectacular losses, leaving his "Goldfinger" reputation more than a little tarnished. Posgate likes to claim that it was his skill in cutting the throats of rival underwriters that led to his downfall, but he could never resist the temptation to cut corners. As he says: "It's human nature to get greedier and greedier and greedier."

THE SCANDAL WIDENS

Lloyd's was to find to its horror that this, the most serious scandal in its history, went still wider. While Deloitte's investigators were poring over Howden's accounts, they came across some odd-looking quota share reinsurances placed by the broker on behalf of PCW underwriting syndicates. Quota share is a form of reinsurance used to lay off part of an underwriter's account. For example, an underwriter will cede 5 percent of his account to a reinsurer who will receive 5 percent of all premiums and pay the same percentage of claims on that class of risk. In return he will receive a 5 percent share of any profits. This is meant to be a hands-off transaction. The PCW quota shares, however, were not just unusually profitable; they had been placed with companies secretly owned by PCW. Tony Shearer of Deloitte's was so concerned by this finding that he alerted the head of Lloyd's audit department, Ken Randall. Two weeks later suspicion had hardened into conviction. On Friday 29 October 1982, the Bank of England and Lloyd's were informed that a massive fraud appeared to have been perpetrated.

The PCW syndicates had been set up in the mid-1960s by Peter Cameron-Webb, who had been a deputy underwriter with the Janson Green underwriting agency. The agency was headed by Toby Green, but after his death in March 1966 his son Peter inherited the chairmanship. Cameron-Webb left to set up his own agency and was joined by Peter Dixon, who had been the financial director of Janson Green. The two men rapidly made their mark. Cameron-Webb, a good-looking charmer, had a weakness for fast horses and even faster women. He also had a reputation for making a lot of money for his Names. Dixon, a qualified chartered accountant, ran the business with cool efficiency. Within the market they were regarded as men with a future, heading desirable and profitable syndicates. In 1973 the agency was bought by Minet, a leading Lloyd's broker, whose chairman John Wallrock, a bluff former merchant navy captain, became a director of PCW.

These three men were summoned by the committee of Lloyd's on Monday 1 November 1982 to provide answers to the riddle of the quota share policies. Peter Cameron-Webb was abroad, so it was left to Dixon and Wallrock to attempt to explain the unexplainable. Dixon was immediately suspended from all his directorships. Wallrock, who continued to protest his innocence, spent the next two days seeking to persuade the Department of Trade that a formal inquiry was unnecessary. His efforts were in vain; within weeks Wallrock resigned his directorships of Minet and PCW, admitting that he had taken part in a reinsurance scheme arranged by Cameron-Webb from which he had benefited.

Three days later the Department of Trade announced an investigation into the affairs of Minet and its subsidiary, PCW. The committee of Lloyd's appointed Peter Millett QC and Nigel Holland from Ernst & Whinney to conduct a separate but parallel inquiry. For the next three years, teams of accountants sought to unravel the extraordinarily complex web of offshore trusts, involving 150 companies in seven countries from Liechtenstein to Gibraltar. These had been used to divert more than $50 million into the pockets of Cameron-Webb, Dixon, Wallrock, and their friends and associates.[7]

Millions were paid out by PCW syndicates in quota share reinsurances to offshore companies controlled by Cameron-Webb and Dixon in Guernsey, the Isle of Man and Switzerland. Many more millions were diverted via "rollers," which were used to finance loans to Cameron-Webb, Dixon and their relations. And another $100 million went to fund excess loss policies. Asked by the Department of Trade inspector about the propriety of these policies, Cameron-Webb replied: "Let's just say this: that in doing the accounts for all the syndicates we always made a decision as to what profit we wanted to pay on all the syndicates, not just the babies. If that required a return from intermediate funds, such return was organized on whatever years that might have occurred. On those years where sufficient profit had been made it was left, and those years where we didn't really want to pay out as much profit as that, we organized the reinsurance to close to produce those figures that we wanted to get to."

Just how corrupt this was is revealed by the Department of Trade's report. In November 1981 a PCW underwriter, Ian Agnew, was called in by Cameron-Webb and Dixon. They explained that they were concerned that the six senior underwriters in the agency were paid less than the going rate.

To remedy this, they told him, they had devised a method of increasing remuneration for key individuals: rather than pay increased salaries, which would merely add to syndicate expenses and be subject to tax, they proposed to take a slice out of a special 5 percent quota share reinsurance from the syndicates. The proceeds would be paid via a Gibraltarian company controlled by Cameron-Webb. Though Agnew was at first delighted that his pay was to increase, he was dismayed when he heard the details. He calculated that after five years each of the six participants in the scheme would be receiving £250,000 a year tax free, a sum so disproportionate to the original intention that it could not be justified.

In January 1982 Agnew asked Dixon for a meeting with the other participants, at which he voiced his objections. How could it be proper, he asked, for the Names' trust funds to be used in this way without their knowledge or consent? It was not a pleasant meeting. Agnew later recalled: "One of the points I made was that the premium trust funds belonged to the Names; that many of the Names on the syndicates were personal friends of theirs; and if the scheme was ever to be found out and made public, how would they ever be able to look these friends in the face again, knowing that they had pretty well stolen directly from their own friends?" Dixon was not prepared to discuss the scheme's merits, and would say only that Agnew's figures were wrong and the proposed profit shares were not unreasonable. But at the end of the meeting he said that, as the participants were not all of one mind, it could not proceed.

Another method used to milk the PCW Names was the creation of parallel smaller syndicates, known as "baby syndicates," which were used to skim off the most profitable business from the main syndicates. Though not all baby syndicates were crooked, it was a device widely used during this era of Lloyd's, by which market insiders enriched their friends and relations. But Cameron-Webb and Dixon went much further. They spawned two babies, the 954 marine syndicate and the 986 non-marine syndicate, for the benefit of themselves and their immediate associates. Each had only seven Names, and they were so profitable that various devices had to be deployed to divert part of their premiums offshore. The declared profits of the two syndicates averaged nearly 50 percent of premium income during the whole of the 1970s, twice that of the main syndicates. But the actual profits were more than 100 percent, as a result of what the DTI inspectors called "a systematic embezzlement of the funds of the main syndicates."

The embarrassingly high profits of the two baby syndicates had to be artificially reduced to avoid passing the benefits to the Inland Revenue. One favoured device was a "tonner" policy, in essence a straight gamble in which the baby syndicate was bound to lose. Tonners were originally an exotic type of excess loss policy; an underwriter wishing to guard against some remote possibility, say the loss of a hundred wide-body jet aeroplanes in a year, could take out a policy guarding against such a series of disasters. But they soon evolved into a form of gambling by which an underwriter would take on a fanciful bet, for example that 500 ships of more than 500 tons would be sunk in a year. Later they evolved into a crooked way of shunting profits from one syndicate to another. In PCW's case, syndicate 954 acted as the reinsurer of Regal, a Guernsey company controlled by Dixon and Cameron-Webb. Twelve "tonner" policies were placed. In each case the number of ships or aircraft which had to be lost before a claim was paid was fixed so low that a loss was inevitable. Nearly $2 million was siphoned out of the baby syndicate by these crude means.

Where did the cascading millions diverted from the syndicates' funds go? The DTI report, which concluded that Cameron-Webb and Dixon were guilty of "systematic, dishonest and cynical plunder," lists an extraordinarily diverse range of their activities and playthings, from yachts and diamonds to villas in the South of France and executive jets. Cameron-Webb bought two large boats, the *Nerine* in 1974, which cost $705,600, and the *N2* in 1977, which swallowed up another $2 million of money diverted from his syndicates. For his third wife, Mrs. Elizabeth Funk, he bought a house on Long Island for $1,250,000, and he paid $250,000 for an extension to her parents' home. He was also generous to his new brother-in-law, supporting his boat-building business in the South of France with a payment of $607,000. And there was a small shareholding in the Banque du Rhône—$202,000, and $333,000 for running a Hawker 125 executive jet. In all, Cameron-Webb's benefits illicitly diverted from syndicate funds amounted to more than $11 million, none of which has been recovered. A further $8 million dollars in assets was eventually recovered.

Peter Dixon also bought a boat, the *Aile Blanche*, which cost him $428,400 plus $1.5 million in running costs, expenses and repairs. Properties in Portugal, Spain, the United States, and a luxury villa at Cap Ferrat in the South of France cost another $4.8 million. He was generous to his mother-in-law, paying off her mortgage and buying her a new house at a cost of $290,000. In addition, she received $161,897 described in the syndicates' accounts as "consultancy fees and expenses." Altogether Dixon's benefits, also illegally diverted, amounted to more than $12 million, of which about $3.5 million was eventually recovered.

Other even more exotic ventures were financed by PCW's syndicates' funds. Dixon and Cameron-Webb invested $3 million in a film company, Shere Productions, whose main claim to fame was a pornographic film, *Let's Do It*, later renamed *Anyone for Sex*. It also made *The Last Horror Film*. Neither made any money at the box office. Then there was a venture to manufacture and sell an orange juice called Sierra, produced in Spain and the South of France. This folded with a loss of nearly $1.5 million. In Holland a company called Techno was founded. It specialized in developing and exploiting new synthetic materials, but it also lost money, and was sold.

The most blatant operation was a bonus scheme operated by Peter Dixon from 1976 with money taken from an account at the Banque du Rhône's branch in London. Varying amounts of cash, ranging from $17,000 to $135,000, were distributed in plain brown envelopes about six times a year to Cameron-Webb and other close associates. Altogether $3 million was handed over in this way. Quite why Dixon and Cameron-Webb were in such continual need of money is unclear. Their basic salaries in 1980 alone amounted to more than $125,000, and that was dwarfed by the profits of their Lloyd's syndicates. Dixon also had the use of three cars: a Rolls-Royce, a Ferrari and a BMW; Cameron-Webb had a Mercedes, a Daimler, and other limousines for his personal use. In addition both had large personal staffs, paid for by the syndicates at a cost of $84,000 a year. These included three gardeners and a chef working for Dixon, and a chauffeur, a yacht captain and a housekeeper for Cameron-Webb. "Why he did it, I just don't know," said the second Mrs. Cameron-Webb. "We had enough, quite enough. A Rolls, an Aston Martin, a mansion in Surrey, a flat in town. But he just wanted more."[8]

When Cameron-Webb was asked by the Lloyd's inquiry how he could justify seeking additional cash benefits for himself, he said he felt that he and Dixon were entitled to bonus payments of at least £250,000 a year tax free. In their report, the Department of Trade inspectors disagreed: Cameron-Webb and Dixon, they said, were "motivated not by any wish to benefit the syndicates for whose well-being they were responsible, but by a desire to achieve and maintain an extravagant lifestyle and to provide lavish benefits to their friends and associates at other people's expense." They added: "We can find no mitigating circumstances to excuse or condone the systematic, dishonest and cynical plunder of the Names' premium over such a period of time and on such a scale."

A Lloyd's disciplinary committee fined Dixon £1 million and expelled him from the market, but could take no action against Cameron-Webb because he had resigned before proceedings could be instituted. Neither of the two men was brought to court to answer the serious charges against them. On 22 December 1988, the Serious Fraud Office announced that warrants for the arrest of Dixon and Cameron-Webb had finally been issued. By then both men were living in the United States and could not be extradited because the offences had occurred more than five years earlier. The Serious Fraud Office blamed the delay in bringing charges on the failure of the Swiss banks to cooperate: "Since 1982 the prosecuting authorities have been seeking evidence from Switzerland. The Swiss authorities have experienced difficulties in meeting requests for certain further important documentary evidence."

This excuse for inaction was not accepted by the Department of Trade inspectors, Stewart Boyd QC and Peter DuBuisson. They tartly observed in the final paragraphs of their report, published in January 1990, that seven years previously they had submitted information to the Secretary of State for Trade indicating that a criminal offence had been committed. Lloyd's blamed the government and the Director of Public Prosecutions for having let it down. Its chief executive, Ian Hay Davison, said the failure to press charges was "an inexcusable lapse by the authorities, which had done great harm to the City." To understand why criminal charges were not pressed, one almost certainly has to seek answers right at the top. Mrs. Thatcher, then prime minister, let it be known that it was probably best if the whole matter was buried, and others down the line took this political cue. "Maggie had no time for the City," said one insider. "She never allowed you to forget that her father had been persecuted by the Midland Bank."[9] Whatever one makes of this, there appears to be no rational explanation for the failure to prosecute Cameron-Webb and Dixon. The fact that they have been allowed to get away with their flagrant dishonesty is, however, a reflection less on Lloyd's than on the Director of Public Prosecutions.

In 1987 Lloyd's made an offer to PCW Names in order to settle what the chairman, Peter Miller, called "one of the most shameful episodes in the long history of Lloyd's." The Names, who faced gross losses of more than $400 million, had to pay about $60 million. The rest was subscribed by Minet, members' agents, and Lloyd's. Dixon and Cameron-Webb, meanwhile, continue to live in style in the United States. Cameron-Webb has been using his insurance expertise, acting as a consultant to companies trading on the Insurance Exchange of the Americas in Miami. At last report he was living in a luxurious apartment in Key Biscayne, and his wife, Elizabeth, has a flat in New York and a house in Vermont. Dixon, meanwhile, is leading the life of a country squire in Warrenton, Virginia, in a white-columned mansion owned by his new wife, Sherrill.

Throughout this whole affair, the only defence that Dixon and Cameron-Webb offered for their dishonesty was that they had behaved no differently from others in the market. There was undoubtedly something in this. The investigators appointed by Lloyd's to inquire into the PCW frauds told the corporation, in a letter dated 20 January 1984, that it was apparent to them that many members of Lloyd's in senior positions had only the sketchiest notion of their legal obligation to act at all times in the best interests of their Names, and not to make secret profits at their expense.

DISGRACE OF A CHAIRMAN

The PCW affair was to cast an even longer shadow over the market. This time the shame was worse, for it involved Sir Peter Green, then chairman of Lloyd's. Sir Peter had had a long and distinguished career, ending with a knighthood and the rare award of the Lloyd's gold medal for services to the market. A member of one of Lloyd's leading families, he served on the committee for four years before being elected chairman in 1980. He was a tough, brusque underwriter of the old school, with a reputation for straight dealing; it seemed inconceivable that he could be involved in anything shady. Sir Peter liked to impress on prospective Names what unlimited liability meant by asking them to write a blank cheque. Stuffing it in his pocket, he would tell them: "That's the risk you are now undertaking as a Name at Lloyd's." The risks turned out to be greater than this unlimited trust implied; few of his Names could have imagined that some of their money might end up literally in the chairman's pocket.

Sir Peter began his term of office by declaring that he was determined to return the market to its old values. At Lloyd's annual meeting in June 1983, he declared: "The relationship between Name and agent is founded on mutual trust, and we must ensure that nothing is done or not done which can undermine that trust."[10] But the chairman admitted that no amount of statutory or self-regulation would stop wrongdoing by "those determined to break the code by which the vast majority of us conduct our affairs." When subsequently asked by the press about the market's perennial conflicts of interest, he retorted: "You don't have to commit incest just because your mother is the only other person in the house." Despite these uncompromising words, the years of his chairmanship witnessed a growing spate of rumours of corrupt practices.

The first indication that PCW Names were being defrauded had come in 1981, almost a year before Alexander & Alexander's take-over of Howden. Complaints were made about a reinsurance policy that had been placed on behalf of Peter Cameron-Webb's syndicates by Seascope, a small Lloyd's broker. As with so many affairs at Lloyd's, the money trail goes back to a social meeting on a racecourse. In the summer of 1977, amid lashings of champagne at Longchamps, just outside Paris, Peter Cameron-Webb was introduced by his old friend David d'Ambrumenil, the chairman of Seascope, to John Nash, a well known banker who represented Warburg's in Zurich. Later that year, the three men agreed to co-operate on a scheme to reinsure PCW syndicates. The contract wording provided that 10 percent of the premiums were to be retained by the syndicates as "an overriding commission"—the jargon used by reinsurers for a discount. In fact this never happened. Instead of the syndicates getting the discount, the money, amounting to nearly $1 million, was paid by Seascope to a newly established Monte Carlo reinsurance specialist called Unimar S.A.M., via Unimar's Panama bank account at Les Fils Dreyfus & Cie S.A. in Basle, Switzerland.[11]

The director in charge of reinsurance at Seascope, Michael Tucker, asked a number of awkward questions about this unusual policy. When they were not answered he resigned, protesting that the syndicates were being defrauded of the commission due to them. Sir Peter Green decided to undertake an unusual one-man inquiry despite his close links with Cameron-Webb, who had begun his career with Sir Peter's underwriting agency, Janson Green. It soon emerged that the Unimar deal was not a normal reinsurance contract; instead it was described by PCW as "an original business concept," under which the Monte Carlo broker received payments of nearly $1 million in advance commission for reciprocal reinsurance business which it pledged it would provide for the PCW syndicates. In fact no such business was ever forthcoming, and critics described the payments as simply "a slush fund." That was a kind description. Most of the money ended up being used by Cameron-Webb as start-up capital for an international intelligence and consultancy firm called IRIS, set up to assess worldwide political risks. Despite a glittering advisory board of directors including a galaxy of international politicians, IRIS discovered there was no market for its services, and went into liquidation. The Names, as always, were kept in ignorance. It was certainly not what they had in mind for their premium funds.

Seascope, whose 10 percent ownership of Unimar was revealed only much later, blamed the controversy on the unfortunate wording of the contract. As a result, it said, "a plan of business development which was original in its conception was made to look unnatural in its implementation." This was the messy affair which the chairman of Lloyd's had volunteered to investigate in January 1982. After a relatively short inquiry, of which the details—as was the practice at Lloyd's—were not published, Sir Peter Green concluded: "I am satisfied that there has been no dishonesty on the part of anyone connected with the transaction." The syndicates, however, were repaid more than £400,000 in commissions, and Peter Cameron-Webb prudently went to work abroad.

Eight months later, when the full horrors of the £40 million PCW frauds were revealed as a result of the Alexander & Alexander take-over of the Howden Group, it was inevitable that Sir Peter's role in what many considered a whitewash would prove controversial. Lloyd's was so worried by the whispers of a cover-up that it commissioned a further inquiry, headed by Simon Tuckey QC, into Cameron-Webb's dealings with Unimar. This confirmed Sir Peter's findings that there had been "no dishonesty" and levelled only the mildest of criticism at Cameron-Webb and his broker friend d'Ambrumenil, saying "they had behaved at times in an over-bearing and unnecessarily secretive manner."

However, when Department of Trade inspectors, with their greater powers to summon and question witnesses, published the results of a third inquiry into Unimar in July 1986, they found evidence of dishonesty on the part of Cameron-Webb, his PCW co-director Peter Dixon, and the chairman of Seascope, David d'Ambrumenil. Though the DTI report noted that Sir Peter's earlier conclusion that there was "no dishonesty on the part of anyone connected with the transactions' went further than was justified by the evidence available to him, they acquitted him of any wrong doing: "The conclusions expressed by Sir Peter were his honest opinion of the matter. We reject the suggestion that he was guilty of a cover-up." But the inspectors noted that they considered the chairman had been "injudicious" in agreeing to conduct the inquiry in view of his relationship with Cameron-Webb. "This was plainly likely, as indeed happened, to expose him and Lloyd's to criticism," they pointed out.

Following the publication of the Department of Trade inspectors' report, Lloyd's instituted disciplinary proceedings against the chairman of Seascope, David d'Ambrumenil. He was found guilty of three charges of discreditable conduct, namely that he had concealed the Unimar arrangements, he had acted dishonestly in advancing money belonging to the PCW syndicates to a company in which he had a financial interest, and he had misled the chairman of Lloyd's in evidence to his inquiry. For these serious offences, d'Ambrumenil was suspended for two years. Once again it appeared that Lloyd's was only too eager to forgive its favourite sons.

Though Sir Peter Green was cleared over his inquiry into Unimar, storm clouds were gathering over his chairmanship. At the beginning of 1983, the Governor of the Bank of England, Gordon Richardson, appalled by the continuing scandals, persuaded Lloyd's to install a chief executive, Ian Hay Davison, from outside the market. One of his first actions was to implement a requirement that working members of Lloyd's disclose all their financial interests. In June that year, Sir Peter wrote to the 1,000 Names for whom he acted as underwriter, disclosing for the first time the existence of reinsurance policies placed with Imperial Insurance, a Cayman Islands company in which he had a 7.59 percent interest. "These funding policies are really part of syndicate reserves," he explained, adding that "a more constructive approach by the Revenue would remove any necessity for these somewhat esoteric policies. . . The problem from the underwriting agents' point of view has been to justify to the Revenue, if challenged, that reserves for unreported losses are proper reserves and not tax avoidance. Thus schemes to overcome this problem had great attractions."[12]

Sir Peter's letter was less than frank. In particular, his disclosure skated over his obvious conflict of interest in the placing of "funding policies" with a company from whose earnings he stood to gain. The letter further claimed that "a large part of the investment earnings on the fund were credited to the policy thus increasing its value further," and added: "This of course is most unusual, as investment earnings usually belong to the insurer or reinsurer and not to the insured." In fact, it was not unusual; the crediting of investment earnings was a normal feature of roll-overs and, as it later emerged, only half of the investment earnings were credited to the Names' policy, less than fair dealing would have required. Another puzzling aspect of the letter was its claim that "a very major part" of the £34 million increase in the reinsurance to close on the Janson Green syndicates had been met from the funding policies. In fact only 15 percent of the increase—a relatively small fraction—came from these policies.

Sir Peter's letter may have been less than forthcoming, but it triggered off inquiries by the Inland Revenue who wanted to know more about the "esoteric" policies and the extent to which the chairman of Lloyd's had personally benefited from them. In the autumn of 1983, following discreet talks with the governor of the Bank of England, Sir Peter announced his resignation. At the end of the year the Lutine bell was rung twice, and work stopped as Lloyd's honoured its outgoing chairman with the award of its gold medal for his services to the market. It was only the thirteenth time since the medal was instituted in 1913 that such an honour had been awarded, and it appeared to be a just reward for Sir Peter's long and distinguished service. It seemed he was to be allowed to retire in peace and honour.

There the matter might have rested, apart from a quiet settlement with the Inland Revenue. Two years later, however, Sir Peter was publicly attacked in the House of Commons by the Labour MP Brian Sedgemore, who has close links with the satirical magazine *Private Eye*. Using the protection of parliamentary privilege, he accused the former chairman of Lloyd's of having failed "to account for the interest on £34 million placed in Imperial Insurance which has gone to benefit his firm." A second motion stated that Sir Peter had "a close business relationship" with Peter Cameron-Webb and Peter Dixon, the two leading fraudsters in the PCW affair. Sir Peter immediately denounced the allegations as "false and misleading," and in a letter to Names stated: "The suggestion that my firm benefited from Imperial derives from reports that are wholly untrue."[13]

Despite Sir Peter's denials, it was evident that Sedgemore, whose reputation as a bruiser is enhanced by the physique of an ex-rugby prop forward, had succeeded in his aim of "rattling the cage." Moreover it was obvious that the source of the attack was a market insider with access to confidential documents. Speculation about who was responsible was rife within the market; Sir Peter was not without his enemies, particularly those such as Ian Posgate whom he had ousted. Others were even more determined to show that the conduct of Lloyd's chairman was not very different from that of those he had disciplined. At this point, it is worth recalling the case of Christopher Moran, the ambitious young broker who became the first member to be expelled from the market in October 1982. He does not attempt to hide his hatred of Sir Peter. The original source of their quarrel, according to Moran, was a large sum of money that he claimed was owed to him by Sir Peter's brother, John Green, who ran the Lloyd's broker Thomas Nelson. After Moran issued a writ for non-payment, he was summoned by the then chairman of Lloyd's, Paul Dixey, who asked him to drop it and submit his claim to arbitration. Moran replied: "I prefer to take my chances in the Temple." The case was settled at the doors of the court but from then on Moran and Sir Peter were sworn enemies. According to Moran, at the height of his disciplinary troubles in 1979 he had a stormy meeting with Sir Peter which ended in his being thrown out of the chairman's room. Moran threatened that if he was brought down it would not be the end of the affair: "I told him, you will never get me and if you do, I'll take you with me."

Whatever the truth of this, Moran was clearly not a man to cross. The information he acquired through his wealth and contacts in the market was very damaging to Sir Peter. "When I started this thing," he recalled, "I was determined to get him. It's a big task to bring down a chairman." Moran claimed he was helped in his pursuit of revenge by an informant in a firm of accountants which audited Sir Peter's syndicates, who gave him an entire file of documents. "I knew where all the bodies were," he said with a grin. "I probably changed the market more than anyone else. I flushed out a lot of the rotten players. When you do what I did, you don't make friends. They tried to truss me up and despatch me, but I wasn't prepared to let them do it."[14]

The situation was so serious that Lloyd's let it be known that an informal inquiry into Sir Peter's relationship with Imperial had begun. A year later, a disciplinary tribunal chaired by Richard Southwell QC began a tortuous legal process that lasted ten months. A complicated tale emerged. Imperial Insurance, in which both Sir Peter and his brother John were shareholders, was originally established in the Bahamas at the end of the 1950s to provide insurance for the American Railroad Association. It was what was known in the insurance business as "a captive," a company that conducted little or no outside business. When the Bahamas gained independence in the early 1970s, the headquarters of Imperial were transferred to the Cayman Islands. At about that time Sir Peter decided that it was in the interests of his syndicates to have "a funding policy" to cover his Names against the large risks of insuring oil and gas drilling rigs in the Gulf of Mexico. His broker, Derek Steel of Bland, Welch & Co, suggested that this oil rig policy should be placed with Montagu Insurance and Reinsurance Co (Mirco), a Bermuda-based company, but Sir Peter insisted that the premium should be placed with Imperial. To ensure that the terms were fair, and to avoid the obvious conflict of interest inherent in Sir Peter's being both the Names' underwriter and a director of Imperial, it was agreed that the amount of interest credited to the policy should be the same as if it had been placed with Mirco.

In 1976 this hands-off arrangement was ended and a new contract was drawn up with Sir Peter's agreement, under which the syndicates were to receive half of the interest earned in the premium fund. A minor variation of this arrangement was later agreed, by which the syndicates would get an amount equivalent to 50 percent of the relevant Eurodollar bank deposit rate. This second deal was less favourable to the syndicates than the parallel Mirco arrangement, which would have paid at least 75 percent of the interest in the premium fund. Large sums were at stake. By 1978 the oil rig premium fund was worth over $5 million; by 1982 it was valued at over $9 million. From Imperial's standpoint, it was a lucrative no-risk contract from which it earned nearly $2 million in seven years, but as far as the syndicates and Sir Peter's Names were concerned, the amount credited to the policy was at least a third less than would have been earned under the previous parallel arrangement. Sir Peter had a 7.59 percent shareholding in Imperial; the benefit he received from the deal was just over $182,000.[15]

No one—least of all the Names—would have known about the oil rig deal if the PCW bombshell had not burst, bringing with it an avalanche of adverse comment about "roll-overs" and "funding policies." As a result of this publicity Sir Peter, prompted by his investment manager, decided to cancel the oil rig policy, and ordered that the syndicate's share of the return on the invested funds should be increased from 50 to 90 percent of the Eurodollar rate for the final year. In January 1983, $10,615,527 was repaid to the Janson Green syndicates, which was referred to in Sir Peter's letter to his Names that summer as "a final settlement."

It was not the final act as far as Sir Peter was concerned. Ever since his early retirement as chairman at the end of 1983, the slow wheels of the Lloyd's disciplinary machine had been grinding. Finally in 1986, after sifting evidence for nearly a year, a Lloyd's tribunal found that he had acted discreditably in failing to safeguard the interests of his Names. The three-member disciplinary tribunal accepted that Sir Peter had not acted dishonestly or in bad faith, but said that his repeated failure over a period of five years to make sure that the terms of the funding policy were fair to his Names was "such serious or gross negligence" as to constitute "discreditable conduct." A fine of £37,500 was imposed as well as a notice of censure in the underwriting room. In addition, Sir Peter was fined £5,000 for conduct "detrimental to his Names" in failing to disclose the $182,160 he earned from the oil rig policy as a result of his 7.6 percent shareholding in Imperial. Further fines of £7,500 were imposed on Sir Peter for writing misleading letters to the committee of Lloyd's and his Names about his involvement with Imperial.

To be found guilty of serious professional misconduct after a distinguished career at Lloyd's, first as an underwriter and then in the market's highest office, was, as the disciplinary committee pointed out, "a severe penalty." Lord Wilberforce, the chairman of the tribunal to which Sir Peter appealed, upheld the verdict: "The responsibilities of one in a position at Lloyd's such as Sir Peter's are very great. His syndicates had complete trust in him: the whole relation of Name and active underwriter and Name and managing agent at Lloyd's depends upon trust. Sir Peter was responsible for the management of very large sums. He committed the Names to arrangements (*viz.* offshore funding policies) which most of them had probably never heard of and which they would probably not understand, which were not controlled by rules or even publicity, as to which they were entirely in his hands. A failure of duty on the part of a person highly regarded, charged with such responsibilities, has to be regarded with great severity."

When the verdict was announced, Sir Peter wrote to his Names offering to repay any money owing to them. He said he was "deeply distressed, saddened, and sorry that after forty years working for you and the other Names, I should have to write such a letter."[16] But he dissented from the tribunal's verdict: "I could not agree that my conduct could properly be described as discreditable. My view is no doubt coloured by the fact that I was the first and only chairman of Lloyd's who had to summon a general meeting to decide whether to expel two members who had been found guilty of discreditable conduct under the 1871 Act."

Sir Peter modified that dissent when interviewed five years later: "I may have been sailing a bit too close to the wind. I don't really know. I wasn't trying to do anything dishonest or anything like that—I thought I was trying to do my Names a lot of good but, you know, you learn by your mistakes."[17] The mistake, according to one leading member's agent, was in essence trivial: "Peter is an honourable man. Of course he was wrong to keep his shareholding and the involvement with Imperial when he became chairman of Lloyd's. It was utterly stupid but I have an idea why he did so. He liked to go each winter on business to the Bahamas and then go deep sea fishing. I don't think it is any more complicated than that."[18] Another managing agent describes the whole affair as a tragedy: "This is one of the saddest stories, all because Peter ignored the law of agency in his arrogant way. I do not believe he was motivated by the desire to take money from his Names unlawfully."

Some outside commentators took a much harsher view. They felt that the chairman of Lloyd's had got away altogether too lightly. *The Financial Times* noted acidly: "The case of its former Chairman suggests that, even after the various attempts at reform, Lloyd's enjoys a much more relaxed regulatory environment than the rest of the business community." Brian Sedgemore, the Labour MP for Hackney South who had originally raised the issue in the House of Commons, was bitter: "I am sure that anyone else who had done what Sir Peter has done would have been expelled. I think he should have been expelled and his knighthood taken away." Whether or not Sir Peter's sentence was too lenient, it is absurd that it should have taken more than four years to bring him to justice. Without the parliamentary stink raised by Opposition MPs under the protection of privilege, it is doubtful whether his "discreditable conduct" would ever have been revealed. It is also odd that the disciplinary tribunal failed to focus on the basic impropriety—the conflict of interest inherent in the placing of his syndicate's policy with a company in which he had a key management role and an important shareholding.

THE NEILL REPORT

In 1986, in response to parliamentary concern that Lloyd's was still a loose cannon on the financial stage, a high-level committee headed by Sir Patrick Neill, vice-chancellor of Oxford University, was appointed to look into the regulation of the market. A further spur was the government's decision to exempt Lloyd's from the provisions of the Financial Services Act. This had provoked sharp criticism in the House of Commons whose members were disturbed by the spate of scandals. The resignation of Lloyd's chief executive, Ian Hay Davison, at the end of 1985 had also revived suspicions that all was far from well. Hay Davison's appointment had been forced on Lloyd's by the governor of the Bank of England, Gordon Richardson, when the publicity over the PCW scandals was at its height. He was shocked on his arrival in 1983 to find that it was not just a question of a few rotten apples. The disease, he found, had gone much further: "It was the barrel itself that was in some danger of being tainted, in the sense that the corruption and malpractices touched a number of members of the committee—the regulating body—as well as ordinary underwriters."[19] Hay Davison did not make friends when, at a council meeting to discuss the succession to Sir Peter Green as chairman, he pointed out that nearly all the potential candidates had to be ruled out because they were the subject of investigation by the Inland Revenue into the use of offshore funds. Nor was his vigorous pursuit of fuller disclosure at Lloyd's welcome to many market insiders. His enemies seized their chance when an error was made in Lloyd's global accounts, for which he was responsible. The council agreed that a working party should be set up to review the procedures. Shortly afterwards Hay Davison resigned.

Sir Patrick Neill's report, published in February 1987, while acknowledging that attempts at reform had been made, drew attention to the conflicts of interest that plagued Lloyd's. Quoting the PCW inspectors' conclusion, the report noted: "Many members of the Lloyd's community in senior positions were not even vaguely aware of the legal obligations on agents to act at all times in the best interests of their principals, not to make secret profits at their principals' expense and to disclose fully all matters affecting their relationship with their principals."[20] A particular example of this was the widespread practice of baby syndicates creaming off the best business from a main syndicate. In 1978, the report noted, some ninety-nine out of 360 syndicates had fewer than fifty members, and more than half of all syndicates in the market were being operated in parallel. The profits which resulted from this practice were sometimes truly remarkable. In 1981, syndicate 485 racked up profits of 380 percent for its three members. For every £10,000 premium, it produced a return of £38,280. In the same year, Peter Cameron-Webb's syndicate 954, which had seven members, produced profits of 270 percent. Not all baby syndicates were corrupt. In the non-marine market, they were sometimes used as a way of enabling a successful underwriter to expand without diluting the profits of the main syndicate. But the practice was clearly open to abuse. Baby syndicates were too often a way of putting additional profits in the pockets of the professional underwriters and their friends at the expense of external Names. The problem was that membership of baby syndicates was not confined to a dubious fringe of the market; they were embraced by many of its leaders, who appeared to believe that it was perfectly acceptable. One example was syndicate 973, managed by Bellew and Raven underwriting agencies. It had only five Names in 1982, among them David Coleridge, later to become chairman of Lloyd's. His response to the conclusions of the Neill report is oddly revealing: "I don't think underwriters ever understood the law of agency. Not because they were stupid but because it never came across their desks." One of his companions on syndicate 973, which, in fact, was not particularly profitable, was Ian Posgate, star underwriter for Howden. Posgate was later to recall: "I think when baby syndicates came to be discussed when I was on the committee of Lloyd's, eleven out of the sixteen members on the committee had to declare an interest. . . I was not considered the respectable end of the committee but extremely respectable people would argue passionately that it was totally fair for them and their father-in-law to be on the baby syndicate whilst all the Names that were on the main syndicate lost money."[21]

As a result of the flagrant abuses disclosed by the PCW scandal, Lloyd's set up a working group which recommended that baby syndicates should cease. But the practice was not formally banned until two years later, a delay adversely commented on by Sir Patrick Neill, who was also critical of the fact that the standard underwriting agreement failed to protect the interests of Names. His report also highlighted Lloyd's failure to honour its commitment to Parliament to publish a register of agents' charges. Both Cromer in 1969 and Fisher in 1980 had recommended that such a register should be set up, but it had been blocked by a powerful cabal of managing agents and underwriters.

To deal with these persistent underlying conflicts of interest, Sir Patrick recommended that the composition of the Lloyd's council should be changed, doubling the number of independent nominated members from four to eight, which meant that working members no longer had a majority. The power of insiders to control the market in their own interest was thus finally eroded. It was the end of a shameful era at Lloyd's which, more than anything else, buried the myth that "utmost good faith" still held sway. As Ian Hay Davison put it in his account of his period at Lloyd's, *A View of the Room*: "The admiration and respect of staff for their betters—the working members of Lloyd's—had been destroyed by the speculation and wrongdoing exposed in 1982. The old attitude had been one of respect for a fine old institution and the Lloyd's men who had led it down over the years. The events of 1982 changed that: the staff could no longer feel respect for a committee which included members who had been involved in dis-creditable practices." The Names were no less disillusioned. For the traders who provided the risk capital, the spectacle of a Lloyd's chairman judged by his peers to have behaved "discreditably" was yet another shock to their fast waning confidence.

6

Asbestos: The Fatal Legacy

"Ask not for whom the Lutine bell tolls. It tolls for Lloyd's."
Economist *leader*

The history of asbestos is a shaming saga of medical negligence and managerial cover-up which has resulted in the premature deaths of millions of industrial workers. Stretching back more than half a century, this corporate scandal brought its own nemesis—a torrent of litigation, punitive jury awards, and the bankruptcy of many of the leading American asbestos manufacturers. Lloyd's and other insurers were left to pick up the bill—£5 billion and still increasing—as the greatest explosion of toxic tort legislation in the history of jurisprudence jammed US courts for a generation. For those syndicates which specialized in insuring and reinsuring American liability risks between 1940 and 1970, the exposure to claims from victims of asbestosis and asbestos-related cancer was to prove disastrous.

The danger of asbestos (the name is derived from the Greek adjective for "inextinguishable'), was first recognized by the Greek geographer Strabo and the Roman naturalist Pliny the Elder. Both mentioned "a sickness of the lungs" in slaves who wove the raw asbestos fibres into fabric. But labour was cheap, materials valuable. Plutarch noted that the wicks of the sacred lamps of the vestal virgins were made of an unusual fiery substance. In ancient Rome "linum vivum," the immortal linen, was used to wrap the bodies of those who were to be cremated. The Emperor Charlemagne liked to impress unsophisticated rivals by throwing a cloth woven from asbestos into a fire and then recovering it unmarked and uncharred. The Tartars tried to convince Marco Polo that asbestos came from the wool of a salamander, but the Venetian discovered that it was made from crushing the ore of a rock found in the mountains.

It was not until the Industrial Revolution that the commercial uses of this mixture of silicates of magnesium and iron, which could be mixed with many different forms of material, were widely recognized. At the beginning of the twentieth century, asbestos was regarded as a wonder mineral whose ore, on being crushed, produced strong, pliable fibres able to withstand temperatures of up to 500 degrees centigrade. These heat-resisting qualities were to find a use in thousands of industrial products, ranging from construction to car manufacture. Only decades later did the effects on the lungs of those who worked with it become apparent. There are three distinct types of asbestos: chrysotile, which constitutes 95 percent of world production, is a very short whitish fibre; amosite, a longer fibre, comes mainly from South Africa; blue crocidolite is inferior only to steel wire in tensile strength and is the most toxic. All three, particularly chrysotile, were used in hundreds of products, from insulation and building construction to brake linings and mattresses.

Strabo's and Pliny's health warnings were forgotten for many centuries, because asbestos in all but the highest dust concentrations is an insidious killer. It is usually many years before the inhalation of its minute, insoluble fibres produces a noticeable scarring of the lungs. During the latency period of asbestosis, which can stretch over decades, there are few warning signs; the worker usually feels no ill effects until one day he is suddenly short of breath. There follows a rapid and progressive deterioration of health. Victims find breathing more and more difficult, the worst affected waste away and eventually die in a choking spasm. There are two even more deadly primary diseases directly related to asbestos. Mesothelioma is a malignant tumour occurring in the lung or abdominal cavity lining, extremely rare in the general population but common among workers exposed to asbestos. Bronchogenic carcinoma is another type of malignant tumour in the upper portion of the lungs. Both are usually fatal within a short time.[1]

The Industrial Revolution brought home the dangers of using asbestos. As early as 1898, the annual report of women inspectors of factories in

Britain warned that the "sharp, glass-like, jagged" fibres were potentially lethal. Two years later, during an autopsy at Charing Cross Hospital in London, Dr. Montague Murray found spicules of asbestos in the lungs of a male textile worker. One of the first modern scientific records of the disease appeared in the *British Medical Journal* in 1924. Dr. E.W. Cooke, who had performed a postmortem on a thirty-three-year-old textile factory worker, described the classic signs of asbestosis—the slow destruction of lung tissue caused by the inhalation of fibres.

The identification of this disease as "asbestosis" was the catalyst for an intensive study in Britain. The medical inspector of factories for the Home Office, Dr. E.R. Merewether, examined more than 350 asbestos textile workers in 1928 and 1929, and found that more than a quarter had damaged lungs. His report noted that "inhalation of asbestos dust over a period of years results in the development of a serious type of fibrosis in the lungs." These findings were considered so serious that two years later legislation was introduced requiring improved ventilation in textile factories in the United Kingdom.

AMERICAN WARNINGS

American health organizations were slower to act, but the danger did not go unrecognized, as Paul Brodeur notes in his excellent study *Outrageous Misconduct* (Pantheon Books, 1985). In 1918, the United States Bureau of Labor published a report by Frederick Hoffman, a consulting statistician employed by the Prudential Insurance Company of America. This pointed out that many asbestos workers were dying prematurely, and that some insurance companies were refusing to sell life insurance to them because of their dangerous working conditions.[2]

A decade later, a paper published by the Penn Mutual Life Insurance Company of Philadelphia quoted three reports from the *British Medical Journal* on the dangers of asbestos and warned: "Until we have the benefit of our experience with this class of workers, we should continue to look upon those who may be exposed to large quantities of dust . . . as risks to be selected with great care and only at an extra premium that will provide for an estimated extra mortality of 50 percent, disability not to be granted." At about the same time, America's largest life insurance company, Metropolitan Life, also commissioned a survey of health conditions in asbestos textile mills which showed that workers were at serious risk. Due to industry pressure led by the main asbestos producer, Johns-Manville, these results were suppressed until 1935, and then published in a watered down form.

The asbestos manufacturers were only too well aware of the hazards of their trade without having to be told of them by insurance actuaries. In the early 1930s, the industry had campaigned to establish compensation schemes in order to limit the amount of its liability for employees who became sick through working with its products. Such "no fault" schemes provided inadequate levels of damages, but the industry argued that it could not afford to give more. It also prevented asbestos victims from suing their employers in the courts. "The strongest bulwark against future disaster for the industry," noted an asbestos industry executive, "is the enactment of properly drawn occupational-disease legislation which will eliminate the jury . . . the shyster lawyer and the quack doctor, since fees should be strictly limited by law."

The legal barriers against actions for negligence proved remarkably successful. By the late 1950s, the manufacturers and their insurers had paid only minute amounts of damages, with most claimants receiving as little as $5,000 a head in workman's compensation. All this time the use of the mineral was expanding fast. During the Second World War, millions of shipyard employees in naval dockyards routinely worked with asbestos in insulation, construction and wiring. There were hundreds of applications, from cement to boiler jackets. It was effective, durable and, above all, cheap.

Commercial success and freedom from litigation bred complacency. Worse still, it led the manufacturers to turn their back on the growing medical evidence of the link between their product and ill health. Just as the tobacco manufacturers did not—and still do not—want to know the truth of the consequences of smoking, so the asbestos industry preferred to ignore warnings of the health time-bomb they were priming. The dangers were, however, known by medical professionals, who publicly warned of the risks being run.

As early as 1938, the US Public Health Service documented the significant dangers for those working in asbestos textile factories. In 1947, the American Conference of Governmental Industrial Hygienists warned of serious risks to asbestos workers. It issued guidance that a threshold of five million particles of asbestos dust per cubic foot of air was the maximum that should be allowed in the workplace. These levels were established on the crude basis of injecting asbestos dust into guinea pigs; they were later criticized by other scientists as being far too lax. The increased risk of lung cancer run by asbestos workers was confirmed by epidemiological studies conducted by Richard Doll in Oxford in 1955. At about the same time a young South African medical researcher, Dr. J.C. Wagner, conducted a study of thirty-three cancer deaths in a blue asbestos mining community in the Transvaal. His paper, published in London in 1960, showed that those at risk from the rare mesothelioma tumour included not just the miners of asbestos, but also their wives, their children and their servants. The conclusion was that asbestos was a potential killer to all who came into even casual contact with it. Despite the scientific studies and accumulating medical evidence, not a single warning was issued by the industry to alert contractors and insulation workers to the consequences of using its products. The prevailing view was that though asbestos mines and factories were dangerous places to work, the products themselves were perfectly safe.

Two developments exploded this complacency. The first was medical. Dr. Irving Selikoff, director of the environmental sciences laboratory at the Mount Sinai school of medicine in New York, witnessed the horrors of asbestos-related cancer when he ran a medical clinic in Paterson, New Jersey, in the 1950s. Several of his patients, who were employed by a local factory owned by the Union Asbestos and Rubber Factory of Chicago, died of cancer within a few years. Suspecting that asbestos dust was even more lethal than had been realized, Dr. Selikoff arranged with local union officials to conduct a study of workers who used products containing a high level of asbestos. During the next two years, he tested more than 1,000 insulation workers. The results were frightening. The vast majority (87 percent) of those exposed to asbestos dust for more than twenty years had severe and irreversible damage to their lungs. In a further study, it was found that asbestos insulation workers were seven times more likely to die from lung cancer, and three times more likely to die from stomach cancer, than other industrial workers.

When these results were published at an international conference in New York in October 1964, a shockwave ran through the asbestos industry. For the first time it had to face up to the lethal risks which its deliberate neglect of health safety had created. The US Department of Health, Education and Welfare was later to estimate that between eight and eleven million workers had been exposed to asbestos-based products since 1940, and that as many as a quarter of a million would die prematurely. In 1978, Joseph Califano, then secretary of the Department of Health, Education and Welfare warned that as many as 5.6 million Americans might die prematurely as a result of exposure to asbestos in shipyards and other work places.[3]

THE LEGAL REVOLUTION

The second development to shake the industry was a legal revolution. Until the early 1960s, product liability in the United States was limited to consumer products designed for human consumption, such as food and cosmetics. Makers or purveyors of filthy food or poisonous drink could be sued in the courts by the purchaser whether or not a formal contract existed, but other mass consumer products were exempt. In the mid-1960s, however, this doctrine of strict product liability was significantly extended to wherever "the defective condition of the product makes it unreasonably dangerous to the user." This fundamental extension of the civil law, part of the wave of consumerism then sweeping the country, was to prove deadly for the asbestos manufacturers and their insurers. It enabled the victims of its products to bypass the inadequate redress provided by workers' compensation schemes and instead sue the asbestos manufacturers directly.

The first test of the new law came in August 1969, when a fifty-three-year-old insulation worker and father of six, Clarence Borel, visited the offices of a small legal firm in the east Texas town of Orange. Its senior partner, Ward Stephenson, who had a reputation for securing compensation settlements, listened as Borel told how after thirty-six years working as an asbestos insulator, he had been suddenly stricken. He could no longer stand or walk for long periods, his breathing was painful, and he had developed a pain in the right side of his chest. An exploratory operation showed that he had extensive pulmonary asbestosis. Within six months Borel was dead, but his claim for damages did not die with him. On behalf of his widow, Thelma, Stephenson filed suit for $1 million against eleven leading asbestos manufacturers, including Johns-Manville, Pittsburgh Corning, and Eagle-Picher. Borel's sworn testimony was damning. He said that basic safety equipment such as masks had not been provided by his employers, and that his clothes were often stiff with asbestos dust at the end of a working day. He knew so little about the dangers that one Christmas he had brought home a bunch of white asbestos fibres to decorate the family tree. Several of the manufacturers settled out of court for small sums, but when the case of Borel v. Fibreboard Paper Products Corporation came to trial in September 1971, the defence claimed that the manufacturers could not have known that their products were potentially dangerous to insulation workers until after publication of Dr. Selikoff's study in 1964.[4] After a ten-day hearing, however, the jury dismissed this "state of the art" defence, found for the plaintiff, and awarded Borel's widow $79,000. The verdict was appealed, but the Fifth Circuit Court of Appeals in New Orleans confirmed the jury's decision in September 1973. It was a landmark judgment which opened the floodgates to thousands of claims from other victims of asbestos across the United States.

Following the Borel case, a tidal wave of litigation and the ensuing legal process known as "discovery," under which all relevant documents have to be disclosed, finally exposed what the asbestos manufacturers had been seeking for decades to conceal. Hidden in the archives was proof that the industry knew the dangers of asbestos and had recklessly risked the health of millions of workers using their products. The next few years witnessed a desperate struggle, as the industry sought to shore up its tottering defences against an ever-growing band of asbestos victims and their lawyers. Evidence that the manufacturers knew much more about the dangers of asbestos than they were prepared to admit came with the discovery of the papers of Sumner Simpson, one of the founders of the leading asbestos producer Raybestos-Manhattan. They included the results of a survey of 126 asbestos textile workers, conducted by the Metropolitan Life Insurance Company for the industry between 1929 and 1931. More than half the workers had developed asbestosis, and the study recommended that asbestos manufacturers must "seriously face the problem of dust control in asbestos plants."

LEGAL BREAKTHROUGH

An early breakthrough for the victims came with the finding of a crucial witness who could give first-hand evidence of how careless the manufacturers had been of their workers' health. Dr. Kenneth Smith, living in retirement in Windsor, Ontario, was the former medical director of Johns-Manville, the leading manufacturer of asbestos products. Dr. Smith said that, after becoming convinced in the early 1950s that workers using asbestos materials were almost as much at risk as those who worked in asbestos plants, he had suggested to Johns-Manville's corporate safety manager that warning labels should be put on all asbestos insulation products. The advice was ignored.

Dr. Smith also revealed that in 1948 he had conducted a survey of workers at a Johns-Manville plant in Canada where ore was crushed before shipping. Out of more than 700 workers, only four had normal healthy lungs. The rest showed varying degrees of asbestosis; but it was company policy that they should not be told of the fate that awaited them. Dr. Smith's report, which he submitted the following year to Johns-Manville's vice-president for production, explained: "They have not been told of this diagnosis, for it is felt that as long as the man feels well, is happy at home and at work, and his physical condition remains good, nothing should be said. . . The fibrosis of this disease is irreversible and permanent so that eventually compensation will be paid to each of these men. But as long as the man is not disabled, it is felt that he should not be told of his condition so that he can live and work in peace and the Company can benefit by his many years of experience. Should the man be told of his condition today, there is a very definite possibility that he would become mentally and physically ill, simply through the knowledge that he has the disease."[5]

Few more damning medical documents can ever have been made public. And there was more to come. The lawyers representing the victims discovered minutes of several lengthy meetings of a health committee held at Johns-Manville's factory at Manville, New Jersey in the late 1950s. The members of the committee included the company's medical director, Dr. Smith, and the plant physician, Dr. David DuBow. Reviewing the case of a woman weaver who had developed asbestosis after working for sixteen years in the plant, Dr. DuBow advised against any action: "If she is called in, she will get hysterical, and I am sure you will have a claim on your hands." Another case involved a forty-nine-year-old woman who had shown the first signs of asbestosis. Dr. DuBow advised the committee against calling her in for further examination on the grounds: "We may aggravate this into some-thing decisive." The plant manager of Johns-Manville's Pittsburgh plant, Wilbur Ruff, who had worked for the company for forty years, later testified that it was company policy not to tell employees about health checks showing they might be suffering from asbestosis, pneumoconiosis or mesothelioma. The manner in which Johns-Manville executives regarded their employees was revealed by Charles Roemer, a lawyer and friend of the president of the company, Louis Brown. He recalled a conversation he had with Louis' brother Vandiver Brown, who acted as the company's attorney, during which the latter had remarked that the managers at Unarco (another asbestos manufacturer) were "a bunch of fools" for telling employees they had asbestosis. Roemer protested: "Mr. Brown, do you mean to tell me that you would let them work until they dropped dead?" Brown replied: "Yes. We save a lot of money that way."[6]

The evidence that Johns-Manville had deliberately concealed the health risks of asbestos from its employees persuaded shocked juries to award larger and larger punitive damages against the company. In May 1981, the company was forced to pay $500,000 in damages and $350,000 in compensatory damages to the widow of an asbestos-insulator, Edward Moran, who had contracted lung cancer. The verdict was upheld by the Sixth Circuit Court of Appeals, and from then on punitive damages began to be awarded routinely. The only defence which appeared to weigh with juries was that many of the asbestos workers had contributed to their health problems by continuing to smoke cigarettes. The Selikoff study had established that asbestos workers who smoked were ten times more likely than non-smokers to develop lung cancer. But this did not dissuade juries from venting their anger at the industry's cavalier attitude towards its employees' health with higher and higher punitive awards. The legal enemies of Johns-Manville now closed in for the kill. One South Carolina attorney, Ronald Motley, described the company as "the greatest corporate mass murderer in history." In June 1982, a jury awarded a record sum of $2.3 million, including punitive damages of $1.5 million, to a retired boiler-maker, James Cavett, who was dying from asbestosis and lung cancer after working for forty years for the Tennessee Valley Authority.

Two months later, on 26 August 1982, Johns-Manville filed for protection from its creditors under Chapter 11 of the Federal Bankruptcy Code. It was the end of a corporate horror story. More than 16,000 claims for compensation had been filed against the company, and they were growing at the rate of 6,000 a year. The greatest avalanche of tort litigation in the history of the United States had claimed its first victim. When Johns-Manville became insolvent, it had already paid out several hundred million dollars in compensation, damages and legal fees. And the costs were mounting. In 1979 the average cost per claim was $21,000; ten years later it had doubled.

Though Johns-Manville was made to pay a heavy price for its misconduct, it would be wrong to believe that it was unique in behaving as it did. The British asbestos company Turner and Newall, now known as T&N plc, also bolstered profits at the expense of the health of its workers for more than half a century. Among more than a million documents disclosed under discovery proceedings brought by the Chase Manhattan Bank in New York against the company, is evidence that it prevaricated about the known dangers of asbestos and appeared to evade government health regulations. The subject of Dr. Cooke's 1924 paper in the *British Medical Journal*, mentioned earlier, was Nellie Kershaw, who had worked for Turner Brothers' Asbestos Company from the age of thirteen until she was completely disabled a generation later. Two years before she died aged thirty-three, a friendly society acting on her behalf approached the company asking for worker's compensation. Her doctor's certificate described her disease as "asbestos poisoning." Turner Brothers responded tersely: "We repudiate the term 'asbestos poisoning.'" The company, meanwhile, wrote to its insurers: "We feel that it will be exceedingly dangerous to admit any liability whatever in such a case and before referring the matter to you, we considered that we ought to do all in our power to repudiate the claim."[7]

Unable to claim sickness benefit and in desperate straits, the dying Nellie Kershaw wrote to Turner Brothers appealing for money to buy food: "I think it is time there was something from you." But there is no record of any payment. As a result of Dr. Cooke's postmortem on Nellie Kershaw and a subsequent study of Turner and Newall's Rochdale factory, which found that more than a quarter of its workforce had lung damage, new safety regulations were introduced by the Home Office in 1931. These required the use of extractor fans in all plants wherever a worker was exposed to asbestos dust on more than an "occasional" basis—defined as once a week. The founder of the company, Mr. Turner, wrote to his co-founder, Mr. Newall: "I feel this definition of 'occasional' is rather too strict. We must take a small risk by stretching the regulations for our own ends."

Turner and Newall's end was profit, which it continued to pursue at the expense of its employees' health. In 1954, it attempted to suppress a scientific study showing that asbestos workers were ten times more likely than other workers to contract lung cancer. The company's medical director, Dr. John Knox, had commissioned the eminent epidemiologist Professor Richard Doll to conduct research, but then had the embarrassing task of requesting its suppression because the company's management had decided that "the conclusions reached were not supported by medical evidence." Professor Doll, now Sir Richard, was so outraged that he subsequently published the study himself.

One of the most shocking documents disclosed in the discovery process concerned Charlie Coyle, an asbestos insulation worker. He was employed to spray asbestos in ships being built on the Clyde but soon began showing the deadly signs of advanced asbestosis. He was always tired, he had no energy, and he was short of breath. Hardly able to work, he asked his lawyers to make a claim for compensation but was stonewalled. That was because the company's lawyers had written to Turner and Newall's board: "The man has a very poor expectation of life. And, if he does succumb, the claim will not be any more expensive and without his evidence the solicitors will be in greater difficulties. In short, I do not think tactically we have anything to lose by leaving the matter in abeyance."[8]

As more and more medical evidence accumulated about the dangers to those working with asbestos products, not just those working in asbestos plants, Turner and Newall tried to subvert government health and safety regulations. In 1968, a senior company executive wrote this confidential memorandum: "The introduction of the new regulations could result in an even more rapid reduction of the use of asbestos than anticipated. If, however, we demonstrate by a token effort only of ostensible intention to comply with the regulations, it is conceivable that we can ward off the evil day when asbestos cannot be economically applied, i.e. hold on until the 1972-73 period."

THE VULNERABILITY OF LLOYD'S

The brazen misbehaviour of asbestos manufacturers left Lloyd's and other insurers in a vulnerable position, but they cannot escape their share of the responsibility for the tragedy that occurred. Despite the undeniable medical evidence that asbestos was extremely toxic and exposed anyone who worked with it to serious harm, underwriters were either oblivious of, or ignored, the risks they were running. Many Lloyd's syndicates, such as Pulbrook 90 which specialized in North American casualty risks, took on vast amounts of excess insurance business for leading asbestos companies between 1940 and 1970. The underwriters were seduced by the steady stream of premium and investment income which such business produced. Claims were few, the profits were good, and no one at Lloyd's realized that a time-bomb was ticking away. A leading underwriter, Robin Jackson, who was later to head the London market's Asbestos Working Party, confided: "We may have known something about the dangers of asbestos but the fact is there had never been any claims through this route."[9]

The first sign that Lloyd's had miscalculated badly came in the mid-1970s when claims advised by Sedgwick, the brokers for Bell Asbestos, started to hit the London market. By the late 1970s, nearly 5,000 asbestos cases had been reported by direct insurers. Lloyd's, whose syndicates acted mainly as reinsurers and would therefore be liable as soon as asbestos damages breached agreed limits, started to worry. It was of particular concern to those syndicates which specialized in "long-tail" risks which might take many years to manifest. In August 1980, the London market set up the Asbestos Working Party to coordinate information about the deteriorating position. Its first chairman was Ted Nelson, a non-marine underwriter, and it included other leading market figures on long-tail syndicates, such as Charles Skey of syndicate 219, Ralph Rokeby-Johnson of Sturge syndicate 210, Robin Jackson of Merrett, and Don Tayler, underwriter for Pulbrook syndicate 90. This later led to bitter accusations that underwriters on the working party had used inside information to safeguard their own position by taking out reinsurance policies covering their asbestos liabilities from other less well informed underwriters in the market.

Lloyd's was vulnerable, both because of the amount of risks it had underwritten and because of the loose, all-embracing wording of its general liability policies. Although the policies were not written specifically to cover asbestosis, they did cover losses arising from bodily injury or property damage. More important, in common with American insurers, the Lloyd's policies were written on an "occurrence" basis covering "exposure to conditions that give rise to bodily injury during the whole period of the policy." This was later interpreted by the US courts as meaning that claims could be made at any time in the future for accidents or exposures in the past. It thus allowed potential claimants to assert that any policy written during the long latent period of asbestosis provided coverage. The policies were written with no aggregate limits, which meant that an infinite number of individual claims could be made during the lifetime of the policy. These mistakes were to cost Lloyd's and other insurers billions of pounds. The crucial legal issue centred on the definition of "an occurrence." Most Lloyd's underwriters supported the "manifestation" theory, which argued that insurance coverage was restricted to policies sold when the disease was first diagnosed. The asbestos manufacturers, however, backed by some direct insurers, favoured the "exposure" theory. This claimed that the incremental damage caused by asbestos was covered by all the policies in force over the whole period of the victim's exposure. If this definition carried the day, many Lloyd's syndicates faced huge liabilities on policies issued up to half a century ago, for which very small premiums had been charged and of which no proper records existed.

The insurers, unable to agree, were prepared to spend millions of dollars on protracted legal arguments in cases which occupied the US Courts for more than a decade. This split in the market was to prove very damaging. The first crucial ruling came in 1980, after the Insurance Company of North America (INA) declared that it would refuse to indemnify a small asbestos manufacturing company, Forty-Eight Insulations, against any claims which had "manifested" after the expiration of its liability policy. The bitterly contested case went to appeal after a US district judge ruled in favour of the exposure basis of liability. The appellants warned the Court of Appeal that if the lower court's ruling was allowed to stand, it would "plague the nation's trial courts and appellate courts, together with insurers and insured alike, for many years to come."

The Appeal Court, however, upheld the decision by two to one, the majority stating that "insurance policies must be strictly construed in favour of the injured and to promote coverage." The judges were apparently swayed by the fact that by the mid-1970s, Forty-Eight's insurance policies contained such high excess points that if the manifestation theory was upheld, the company would have been, to all intents and purposes, uninsured. That would mean that Forty-Eight Insulations would be bankrupt and the victims who were suing would get nothing. This "deep pocket" approach to the law was fatal for excess insurers like Lloyd's. Nor was the Appeal Court sympathetic to the industry's fear that an exposure ruling would unleash an avalanche of litigation. "The cause of the plague," said the Court dismissively, "is an insurance industry which adopted a standard policy which is inadequate to deal with the problems of asbestosis."

A series of contradictory judgments followed in other state jurisdictions. The only common theme that the courts followed was that they invariably ruled in favour of maximizing insurance coverage. In Eagle-Picher Industries v. Liberty Mutual Insurance, for instance, the court upheld the manifestation argument, seemingly because the asbestos manufacturer had adequate insurance coverage only for the period after the disease had become apparent.

These judgments were followed by what proved to be a decisive blow. In October 1981, the Court of Appeals for the District of Columbia decided to broaden asbestos insurance coverage still further. The Keene Corporation, facing more than 500 claims, had filed suit against INA and three other insurers, calling on them to honour their policies. The judges not only backed both the exposure and manifestation arguments, they took them one stage further by endorsing what became known as the "triple trigger" approach. This held that all periods of insurance cover were liable, from inhalation of the first harmful asbestos fibre to outbreak of the disease, often thirty years later. The insurers sought to persuade the United States Supreme Court that it was grossly unfair that a one-year liability policy could be held to provide coverage for decades of losses. But the court declined to hear the case, despite being warned that the asbestos cases "presented the most costly product liability claims ever to confront American industry."

A LEGAL DEBACLE

These judgments were extremely serious for Lloyd's, but worse was to follow. The Californian Supreme Court decided in 1980 to shift the burden of proof from plaintiffs, who had traditionally been required to show they had been harmed by a particular product, to the defendant manufacturer. In the case of Sindell v. Abbott Laboratories, one of a thousand lawsuits involving the synthetic female hormone drug, diethylstilbestrol (DES for short), the plaintiffs were allowed to plead that they had been harmed by the drug, which had proved to be carcinogenic, even though they were not able to prove which manufacturer had actually produced it. This concept of "market share" liability had an immediate impact on asbestos litigation, particularly on reinsurers such as Lloyd's, who would eventually have to pick up the tab when the primary insurance was exhausted.[10] Soon afterwards Robert Sweeney, a Californian attorney, amended the pleadings in a case involving forty-two asbestos insulators, to cover "market share" claims against fifteen asbestos manufacturers. The defending insurers were forced to settle to the tune of $1.5 million.

The legal arguments over who should pay and what was the period of exposure were to rage for another decade, but the verdicts mostly went against the liability insurers. The issue was eventually resolved in January 1990, in a Californian trial lasting seven years and involving seventy insurance companies represented by more than a hundred lawyers. Judge Ira Browne adopted the "continuous trigger" ruling which was designed to give the insured the broadest possible coverage. For Lloyd's it was the final blow. There were loud complaints that the American judiciary had forgotten its duty to dispense equal justice before the law. A British legal study had this to say: "A substantial part of the losses . . . arises out of the violence done by US courts to policy wordings so as to provide cover where none was intended or foreseen on claims circumstances arising decades ago. It is ironic that the world's champion of capitalism should use its own insurance industry as a surrogate social services department for the relief of injured consumers. Yet this is precisely what has happened in the USA. A substantial part of the burden of these judgments, particularly on asbestosis claims, has been passed on to the Lloyd's market and its Names. This extended coverage far beyond that ever intended by any of the parties to the original reinsurance policies written in the 1940s and 1950s."[11]

The view that Lloyd's had been set up by the American courts was echoed in London. "What is more troubling," said Lloyd's chairman, David Coleridge, "is the determination of the courts in some countries to bend over backwards, sometimes interpreting insurance wordings in bizarre ways, to reach the perceived deep pockets of insurers." But when this point was put to Judge Browne, he retorted: "They [Lloyd's] think it was social engineering but I have to tell them that as a trial judge, it is not my purpose to carve out new areas of the law. This was my first venture into the troubled waters of insurance coverage. I went in with no pre-conceived ideas."[12]

Lloyd's may have had rough treatment in the US courts, but it cannot escape responsibility for its cavalier attitude to the known risks of asbestos. British medical research in this area was, if anything, ahead of the United States. As Professor Irving Selikoff pointed out, any insurer who wanted to know the risks faced by asbestos workers had only to look up the medical literature, notably reports in *The Lancet*, *The British Medical Journal*, and *The British Journal of Industrial Medicine*. "Certainly by 1930 we knew that people could die from scarred lungs if they inhaled asbestos while working," he explained shortly before his death in May 1992. "This information was widely available in the medical literature . . . if anybody wanted to look into this hazard, it was there for all to see."[13]

The Rowland Task Force, which reported to Lloyd's council in January 1992, refused to accept that Lloyd's underwriters had been negligent: "The outcome was impossible to foresee at the time the policies were written . . . it would be unreasonable to accuse the insurance industry of lack of foresight about these latent liability problems." That excuse is altogether too pat. Lloyd's, as one of the principal insurers of North American liability risks, should have been better informed. Some US insurers consistently refused to cover asbestos manufacturers because of the known dangers. The Prudential Insurance Company stated as long ago as 1918 that the company would not issue life insurance policies to asbestos workers. By the mid-1930s, asbestosis was widely recognized as a lethal threat to all those who worked in asbestos plants. The Selikoff report in 1964 confirmed the high risk being run by all workers who came into contact with asbestos products, even on a temporary basis. A US Senate report published in 1970 warned: "Because nothing has been done about the hazards of asbestos . . . 20,000 out of 50,000 workers who have entered on asbestos trade alone—insulation work—are likely to die of asbestosis, lung cancer or mesothelioma. Nor is the potential hazard confined to these workers, since it is estimated that as many as 3.5 million workers are exposed to some extent to asbestos fibres as are many more in the general population."[14] By the late 1970s, the probability of a torrent of insurance claims was apparent and was frequently discussed in the American press. The *New York Times*, reporting the result of the mammoth Tyler Plant case in Texas, which ended in a $20 million settlement in 1978, predicted that it would spark a string of similar legal challenges involving tens of thousands of workers across the country. The trade paper *Business Insurance* carried an article on 11 June 1979, headlined: "Asbestos Claims Deluge Manufacturers and Courts," warning that 10,000 legal actions were likely to be filed in the near future. Yet it was not until 1985 that Lloyd's restricted the scope of the cover of their general liability policies. This was done by replacing the "occurrence" wording with a "claims made" qualification requiring a claimant to make his claim during the period of the policy. If this had been done a generation earlier Lloyd's would have saved itself £5 billion. David Evers, chairman of David Evers Ltd, a small members' agency, is in no doubt where the responsibility lies: "The main reason for these huge losses is that the asbestos manufacturers went on manufacturing asbestos for decades after its harmful effects were known; and, above all, because some insurers were naive enough to insure them."[15]

SOCIAL CHANGE

Lloyd's difficulties, it is only fair to acknowledge, were aggravated by an unforeseeable social change. Americans have always been litigious—their tendency to reach for a writ at the slightest hint of trouble is a well-known national trait. But in the 1970s a revolution in legal rules and procedures and, above all, in attitudes set off an explosion of personal injury actions. The result is that the United States now spends five times as much per capita on personal injury actions as its major industrial competitors. Compared with Britain, the US has three times as many lawyers, ten times as many tort claims, forty times as many malpractice claims, and an astonishing hundred times as many product suits per capita. "Sue and be sued," is the prevailing motto. Nearly 80 percent of obstetricians and reportedly every neurosurgeon in Washington DC have been sued for negligence.[16] By 1990, New York obstetricians with good records were having to pay $100,000 a year for liability insurance, while Miami neurosurgeons were paying more than $220,000. Jokes about lawyers became a mordant national pastime. "What's the difference between a single sperm and a lawyer?" Answer: "The sperm has one-in-a-million chance of becoming a human being." "What's the difference between a dead lawyer on the highway and a dead rat?" Answer: "The rat has skid marks in front of it." The American Bar Association was so worried by its unfavourable image that it set up a $750,000 defence fund, and sought to make anti-lawyer jokes a legally punishable offence subject to the same penalties as incitement to racial hatred.

The causes of this extraordinary torrent of litigation are many. Unlike nearly all other developed countries, the US does not make the loser in a civil action pay the costs of the case. Making losers pay discourages litigation; the American contingency fee system, where lawyers are allowed to recoup their costs by charging a "success fee," often as high as 30 to 40 percent of the court's award, does the opposite. As the US Supreme Court explained: "We cannot accept the notion that it is better for a person to suffer a wrong silently than to redress it by legal action. . . That our citizens have access to their civil courts is not an evil to be regretted, rather, it is an attribute of our system of justice in which we ought to take pride."

Until the mid-1970s, it was illegal for American lawyers to advertise their wares or solicit for clients. But two landmark cases in the late 1970s removed the ban, and from then on it was devil take the hindmost. Americans do not do things by halves. "My custom TV ads can make you millions," shouted an advertisement in *Trial*, the magazine for American injury lawyers. It went on: "Twenty-seven lawyers have become millionaires while running my custom TV commercials; nine are multi-millionaires and twenty-two are close (net worth between $450,000 and $975,000). . . Some started with less than nothing! One borrowed $6,000 to go on the air and took in an off-shore injury case the second week that settled for $3.8 million."

The combination of advertising, aggressive solicitation, and the contingency fee system created a new breed of ambulance chasers. The relaxation of rules on class actions in the mid-1970s also gave a sizeable boost to aggressive group solicitation. A struggling lawyer had only to find a pollution or latent disease sufferer whose background was parallel to those of thousands of other industrial workers, and he had found a goldmine. By grouping potential plaintiffs together under a common banner, attorneys could construct powerful and extremely lucrative collective actions. When the *Exxon Valdez* sank off Alaska in 1989, lawyers from all fifty-two states descended in droves, even before the oil hit the beaches. According to a report in the *Wall Street Journal*: "Liability lawyers and prostitutes fresh from nearby Anchorage are said to prowl the dark, smoky bars in search of clients. Townspeople aren't as concerned about the prostitutes as they are about the lawyers. Sue Laird, a salmon fisherwoman from nearby Cordova, says she got twenty calls from lawyers within hours of the disaster. 'They are like cannibals. They bite into you and they don't let go.'"

Class actions allied to the propensity of juries to pick on the deepest pockets, created an incentive to litigate. The downside for plaintiffs' lawyers was minimal. The upside was often huge awards from which they could extract multi-million-dollar success fees. The consequences for the non-lit-igating consumer were less happy. In March 1986, *Time* ran a cover story titled: "Sorry America, Your Insurance has been Cancelled." It pointed out that after years of huge jury awards, buyers of insurance liability policies faced crippling bills, with increases in premiums ranging as high as 5,000 percent. The New York City subway system found that its insurance bill had increased from $800,000 to $9 million. A sporting goods manufacturer had been paying $8,000 a year for $25 million of product liability insurance; its renewal notice demanded a $200,000 premium for $1 million dollars of insurance.

AMERICAN LAWYERS

American lawyers were not slow to see the potential presented by asbestosis victims. Some sent X-ray equipped vans to park outside factories in order to give on-the-spot diagnoses to industrial workers. Research later found that these mobile tests contained huge numbers of diagnostic errors, but they tripled the number of asbestos law suits in one year. Direct mail was another useful sales technique. "You may be in danger of death," warned a mail-shot from a firm of Detroit lawyers to merchant seamen who might have been exposed to high concentrations of asbestos dust aboard their ships. The note went on to point out that damage awards for asbestosis victims were "in the six to seven figure range." Not surprisingly, thousands of legal actions rolled in.

The resulting trials involving multiple claimants were often of stagger-ing complexity, as manufacturers, insurers and plaintiffs disputed liability. In Cimino v. Raymark Industries, the court signed 373 pre-trial and trial orders, and over 3,000 depositions were taken. The trial lasted 133 days; 563

witnesses testified under oath, and the transcript ran to 25,348 pages. Altogether 6,000 exhibits, consisting of more than half a million pages of evidence, were submitted. The costs of such legal marathons were enormous, most ending up in the pockets of lawyers. A Rand Corporation study found that by the end of 1982, $1 billion had been spent on asbestos litigation, but less than a third had gone to the victims. "In asbestos-damage actions seventy-five cents out of every dollar goes to grey flannel suits, and twenty-five cents goes to blue collars and overalls," admits one policy-holder attorney. Each case on average, according to Rand, costs the defendant manufacturer and its insurers $95,000, of which $60,000 goes to meet legal fees. One manufacturer alone, Eagle-Picher Industries, which was forced to file for protection from its creditors under Chapter 11, faced legal costs of $119 million in 1989 for 137,000 claims against it. By the early 1990s, more than half of the twenty-five largest asbestos manufacturers in the United States, including Amatex, Carey-Canada, Celotex, Forty-Eight Insulations, Manville Corporation, National Gypsum Standard Insulation, Unarco, and UNR Industries had been forced into bankruptcy. By 1990, Manville alone was involved in 149,000 liability suits.

The parties to this legal nightmare blame one another. The plaintiffs' lawyers, representing the policy-holders, allege that it is the deliberate policy of insurers to drag things out for as long as possible, to avoid paying legitimate claims. "The insurance industry has decided to litigate in court to the last dead lawyer. Even if they lose they gain time," said Eugene Anderson, senior partner of Anderson, Koll, Olick and Oshinsky. The defendants, on the other hand, claim that the flood of asbestos litigation has been fed more by the greed of plaintiffs' lawyers than by the urge to right a public wrong. "Contingency fees provide some of these lawyers with a return of well over $10,000 an hour, encouraging them to recruit even more plaintiffs," claims Glenn Bailey, the chairman of Keene Corporation, a leading asbestos producer which is spending $800,000 each week in asbestos-related litigation. In the last three years Keene have settled 35,700 asbestos cases at a cost of $119 million, of which more than half was swallowed up in legal fees. "Unless something is done," Bailey adds bitterly, "I predict in ten years' time that there will be 3,000 defendants and 2,000,000 [asbestosis] cases with 170 bankruptcies, including Fortune 500 companies, and hundreds of thousands of jobs lost."[17] Paul Brodeur, the author of the definitive study cited earlier, regards such special pleading as obscene: "Asbestos litigation was not part of a plaintiff bar conspiracy but a valid effort by victims of asbestos disease to get some compensation before they died. It is right to suggest that there is a lot of invalid litigation in the USA, but God knows, asbestos hardly fits into that category."[18]

If costs are horrendous, trial delays are even worse. By the early 1980s, the US Courts were clogged with 25,000 asbestos cases waiting a hearing. Something had to be done to deal with the log-jam. In October 1982, the president of the Centre for Public Resources, James Henry, set up a meeting between asbestos plaintiff lawyers, insurance company executives and leading asbestos manufacturers, to see if the differences between the parties could be thrashed out. Under the chairmanship of the dean of the Yale Law School, Harry Wellington, lengthy negotiations took place to establish a central facility which would enable asbestos claims to be arbitrated without litigation. "The time has come for traditional and expensive courtroom warfare to give way to a private and equitable settlement of the asbestos tragedy," said Wellington. Eventually thirty-four asbestos manufacturers and sixteen insurance companies including Lloyd's took part in the Wellington facility, but several major insurers and manufacturers refused to participate. For a time the compromise worked as intended, but after three years the Wellington facility collapsed under the sheer weight of claims.

There followed another spate of legal actions, this time relating to property damage from buildings constructed with asbestos. In September 1984, a federal judge in Pennsylvania approved a national class action brought by some 14,000 schools against more than fifty asbestos manufacturers. By 1985, the Environmental Protection Agency estimated that asbestos was likely to be found in 700,000 government, residential and commercial buildings, and in 31,000 schools attended by seventeen million students and staff.

BATTERED LLOYD'S

For Lloyd's and its battered syndicates, this second wave of claims, potentially running into tens of billions of dollars, followed by a third wave from those who had been exposed to asbestos in the affected buildings, was the last straw. The consequences took some time to make themselves felt, but for individual Names they were far-reaching.

Richard Micklethwait, a farmer, married with two children, joined Lloyd's in 1979, writing £150,000 of risks, and was placed by his members' agent on Janson Green's syndicate 932 and two Wellington syndicates, 406 and 448, all with heavy exposure to asbestos and pollution claims. "I decided to go into Lloyd's because the farm income was going down 5 percent a year over the last ten years. I thought this would be a way of generating extra finance," he explained. For a few years things went relatively well, so he persuaded his wife to join too. "At least it paid the school fees." Today, faced by huge and mounting losses of over £200,000 with deficits exceeding 100 percent on his long-tail syndicates, Micklethwait has had to put his 400-acre farm, which his family have owned since 1867, up for sale. "It's completely ruined my life," he says. "We Names have been stitched up. Anybody putting money into Lloyd's needs their head examined."

Looking back on his experience, Micklethwait is ambivalent about whether he was rash in joining the market: "I still think it was the right thing for me to do at the time. I'd got a huge capital asset and there seemed no other way to subsidize it." He recalls that his initial returns from Lloyd's were just under 9 percent. "I've had gains of £17,000 and £18,000 and then tax refunds on top of that. It's been the only thing that kept this place afloat. But I think now that I should have had a much better return, considering the risk I was taking. The full extent of the risk was never explained to me." The failure of Lloyd's to disclose the extent of asbestos claims facing the market has led him to refuse to pay anything more despite the threat of a writ. "I am now being asked to reserve for losses that were concealed for many years. Why should I?" he says.[19]

Tim Powell, a former businessman and champion powerboat racer and his wife, Anthea, have racked up losses of more than £1 million at Lloyd's. They have been forced to sell their much-loved Chelsea house where they had lived for twenty-four years, and move to a smaller house in Wandsworth. "Losing your bloody home is one hell of a wrench," he says bitterly. In the last two years, his losses have accelerated to such an extent that the Powells have been forced to apply to the Lloyd's Names hardship committee. "To think that I'm paying something towards somebody who caught asbestosis fifty years ago, I find quite incredible and certainly it is something that was never explained to me," he says. "I think Lloyd's, who are supposed to be the experts, have been totally wrong-footed and caught on the hop." Powell blames a complete failure of regulation for his plight: "I'm not complaining about losses of properly managed syndicates. What I am complaining about are the unforgivable losses due to malpractices of one kind or another. Frankly, we have been robbed."[20]

Asbestos has also turned Warren Hurst's hopes of a comfortable retirement into a nightmare. The sixty-seven-year-old Canadian retired to eastern Ontario after a career as a chartered accountant and investment adviser. In 1982, on the advice of friends, he joined Lloyd's through the Stewart Wrightson members' agency and was put on two of its long-tail syndicates, Pulbrook 90 and 334, both heavily exposed to latent disease and pollution claims. Hurst says that at the time he had no worries. "All my friends were receiving cheques of $15,000 or $20,000, or more, every year," he recalls. But now, along with sixty other Lloyd's Names in the Hamilton area, he faces demands for more than $500,000. "I never dreamed of that kind of loss," he says. Hurst is bitterly critical of the way Lloyd's failed to regulate the market. "I find my own direct personal experience with the self regulation as practised at Lloyd's to be completely unsatisfactory," he wrote to the minister of Trade, John Redwood. "When my personal experience is potentially duplicated 27,000 times by other Names, I fear for the future of Lloyd's."[21]

Names on long-tail syndicates, such as Micklethwait, Powell and Hurst, know they can expect little public sympathy—the rich and the greedy who gamble and lose must take their chance, is the popular view. Yet if ordinary investors had been treated as Lloyd's treated many of its Names in the 1980s, there would be a public outcry. The scale of asbestos claims was foreseeable by the late 1970s; by 1982 it was clear that the market was facing a very serious problem. But little or none of this was disclosed to the thousands of Names who were recruited by commission agents and per-suaded to join long-tail syndicates in the mid 1980s. Unfortunately the nightmare of asbestos is still far from over.

The best estimate of what lies ahead is a study published by the Yale School of Organization and Management in 1992. Its author, Paul MacAvoy, who a decade ago accurately forecast a huge acceleration of asbestos claims, predicts that there will be nearly 200,000 asbestos-related deaths over the next quarter of a century at a cost to asbestos manufacturers and their insurers of $50 billion.[22] That sum is almost ten times the combined net asset value of the asbestos producers, and is roughly equal to the assets of their liability insurers. The net worth of the twenty-eight leading American asbestos companies is approximately $6 billion, while the combined book value of their forty-five primary and excess insurers is estimated at only $50 billion.

The conclusion is inescapable—large numbers of manufacturers and their insurers, both American and European, are headed for liquidation. For the victims of asbestos, this will mean that hundreds of thousands of them will be denied proper compensation unless governments intervene. The consequence of such an industry-wide meltdown for other types of policy-holder is hardly less serious. As the Yale study points out: "These estimates show that it is probably beyond the ability of the asbestos and the insurance industry to pay out the total claims that will be made. Unless action is taken to spread claims, a group of future claimants will remain uncompensated as a large number of insurance firms take bankruptcy proceedings." So far such blunt warnings have gone unheeded. But it cannot be long before a devastating series of financial failures drives home the message.

7

The Outhwaite Affair

"Our industry was built on 'Good Faith' and until all our contracts
are placed and honoured in accordance with 'Utmost Good Faith'
we do not deserve the reputation of an honourable profession."
Robert Kiln

At the centre of the asbestos disaster that was to wreck the fortunes of
thousands of Names was one of the cleverest men in the market, a dark-
haired, intense underwriter, Richard Henry Moffit Outhwaite. A taciturn
Yorkshireman, he had the reputation of an entrepreneur who ploughed his
own furrow and, in so doing, made a lot of money for his Names. He had
had a long career at Lloyd's, having joined the Merrett Group in 1956 as a
trainee. Merrett was one of the leaders in the marine market, insuring a wide
variety of direct marine business—hull, cargo and drilling. Its syndicates
also wrote large amounts of excess of loss and other specialist reinsurance,
accepting risks which other underwriters wanted to lay off, or deemed too
great. The Merrett style of underwriting was in the classic Lloyd's tradition
of being prepared to take unusual risks for high premiums.[1]

Outhwaite thrived in this milieu, and in 1970 was promoted by Roy
Merrett, the group's founder, to be joint underwriter. It seemed he was being
groomed as the heir apparent, but Roy's son Stephen, another determined
character, had other ideas. In 1974 Outhwaite left to form his own agency

where, as underwriter of a linked syndicate, Marine 317 and Non-Marine 661, he began to attract a following. Within five years the numbers of his Names had quadrupled to nearly 1,600, a quarter of whom, a higher proportion than average, were professionals in the market. The external Names were equally prestigious, ranging from the former prime minister Edward Heath to the tennis star Virginia Wade.

One of the areas in which the Outhwaite syndicate specialized was "run-off" reinsurance. A word of explanation is called for. When a syndicate's year is closed at the end of its three-year accounting period, the most crucial decision that has to be taken by the underwriter is the internal reinsurance to close (RITC). This is the amount required to reinsure any risks still outstanding, and is paid to the successor year by the syndicate whose accounts are being closed. Syndicates specializing in insuring long-term risks such as latent disease will have taken on liabilities of which the final outcome may not be known for decades. The RITC of these "long-tail" syndicates is therefore large, and the underwriter has to be careful to be fair to the Names (some of whom may be different) on both the old and the new years of account. If the RITC is too low, those Names who inherit the risks will lose, because the premium paid will be insufficient to meet future claims. If, on the other hand, it is too high, the losers will be the Names on the old year who will have paid too much. A "run-off" policy is similar to an RITC in that it covers all prior year risks. But whereas the RITC is an internal syndicate transaction, a run-off is an arms-length policy underwritten by another reinsurer. Most of these were commercial transactions but occasionally there were other motives.

An example of a "charity" run-off policy came in the early 1960s, when Lloyd's sponsored a rescue operation to protect Names on a syndicate which had failed. Lieutenant-Colonel Robert Roylance, a former chairman of Lloyd's, retired leaving more than a hundred on his syndicate, including several MPs and peers, facing losses of more than £2 million, a large sum in those days. The committee of Lloyd's, scenting trouble, proceeded to twist the arms of the market's leading underwriters, persuading them to take small lines on a policy which took over the liabilities of the failed syndicate. In the following years, a number of similar policies were placed to rescue syndicates whose underwriter had retired, died, or got into trouble.

Until the late 1970s, run-offs were relatively uncommon. But as the claims for asbestos mounted, matched by the growing concern of syndicates which had specialized in long-tail North American liability risks, the demand for a "sleep-easy" policy increased. Underwriters wanted to be able to tell their Names that, though current results were bad, past risks would not come back to haunt them. Some underwriters were more far-sighted than others. Roger Bradley, a Janson Green underwriter, recalls a conversation in October 1973 with Sturge's leading non-marine underwriter, Ralph Rokeby-Johnson. In the course of an amiable game of golf at Walton Heath, Bradley was taken aback when asked by Rokeby-Johnson: "Has Green [Peter Green] got his asbestos reinsurance in place and has he got enough of it?" When he asked what that meant, he was startled by the reply: "What I can tell you, my friend, is that asbestosis is going to change the wealth of nations. Lloyd's will probably be bankrupted in the final chapter unless something happens to intervene." Pressed further, Rokeby-Johnson predicted that asbestos claims would result in losses rising to $120 billion by the end of the century. It turned out to be a remarkably prescient forecast, as the most authoritative estimates now suggest that asbestos will cost insurers $50-$100 billion. Shortly after this conversation, Rokeby-Johnson reinsured most of his long-tail liabilities with the American insurance company Firemans Fund, thus safeguarding the future of Sturge syndicate 210.[2]

By the end of the 1970s the warning signals, even for the doziest underwriters, were getting louder. At a private dinner held in New York by Citibank in 1979, one of its senior executives, told one member of a visiting group of Lloyd's brokers and underwriters: "There are not enough dollars in the Lloyd's American Trust Fund to pay for asbestosis."[3] Shortly afterwards, US Attorneys representing Lloyd's in Illinois, Lord, Bissell and Brook, warned that it was impossible to predict the number of claims that might be brought: "There are numerous well-informed people who profess to believe that the claims filed to date represent only the beginning of a potential flood of asbestos litigation. We recall that the Secretary of Health, Education and Welfare of the United States reported in 1978 that 67,000 people each year will die from exposure to asbestos products during the rest of the twentieth century. We know that between eight and eleven million workers have variously been exposed to asbestos in the United States since the beginning of the Second World War, and that of these 4.5 million have worked with asbestos-containing insulation materials in shipyards. Most of the shipyard workers have been exposed to asbestos and it is estimated by the US Government that one third of all those heavily exposed to asbestos have died or are likely to die of asbestos-related diseases."[4]

In August 1980, the London market responded to these danger signals by setting up the Asbestos Working Party, chaired by Ted Nelson of K.F. Alder, to monitor developments. Its first action was to send a circular letter to all managing agents advising them how serious the asbestos threat was: "It must be emphasized that the potential losses involved here are so large and the issue is so complicated that we cannot allow a muddle-through-some-how approach." The letter quoted a prediction by one of the largest producers, Johns-Manville, that 30,000 asbestosis actions could be filed over the next decade, and suggested that underwriters should reserve on the basis of $75,000 a claim. It added a blunt warning: "Bearing in mind the substantial increases in costs over the coming years, it will be immediately apparent that reserve projections in this manner will have a serious impact on the market as a whole and yet, on the other hand, not to acknowledge the fact that reserves will inevitably increase would be irresponsible."[5]

Three months later another firm of US Attorneys, Wilson, Elser, Edelman and Dicker, advised Lloyd's that the claims position was continuing to worsen: "Of additional concern is the fact that discovery in pending litigation continues to develop information regarding industry's knowledge of the dangers of asbestos and its sometimes callous disregard of the untoward effects of the product upon unprotected workers. Evidence of this nature, as underwriters are well aware, serves to infuriate juries in the US and leads to shock verdicts and awards of punitive damages."

In February 1981, the Asbestos Working Party sent a second circular to the market, advising underwriters of "a rising trend in settlement figures" and warning: "At this stage it is not possible to predict how many claims will be filed." Shortly afterwards a leading American attorney, Victor B. Levit, whose firm specialized in defending insurance companies, spelt out the gravity of the situation to a meeting in London organized by the Lloyd's Underwriters' Non-Marine Association. Citing an industry estimate that asbestos lawsuits would cost insurers more than $1 billion annually over the next decade, he warned that this situation might reflect only a fraction of the problem, and that it was possible that an avalanche of claims could eventually force some insurance companies into liquidation. He concluded gloomily that "there will be many more claims than we can possibly anticipate from toxic substances, that such claims will often take many years to manifest themselves, and that the pounds and dollars involved will be far greater than we can possibly imagine." An equally pessimistic view was reflected in a study, "Asbestos: A Social Problem," published by Commercial Union's US subsidiary company in 1981. It noted that ever-increasing asbestos claims were already endangering the financial stability of many insurance companies, and predicted that several million more claims might eventually be filed. If so, it warned, "the damages that will be ultimately awarded will exceed the combined assets of the insurance and asbestos industries." Proof of the deteriorating position of asbestos producers came with the decision of Johns-Manville's auditors in February 1981 to qualify the company's accounts because of its potential huge liabilities.

By the end of 1981, the select group of accountancy firms who specialized in the auditing of syndicates at Lloyd's were concerned as to whether they would be able to approve the 1979 accounts of those underwriters heavily exposed to asbestos. More than 15,000 claims had already been filed, and they were increasing at a rate of 400 a month. On 16 February 1982 Don Tayler, then chairman of the Asbestos Working Party and underwriter of Pulbrook syndicate 90, wrote a further letter to underwriters: "It was emphasized to you in the circumstances of year end reserves that, in view of the uncertainties of the future, it is difficult at this stage to provide the market with any meaningful projection of the developments that are likely to take place over the coming years in regard to this problem. However, the number of claims is likely to escalate and for this reason I must emphasize that future deterioration is inevitable."

A REINSURANCE PACKAGE

Long-tail underwriters, faced by this deteriorating position, began to look for a way of dealing with the problem of their old years. Though almost all external Names remained in complete ignorance, the underwriters needed to be able to satisfy their auditors that they had made adequate provision for latent disease claims. Winchester Bowring, a broker which specialized in reinsurance, seeing an opportunity to generate profitable business, devised a reinsurance package for troubled long-tail syndicates. The key features were coverage of a first layer, say the first £25 million of loss, by a time and distance policy while a run-off contract would cover all prior-year risks above that figure on an unlimited basis.

Richard Outhwaite was the leading underwriter for such run-off business, often writing 100 percent of the risk. Other highly regarded underwriters, such as Stephen Merrett of syndicate 418 and Michael Meacock of 727, wrote similar run-offs. Premiums were high and potential profits appeared to be good at a time when margins on conventional policies were falling. Yet with hindsight, these run-off judgments were not just wrong, they were very rash. It was likely at the time the policies were written that there would be heavy claims. But the view of the run-off reinsurers was that such claims as might be made would arise only over a very long period, allowing profits to be made from the investment income. Outhwaite was by far the largest player in the run-off market, writing nearly fifty policies for the 1982 account. The gross income from these policies was $24.3 million, 15 percent of his syndicate's turnover for the year.

The run-off premiums proved to be completely inadequate for the risks that were being carried—the policies turned out to be the most disastrous insurance deals ever underwritten at Lloyd's. Within five years, Outhwaite's Names had had to pay calls of more than 100 percent, and the sum of known outstanding claims was nearer 1,000 percent. But that was only the beginning. By 1994, syndicate 317/661 had paid out 600 percent and, according to Chatset's *Guide to Syndicate Run-Offs*, the overall loss on the open year might eventually reach 2,500 percent. When Outhwaite was later asked why he had exposed himself and his Names to such an accumulation of risk, he replied: "The reason why I wrote the run-off contracts was that this business seemed to be a good risk at the time." One member's agent whose Names lost heavily on Outhwaite's syndicates was less charitable: "It was a mixture of arrogance and ignorance. I believe he knew the risks he was running but simply thought they would not come home to roost." Outhwaite nowadays has few defenders in the market, but what led him to risk his Names' fortunes is still a mystery. Certainly some of his fellow underwriters realized the dangers. Robert Kiln, who resigned from the committee in 1981, in part because he was disgusted by its failures to check the excesses of the market, suggested, in a lecture to the Insurance Institute of London at the end of 1984, that many long-tail syndicates were fundamentally under-reserved. The final loss ratios on such business were likely to average 400 to 500 percent at the end of the fifth year of an account, far more than the market had reserved. The situation, he noted, had become "very acute indeed," and experience pointed to the fact that audited reserve positions were unreliable. The run-off of the 1978-83 accounts could be devastating: "We are on a roller-coaster," he warned.

The first sign of trouble came with the decision of Ernst & Whinney to qualify Outhwaite's 1982 accounts when they were closed at the end of the normal three-year cycle in May 1985. "We are unable to express an opinion on the accuracy of the reinsurance to close and therefore the result of the 1982 account," said the auditors, referring to the uncertainties surrounding the run-off liabilities. Outhwaite despatched syndicate 317's annual report routinely, though he acknowledged that the run-off contracts were causing concern: "It appears that the accumulated social and environmental problems of the last forty years in the USA are being corrected at the expense of the insurance industry. . . After the experience of the last twelve months it would be unwise not to take a pessimistic view of future liabilities." Despite these warnings and the auditors' qualification, Outhwaite decided to announce the closure of the account. This was a crucial step for it meant that the old-year claims would be inherited by Names on the succeeding year who would be vulnerable if the reinsurance to close proved inadequate.

The response from the market was immediate. Colin Murray, chairman of Kiln, a leading member's agency, wrote to Outhwaite to say that he was withdrawing all his Names from syndicate 317/661: "We understand that your syndicates may have taken on very substantial gross commitments by way of so called run-off protections. . . The effect of writing a run-off stop loss is that the burdens of the many are carried by the few." When other agents, including John Donner, Frank Barber and David Evers, also warned that they would have to withdraw their Names, Outhwaite was forced to give in and leave the year open. As he later admitted: "If these threats were carried out, my perception was that syndicates 317 and 661 would have to stop writing business."[6]

Leaving the 1982 year open was a clear signal of trouble. But Outhwaite was determined to show a brave face. In a letter to Names on 1 July 1985, he wrote: "It is our considered view that despite the common assumption that an open account usually arises because of a significant loss, the 1982 account will prove to be profitable. The closing reinsurance, as originally agreed by our auditors, took a pessimistic view of the situation and it may be felt that it is only fair to the 1982 Names that they should benefit accordingly should this prove correct." This prediction was soon shown to be wildly wrong. Less than eighteen months later, Outhwaite was obliged to call £10 million, approximately 25 percent of line, quickly followed by a demand for a further £20 million. These were the first of a long series of demands for money from his unhappy Names.

THE INQUIRY BEGINS

During the summer of 1987, members' agents who had placed Names on the Outhwaite syndicate became increasingly concerned as one cash demand succeeded another. A steering committee led by John Heynes was formed, whose first action was to secure a standstill agreement. This allowed time for an investigation into the losses, while ensuring that any subsequent legal action would not be "time-barred"—prevented from being brought because of legal time limits. At the beginning of 1988 Freshfields, a leading firm of City solicitors, was instructed by the agents' committee to carry out an independent inquiry. Its report, completed in less than five months, was a model of clarity. It acquitted Outhwaite of underwriting recklessly or being "a soft touch," but it noted the underwriter's ignorance of the extraordinary risks he was undertaking on behalf of his Names. The transcript of Outhwaite's evidence to the inquiry reveals how little he knew of the dangers of asbestosis:

Q. "Did you look into the asbestos situation yourself in any detail before allowing the business to expand?"

A. "Not in great detail. You see, I would always have to rely very much on the people that we were reinsuring, their knowledge of their account and the effect of asbestosis . . . and the figures which they gave us to establish a reinsurance contract."

Q. "As I understand it, from about 1979 there were beginning to be some scares about asbestos, there were articles written by professors in the United States and the like?"

A. "Yes."

Q. "To what extent were you aware of the scare developing?"

A. "Of course, one is always talking in hindsight here. At the time one knew the non-marine market was concerned about it because they had set up the Asbestos Working Party. . . My direct knowledge of asbestosis was limited."

Q. "Did you make any specific additional inquiries other than what you knew about market gossip, if I can put it that way, about the asbestos situation with loss adjusters?"

A. "Not external to the market, no. You can get loss adjusters and reports and things which come through which one reads but I did not institute any independent inquiry about it."

Later Outhwaite was asked by one of the expert assessors to the inquiry, Christopher Rome, a leading underwriter:

Q. "I suppose this is almost the nub of the inquiry. Here was a situation where the non-marine market was extremely concerned and active underwriters in the market would have known of that general concern. The point, presumably, therefore, is why did you feel able to write these policies at a time when there was very great concern generally felt in the market about asbestosis. . . Were you more confident of the outcome than the reinsuring underwriters?"

A. "No. I was confident on the policies I wrote that the reinsuring underwriter had done sufficient research and had knowledge and was aware of the sort of costs that asbestosis were going to bring to bear on the syndicate and they were being reflected in the figures we were shown which meant one could work out some sort of policy for them. I did not see the policies in the light of the deterioration of asbestosis, I saw the policies in the light of something else which had not yet occurred, which they did not know of being safe-guarded against."

Q. "You were therefore confident that the asbestos problem was identified and properly catered for?"

A. "Yes."

Q. "Why, what led you to that conclusion given the situation was developing strongly? Why did you really think the asbestos problem was fully identi-fied?"

A. "Well, one has to choose one's words carefully. I do not say necessarily 'fully' because we always deal in what I think are reasonable margins. 'Adequately' is a better way to put it. One would enquire of the brokers and underwriters we were reinsuring what they had done and what provisions were being made in general terms for all of this. We were always getting the answers they had taken full account of what their liabilities were as far as they could foresee them for asbestosis."

Freshfields, unimpressed by these answers, concluded that Outhwaite was open to criticism for not investigating the risks he was assuming on behalf of his Names, and for writing a large number of policies without giving sufficient weight to the consequent aggregation of risk. "A substantial case could be made out for breach of duty," it stated. But, apparently swayed by the evidence of expert underwriting assessors, the report concluded paradoxically: "Any action that might be started by a Name on syndicates 317/661 against Outhwaite's or Mr. Outhwaite is unlikely to succeed. The expert evidence that would be brought on Mr. Outhwaite's behalf [from fellow underwriters] would, in our view, be likely to persuade the court that there was a good defence."

While the Names, who had by now banded together into a steering committee, mulled over this opinion, another defender of Outhwaite came forward. John Donner, chairman of Donner Underwriting Agencies, a tall, distinguished figure, had spent his whole career at Lloyd's as had his grandfather. He believed in the old verities of utmost good faith and full disclosure. He had known Richard Outhwaite for many years, and held him in high regard. "I had broked to him. He was professional, straight and tough. When he split away from Merrett, I backed him. The question I kept on asking myself is, what happened to that man, why did he write these risks?" he later recalled.[7]

Donner, who had been responsible for placing a number of Names, including his wife, on the Outhwaite syndicate, came to the conclusion that something was rotten. "I have never used the word conspiracy but what I do say is that information which was privy to a handful of people at the very top of Lloyd's was not properly disseminated." At the centre of his suspicions was the role of the Asbestos Working Party. Its members, he believed, had taken advantage of their inside knowledge of the developing asbestos crisis to transfer their syndicates' liabilities to Outhwaite. Donner publicly voiced his suspicions at the Lloyd's annual meeting in 1989, shortly afterwards writing to the chairman of Lloyd's, Murray Lawrence, demanding an inquiry. He pointed out that more than half the huge claims which had fallen on the Outhwaite syndicate were accounted for by just four contracts, two of which had been secured by leading members of the Asbestos Working Party acting through the same broker.[8] The implication of all this was plain. Utmost good faith had been notably lacking.

Donner was subsequently to broaden his allegation that Outhwaite had been cheated into the charge that there had been a market-wide agreement to hide from Names the seriousness and extent of the asbestos claims. At a meeting with Lloyd's chief executive, Alan Lord, and the head of Lloyd's regulatory department, Bob Hewes, he spelt out his suspicions: "At the time that the 1979 account was being closed at December 1981, there were two practical alternatives available to underwriters with an asbestos involvement. The first was to make full provision for the losses in line with information then available which would have resulted in many syndicates remaining open and some going out of business. The alternative was to roll the losses forward so that claims arose in the future, and future Names had to pay. This involved massaging the audit at December 1981. The Lloyd's panel of auditors made clear their view of the gravity of the situation to some individuals in senior positions of authority at Lloyd's. Senior people in the Market concluded that they could not face this and there was a considered decision by some of those in authority, underwriters and auditors, to view the 1979 account as far as asbestos claims were concerned in the most favourable light possible. The result of this would have been to roll forward the losses to later years."[9]

This was a damaging charge, for if true it meant that thousands of Names who had been persuaded to join Lloyd's in the mid-1980s had been seriously misled, because they had not been told of the risks to which they were being exposed. Faced by a leading members' agent crying foul, the council of Lloyd's decided to kick for touch. It announced that a full inquiry was warranted only if prima-facie evidence of misconduct could be produced, and appointed four of its nominated members who had no financial or other conflicts of interest to consider the Donner allegations. They made a high-powered group: Sir Maurice Hodgson, former chairman of ICI, Matthew Patient, a partner in Coopers & Lybrand Deloitte, David Walker, chairman of the Securities and Investments Board, and Alan Lord, deputy chairman and chief executive of Lloyd's.

During the next few months, the group held lengthy but inconclusive meetings with Donner and his solicitor. The evidence produced undoubtedly pointed to the fact that an inner circle had a shrewd idea how bad the asbestos claims position might become. The minutes of a senior partner present at a meeting of the Lloyd's advisory panel of auditors on 10 November 1981 noted: "It cannot be over-emphasized how serious the losses will be as a result of asbestosis and Mr. Murray Lawrence felt that where syndicates had reinsurance protection the scale of the losses may be sufficient to bankrupt the reinsurers." A further auditors' meeting on 25 January 1982 said it was impossible to estimate the final number of claims, but suggested that by the mid-1980s, "we should expect some 75,000 in total." A month later a letter was sent by the accountants, Neville Russell, on behalf of the five other panel auditors, to the manager of Lloyd's audit department, warning that many

syndicates faced unquantifiable losses from claims in connection with asbestosis and related diseases. It noted that there were already 15,000 individual claimants, and that the total number would be "considerably in excess
of this figure." Most syndicates, it added, were uncertain of their recoveries
and would incur losses on their writing of reinsurance business. It noted:
"Very little of this has been advised so far." After this series of warnings, the
auditors' letter concluded: "The Audit instructions require that if there are
any factors which may affect the adequacy of the reserves, then the auditor
must report to the Committee and obtain their instructions before issuing his
Syndicate Solvency Report. We consider that the impossibility of determining the liability in respect of asbestosis falls into this category and we
accordingly ask for your instructions in this respect."[10]

The Lloyd's committee's response to this highly embarrassing missive
was to pass the buck smartly back to the market. In a letter to underwriters
and managing agents on 18 March, the deputy chairman, Murray Lawrence,
pointed out that "the responsibility for the creation of adequate reserves rests
with managing agents who will need to liaise closely with their Auditors."
He added: "Managing and members' agents are strongly advised to inform
their Names of their involvement with asbestosis claims and the manner in
which their syndicates' current and potential liabilities have been covered.
Where reserves for asbestosis represented a high proportion of the reserves
of a syndicate, agents should consider whether or not to leave the account
open. It is the agent's responsibility to ensure that the reserves provided for
asbestosis are sufficient to meet the syndicate's liabilities regardless of
whether the account is closed or left open."

Ken Randall, who at the time was head of Lloyd's audit department,
later told the four-man independent inquiry that the letter of 18 March
contained a clear warning which was largely ignored by the market: "Many
underwriters had already decided to close 1979 using figures that did not
reflect what they knew about the risks, the liabilities for which they were
supposed to be reserving." He also recalled the grave concern of panel
auditors: "They considered that if a proper view was taken of reserves needed
by syndicates at December 1981 they would not be able to sign off the
accounts and many years would be left open or there would be such large
provisions that the Market would effectively be bankrupt."[11]

An important piece of evidence produced by Donner in support of his
charge of collusion was a draft affidavit from the former secretary of the
Asbestos Working Party, Stephen Mitchell, a solicitor who worked for

Elborne Mitchell. This confirmed that information available to members of the AWP on potential asbestos claims was so serious that if it had been fully taken into account, it would have meant that syndicates would have had to declare substantial losses in closing the 1979 year or else leave the year open: "In practice, I do not believe that even had the Working Party attempted to quantify the future cost to the market, they would have produced the correct figure. What I do know is that the Working Party realized that it would not be practical for any syndicate to attempt to reserve at the level they knew would be necessary if a proper attempt was to be made to cater for the problems as at 31st December 1981. I understand it would have been virtually impossible for any Syndicate with an asbestos exposure to have closed the 1979 account had they done so."[12]

Whether this represented Stephen Mitchell's considered view is not clear, as the affidavit was unsigned. However, in a subsequent letter to John Donner he wrote: "I think that some, maybe many, syndicates were in an intolerable dilemma as to whether to 'massage' the reinsurance to close or admit to large losses and, in some cases, go out of business. I do not say which of those alternatives was right. . . The point, however, is not whether, generally speaking, the asbestosis market did the right thing, but whether the fact of what it did was disclosed to Outhwaite and, if it wasn't, whether it would have affected his mind if it had been."[13]

Did Donner's evidence support the view that there had been a conspiracy to conceal information? Some underwriters certainly knew much more than others about the potential of asbestos claims to bankrupt the market. As for the Names, they were almost all blissfully ignorant of the gathering storm. The majority were told almost nothing by their members' or managing agents of the huge risks they were running. But the four nominated members of the Lloyd's council were unimpressed by Donner's claim of a market-wide plot. Six months after beginning their inquiry, they dismissed his allegations and concluded that there was nothing to merit a formal investigation: "No evidence has been provided which supports the suggestion that in placing their contracts the underwriters took advantage of information which was available to the AWP but was not made available to the market."[14] Despite this summary dismissal, the issues of non-disclosure and bad faith were not put to rest. The Lloyd's Names Associations' Working Party (LNAWP), representing the worst hit Names, was later to use the Donner allegations to claim that Lloyd's insiders had deliberately withheld information from Names in order to lure them into the market.

"Since 1979," it noted, "nearly 10,000 Names have joined Lloyd's while successive Chairmen and Committee members knew that asbestos could break Lloyd's. Can any Name recall having these facts drawn to his attention by the Rota Committee? A recent court case was told that untruths were better described as being economical with the truth. In relation to asbestos, Lloyd's economy was downright parsimonious." The chairman of the LNAWP, Christopher Stockwell, said: "What happened in 1982 was a disgraceful cover-up. Information known to Lloyd's was withheld from the external Names." Few Lloyd's professionals are persuaded by these arguments. "Of course Names were suckered into joining Lloyd's," said one former council member. "But they were suckered through snobbery and greed, not because they weren't told about asbestosis."

Though Donner had been unable to prove a market-wide conspiracy, he had shown that individual syndicates seeking run-off policies had not always been as frank as they should have been. Richard Outhwaite used this weapon of material non-disclosure to dispute claims on twenty-five of the thirty-two run-off contracts. Several of the disputes went to arbitration; others, encouraged by a mediator appointed by Lloyd's, Mark Littman QC, were renegotiated. As a result Outhwaite was successful in avoiding unlimited liability in many of the run-offs, thus saving his Names millions of pounds. Typical was the deal done with Pulbrook syndicate 90, which had huge exposure to both asbestosis and pollution and was one of the largest claimants under the run-off policies. After a protracted arbitration in which it was alleged that Don Tayler, syndicate 90's underwriter, had failed to disclose that reserves against asbestosis had had to be sharply increased, a compromise was struck in which Outhwaite's share of the ultimate loss was capped at $250 million. Another big claimant, the Murray Lawrence agency, also agreed, under pressure from Outhwaite, that syndicate 362 would resume the liabilities on its unlimited run-off in exchange for $62 million over six years. This run-off policy had been placed with Outhwaite seventeen days after Murray Lawrence signed the Lloyd's letter to managing agents on 18 March 1982, advising them to make adequate reserves for asbestos claims.

THE OUTHWAITE LITIGATION

The result of this and similar deals was that a large proportion of the Outhwaite losses was spread across the market. There was undoubtedly an element of rough justice about this mutualization—Outhwaite Names were facing losses of £200 million, equivalent to 450 percent of their line. For an average Name subscribing £25,000, this represented a cash call of £116,000. Over the next twenty years, it was predicted that pollution claims would double, or possibly even triple, this deficit.

At the beginning of 1988, a large majority of the 1,600 Outhwaite Names decided that they had had enough. A steering committee, headed by an amiable but tough-minded Old Etonian businessman, Peter Nutting, was formed. It sought legal advice which, contrary to the original Freshfields opinion, concluded that the Names had a winnable case. The view of Anthony Boswood QC and Michael Hart QC was that Outhwaite's professional performance in taking on such huge asbestosis risks "fell far below the standard of skill and competence reasonably expected of him in the conduct of the syndicate's affairs." Nearly 1,000 Names stumped up an initial £250 plus 4 percent of their premium line to fund the action. The Outhwaite Action Group soon had a kitty of more than £2 million. The hierarchy of Lloyd's harrumphed, deplored the rush to litigation, and said the Names did not have a chance. Outhwaite, they said, had not been negligent. It was just the bad luck of the draw. David Coleridge, later to become chairman of Lloyd's, unwisely predicted that when the Outhwaite Names lost, all the other legal actions started by Names against their members' and managing agents would "drop into the sink." At an initial meeting of Outhwaite Names at the Baltic Exchange, Sir Peter Miller, a member of the syndicate, warned his fellow Names that they were wasting their time. Lloyd's would sort out everything, he said.

Despite this advice from on high, a writ alleging negligence was issued against the Outhwaite agency by 987 out of the 1,614 Names on the syndicate. They included a roll-call of the prominent: Edward Heath, Robert Maxwell, Rocco Forte, Adnan Khashoggi, Lord Weidenfeld, Patrick Sheehy, chairman of BAT, John Ritblat, chairman of British Land, and the sports stars Tony Jacklin and Virginia Wade. When the case opened in the High Court before Mr. Justice Saville in October 1991, much was at stake, not least Richard Outhwaite's reputation as one of the market's leading underwriters. Had he been negligent in writing the run-off contracts and thus exposing his Names to huge and unquantifiable liabilities running into the twenty-first century? No less important was the issue of duty of care.

The main target of the Outhwaite Names' action was not the Outhwaite managing agency but some eighty members' agencies which had been responsible for placing Names on his syndicates. That was because the Names' formal contractual relationship was with the members' agent, not the managing agent. An additional reason for targeting the members agents was that the only hope of recovery of the £150 million claimed in damages lay in the professional indemnity policies, known as errors and omissions or E&O for short, which each agent was obliged to carry. The members' agents themselves had few capital reserves—the only deep pockets were the E&O insurers. But were members' agents responsible in law for the actions of an underwriter over whom they had virtually no control?

The documentary evidence took up so much of the small Court One that the witnesses barricaded behind huge box files could hardly be seen. Nor were conditions any more comfortable for the 150 barristers, solicitors, journalists and other hangers-on, many of whom had to half sit, half lie on the floor. Anthony Boswood QC acknowledged the wide public interest when he opened the case for the plaintiffs: "Never in the commercial history of the City of London has so much of other people's money been lost by the single-handed negligence of one man." The first principle learned by every school leaver starting his first job in an insurance firm, he told the court, was that the whole object was to transfer the risk of loss from the shoulders of the few to the shoulders of the many. "What Mr. Outhwaite did was precisely the opposite." The plaintiffs' counsel levelled three charges against the underwriter: Outhwaite's lack of knowledge of, and failure to inquire into, the fast growing tide of asbestosis claims; his recklessness in accumulating so many risks in an unquantifiable area; and his failure to keep proper records. The files relating to the run-off contracts, he said, could only be described as "an absolute nightmare."

Outhwaite's defence, set out by Kenneth Rokison QC representing the errors and omissions insurers, was straightforward. First, Outhwaite's understanding of asbestos in 1981-82 was no different from the rest of the market's. The underwriter "neither was nor is a sucker and a pushover." No one at that stage, he said, foresaw the extraordinary escalation of claims that would follow US court decisions. A graph of claims against the leading asbestos producer Johns-Manville was produced, showing that actions filed for asbestosis had soared from less than 1,500 in 1977 to nearly 45,000 in 1989. Second, that Outhwaite was entitled to rely on the reserve figures for asbestosis given to him by syndicates seeking run-off policies. Business at Lloyd's, particularly reinsurance, was conducted on a basis of trust. Rokison claimed that Outhwaite's actions were entirely consistent with the practice of the market, and had indeed been matched by those of other leading underwriters who had also written run-off policies in 1981-82. "What the plaintiffs have to show," said Mr. Rokison, "is that no reasonable, competent underwriter would have done what Mr. Outhwaite did." He added that the plaintiffs could not ignore "a substantial and probably insurmountable hurdle that other underwriters did write similar risks."

The first dent in this defence came when Outhwaite, under cross-examination, was forced to admit that his experience of American long-tail business was limited. But he claimed this was less important than his knowledge of the syndicates seeking the run-off policies. He also conceded that he had not seen reports from the Asbestos Working Party and had not read any of the insurance trade papers which dealt with US casualty risks. Nor had he read any of the four reports commissioned by Lloyd's from US attorneys, circulated to all underwriters, which had warned the market of the gathering asbestosis crisis. This led the plaintiffs' counsel to comment: "Mr. Outhwaite kept himself in what can only be described as a state of wilful ignorance."

What was decisive to the outcome of the case was not, however, damage done under cross-examination but the evidence of the expert witnesses. The key witness for the plaintiffs, Heinz Ulrich Von Eicken, former executive manager in London of the leading German reinsurance company Munich Re, proved unshakeable. He said that Outhwaite must have been living in "cloud-cuckoo-land" when he wrote the thirty-two run-off contracts. It was "pure folly" to write such contracts without thorough research. In his expert report he said: "One simply has to assume that a man who is writing 100 percent shares of unlimited covers in a specialized field knows much more about the field than individual cedants." Outhwaite had been "astonishingly uncritical" in his treatment of the brokers' material in support of the run-off contracts. His record keeping had been "sloppy and incompetent." Von Eicken pointed out that Outhwaite was not a specialist in casualty risks, knew little about asbestosis, and had not even seen it as part of his task to monitor the accumulation of risk. He was open to serious professional criticism on any one of these counts, but when viewed collectively "I would go so far as to say that the case against him is unanswerable."

Faced by this onslaught, all that the defence could do was to seek to undermine Von Eicken's evidence by suggesting that he was ill qualified to comment. It was pointed out that Munich Re had also written its share of asbestos risks in North America. When Von Eicken suggested that if Outhwaite had visited American attorneys before underwriting the thirty-two contracts, it would have "put the fear of God in him," Kenneth Rokison QC for Outhwaite responded that the syndicate seeking the run-off policy was in "a much better position" to assess the impact of asbestosis. Outhwaite was entitled, he said, to trust the ceding syndicate and the broker to present "a full and fair picture."

If Von Eicken was damaging to Outhwaite's cause, the defence was not helped by its own expert witness Dick Hazell, underwriter of syndicate 190 and a leading member of Lloyd's council. He was forced into a number of admissions, not least that Outhwaite had been "imprudent in some respects." Hazell claimed, however, that Outhwaite had been "perfectly justified" in writing the run-off contracts. No one had been able to predict the explosion of asbestos claims. As a result, underwriters had calculated their potential liability on the basis of past claims. But when asked under cross-examina-tion: "How could this be a sound methodology in relation to asbestos, which everyone agreed was a new phenomenon in which the past could not be regarded as a guide to the future?" he virtually admitted that the approach had been unsound: "None of us at the time recognized how big the problem was." At one point Anthony Boswood QC for the plaintiffs said that although Outhwaite had claimed that he had asked for predictions of potential ultimate losses, he had accepted some contracts without receiving such a forecast or a detailed breakdown of asbestos claims. In reference to one particular contract with Fireman's Fund, Boswood asked: "Do you have any explana-tion consistent with prudence and competence as to why he did not?" Hazell responded: "No, I do not."

PEACE TALKS

After this damaging encounter, Mr. Justice Saville announced that there would be an adjournment for a week to permit "administrative details" to be tackled. On the day the trial was due to resume, the parties concerned, the Outhwaite Names Association and the errors and omissions insurers, an-nounced that they were in negotiation. It had taken five months and forty-nine days of hearings, with costs estimated at more than £5 million, to get to this point. As Stephen Merrett was to remark: "Litigation is the most expensive means of settling a dispute, short of warfare."[15]

The initiative for talks had come from the chairman of the Outhwaite Names Association, Peter Nutting, who spoke to Merrett after Von Eicken's marathon cross-examination. Nothing came of this first approach, but while Nutting was in court listening to Hazell's evidence in the witness box, he got a message that the chairman of Lloyd's wished to see him. In David Coleridge's office he found Stephen Merrett and the lead E&O underwriter, Malcolm Cox. The opening offer was £90 million, which Nutting later privately admitted he was minded to accept.[16] The eventual terms of the settlement were £116 million, of which £80 million was for compensation and interest, £34 million for future deterioration of the account, and £2 million for legal costs. It was hailed as a victory for the Names. The chairman of the Outhwaite Names Association called the settlement "a thoroughly satisfactory outcome to what has been a long and difficult road." Initial euphoria soon, however, gave way to doubts. The 1982 year still remains open, and it is by no means clear how much Outhwaite Names will have to pay in future years for cash calls. Three months after the case, they were asked for another 50 percent of line, an average of £15,000. They now face further losses which, Chatset estimates, could be as high as 2,100 percent. Peter Nutting defends the out-of-court settlement on the grounds that even if the Names had won on liability, arguments over quantum (the amount of damages) would probably have been appealed right up to the House of Lords.

The 600 Outhwaite Names who had not taken part in the litigation and were thus excluded from the financial settlement were distinctly unhappy with the outcome. Some had taken this course because they did not believe in suing, others because they felt the action had little chance of success. Many, particularly working Names, had felt under pressure not to rock the boat, having at the outset received a letter from the then chairman, Murray Lawrence, urging them to desist from premature and possibly unnecessary litigation. After the settlement, they found that they were time-barred from pursuing their own legal action. Their bitterness was summed up by Richard Outhwaite: "If anyone had suggested to me a few years ago that Names who were loyal to the Lloyd's ethic, who stood by the advice of their agents and the Lloyd's authorities, would be worse off financially than members who sued all and sundry, I would not have believed it. Apparently the Council of Lloyd's believes this to be none of their business. I would have thought that the equitable treatment of Names on a syndicate was fundamental to the business."[17]

The decisive outcome of the Outhwaite case had a dramatic effect on other groups considering litigation. Their ranks swelled as the implications of the settlement sunk in. Those who sued, it appeared, had a good chance of recovering some, if not all, of their losses; those who did not would be ignored. It was a lesson that was mercilessly rubbed in by the steering groups conducting the actions on behalf of nearly a dozen syndicates including Pulbrook 334 and 90, Merrett 418, Aragorn 384, and Poland 105 and 108.

The impact on the market and its authorities was also profound. The chairman and the council now knew that a decade of litigation by Names against syndicates, members' agents, brokers, and auditors was inevitable. The sums at stake were so huge, running into billions of pounds, that it was difficult, if not impossible, to settle outside a court room. When the Outhwaite Names Association met to approve the terms of the settlement agreement, its counsel, Anthony Boswood QC, said three particular lessons had emerged. First, the notion that underwriting was a mystery so shrouded in obscurity and inherently risky that ordinary standards of skill, competence and prudence were not applicable and would not be enforced by the court, was a myth. Second, Lloyd's had learnt that it could no longer afford to treat Names with the lofty disdain that the Outhwaite litigants had been subjected to. When Names grouped together and had adequate funding for a legal action, they were a force to be reckoned with. Lastly, it was a recipe for disaster for the conduct of a business which involved risking other people's money to be in the hands of one powerful individual without proper management systems.

A direct consequence of the Outhwaite settlement was the collapse of the professional indemnity market at Lloyd's. This forced the council to exempt syndicate managements and members' agents from having to have such cover as a condition of trading. There could hardly have been a more embarrassing public acknowledgement of the depth of the crisis facing the market. The world's leading market in errors and omissions cover was no longer willing to insure the competence of its own underwriters and managers. If Lloyd's had so little trust in itself, why should anyone else have faith in its abilities to conduct a well-ordered market place? Sadly, it was a question to which there was apparently no satisfactory answer. Lloyd's deputy chairman, Robert Hiscox, has, however, attempted one: "First, E&O was never meant to cover bad underwriting decisions, only clerical errors. Second, it is daft for any syndicate to cover the stupidity of other syndicates."[18]

For Richard Outhwaite the settlement, which was concluded by the E&O insurers over his head, was a bitter pill. Inevitably, Names drifted away from his syndicates. Outhwaite was philosophical about his own future when I went to see him just before he surrendered control. He remained convinced that he was right to have written the run-off contracts and, though he regretted the resulting losses for the Names, he said the underwriting had been conducted with diligence and in good faith. "There was certainly no negligence," he insisted. Sanguine about his own future, he was much more gloomy about the prospects for Lloyd's. "I am not confident that the market will survive," he said. Whether it would or not depended, he believed, on changes to its capital structure. There was no future for unlimited liability. "We will never get any significant new capital in Lloyd's unless the basis of membership is a limited one in both time and money. Unless drastic changes are made, the capital base will simply erode. We have to devise a system which will put a final line."[19]

Outhwaite's pessimism about the future of the market is closely linked to his view that the council has shown little leadership. "Too many decisions have involved the quick fix," he wrote in his report to Names. "There has been little perception of any grand strategy. There are times where the market is facing a crisis and at such times inspired leadership is required, and where else should we look other than to the Chairman and Council?"

Such comments provoke a bitter reaction from those he criticized. They point out that Outhwaite remains a very rich man, unlike many of the Names he ruined. The fact that he and other underwriters who caused so much mayhem by writing unlimited run-off policies were able to escape the financial wreckage is a cause of much anger. But though Outhwaite is the most spectacular example of misjudgment, he was by no means the only loser from the disaster of asbestos. In retrospect, it is extraordinary that the majority of underwriters at Lloyd's were for so many years ignorant of the huge risks they were taking by writing general liability policies without aggregate limits. The medical evidence of the dangers of latent disease had been accumulating throughout the twentieth century. The rapid acceleration in US civil litigation, and the consumerist approach taken by US courts of searching for the deepest pocket, were obvious to anyone who read court reports and medical journals. Lloyd's failure to spot these danger signals was to cost its Names dear. At the latest count, asbestos is estimated to have lost the market more than £5 billion, an average of £170,000 per Name. The future could be worse. Robert Sweeney, an American lawyer specializing in asbestos claims, estimates that Lloyd's liabilities from asbestosis will amount to £30 billion over the next two decades.

Who goes bust will be decided by the courts. But it is, at the very least, disturbing that so few managing and members' agents followed the advice of Lloyd's deputy chairman, Murray Lawrence, in his letter of 18 March 1982 that they should "inform their Names of their involvement with asbestosis claims and the manner in which their syndicates' current and potential liabilities have been covered." The failure to do this led many thousands of unwitting Names to join long-tail syndicates throughout the 1980s. Many professionals at Lloyd's realized the dangers. Very few outsiders did.

8

Pollution: An American Nightmare

"We don't have deep enough pockets
to clean up the Western World."
Tim Holloway, chairman of Lloyd's Non-Marine Association.
September 1989

One June morning in 1960 Marvin Smith, a game warden from the Colorado Department of Fish and Game, was out watching wildfowl on a lake near a chemical plant on the outskirts of Denver. What he saw worried him: "Some of the movements looked very strange to me. I had never seen a duck swimming in a circle—with one wing drooped. One or two other ducks with outstretched necks had the appearance of feeding but they appeared to be very nervous, almost uncontrollable. Worst of all, I remember seeing one duck that simply could not hold its head up, and every time it tried, it had to drop its head into the water. It was drowning itself."

Angered by what he had seen, the game warden confronted the plant manager at the Rocky Mountain Arsenal, where Shell manufactured a range of powerful insecticides. His fears were brusquely dismissed: "That's just the price of doing business if we are killing a few birds out there." Subsequently the plant manager, Mr O. M. Williams, was reported in the *Denver Post* as saying: "These are industrial lakes and we have no control over use of the lakes by ducks. . . As far as we're concerned, this situation is all right and we have no plans to change our operations."[1]

Two decades later the disregard which Shell, along with many other American companies, showed for the environment reaped a bitter, hugely expensive harvest. The Rocky Mountain Arsenal had by then become notorious as the "most polluted site on earth." The consequence came in 1980 when Congress passed the Comprehensive Environmental Response, Compensation and Liability Act. The most far-reaching environmental legislation ever enacted, CERCLA requires polluted sites to be cleaned up irrespective of cost; it is retroactive in that it makes corporate polluters pay for the past. But its legislative sweep goes further. The liability is "joint and several," which means that any company, however small its role in the pollution, can be held responsible for the entire cost of reclamation. A company may have deposited only 1 percent of the waste at a municipal dump site, but can be held liable for 100 percent of the costs unless it can find others to share the bill. Congress was determined that whoever was going to pay for the clean-up, it would not be Uncle Sam. Under the terms of the act, not only the past and present owners of the site, but also anybody else who manufactured or transported toxic materials found at the site is "strictly liable." This means that the government does not have to prove negligence or failure to exercise due care, merely that those held responsible are properly identified as owners, generators, or transporters.

The impact of the legislation on corporate America has been stunning. The Rocky Mountain Arsenal is just one of thousands of contaminated areas throughout the United States which are having to be cleaned up at a cost of hundreds of billions of dollars. Given this huge liability, it was inevitable that companies would seek to shift the burden and look to their insurers for compensation. The result has been an avalanche of litigation at the heart of which stands Lloyd's, one of the major insurers and reinsurers of North American liability policies. So vast is the scale of the pollution—there are estimated to be 400,000 sites requiring reclamation—that it threatens not just the London market but the survival of much of the American property-casualty insurance industry.

At about the time Marvin Smith spotted the dying wildfowl on the Rocky Mountain Arsenal lake, a warning was published by a young scientist, Rachel Carson, whose book *Silent Spring* was to become a seminal study for the environmental movement. "In the entire water-pollution problem there is probably nothing more disturbing than the threat of widespread contamination of groundwater," she wrote. "It is not possible to add pesticides to water anywhere without threatening the purity of water everywhere. This groundwater is always on the move, sometimes at a pace so slow that it travels no more than fifty feet a year, sometimes rapidly, by comparison, so that it moves nearly a tenth of a mile in a day. It travels by unseen waterways until here and there it comes to the surface as a spring or perhaps it is tapped to feed a well but mostly it contributes to streams and so to rivers. Except for what enters streams directly as rain or surface run-off, all the running water of the earth's surface was at one time groundwater. And so, in a very real and frightening sense, pollution of the groundwater is pollution of water everywhere."

Its failure to heed this warning was to prove expensive for Shell. In October 1983, after years of prevarication, the company was told by the US Environmental Protection Agency to clean up the Rocky Mountain Arsenal. The federal order set off one of the largest single day's falls in the company's share price. The next day Shell began legal action in San Mateo Superior Court, California, against 220 insurance companies and 400 Lloyd's syndicates which had acted as its liability insurers between 1946 and 1983. At stake was the question of who was to pay clean-up costs estimated at nearly $2 billion.

The marathon litigation was so complex that it was split into two stages. The first phase, which dealt with issues of policy interpretation, took more than four years to get to trial. The case eventually began on 4 November 1987 and lasted seventy-six days, including six weeks of closing arguments. The second phase, the decisive jury trial, began nine months later and lasted sixty-seven days. The issues which the jury had to decide were whether Shell knew of the damage its operations were causing, whether that damage was deliberate, or whether Shell was an innocent victim of changing public attitudes to the environment.

Pollutants had been seeping from the Rocky Mountain Arsenal for nearly half a century, from the time it was built by the US Army during the Second World War as a secret chemical warfare plant to produce nerve gas, blistering agents, and incendiary devices. Such a facility would normally have been sited by the sea, far from residential and farming developments but, because of the need for wartime secrecy, the plant was constructed with little concern for the environment. In 1952 Shell took over the lease of the South Plants area, part of the Arsenal which had been rented to a small chemical company by the army at the end of the war. Right from the start, it was apparent that the chemical facility was poisoning the surrounding countryside, killing everything it touched—plants, animals and crops.

If Shell did not know this when it began producing pesticides in the early 1950s, its executives had only to read Rachel Carson's book a decade later to be left in no doubt about the lethal character of its manufacturing site. "It must have been by such a dark underground sea," she wrote in 1960, "that poisonous chemicals travelled from a manufacturing plant in Colorado to a farming district several miles away, there to poison wells, sicken humans and livestock and damage crops—an extraordinary episode that may easily be only the first of many like it. . . Farmers miles from the plant began to report unexplained sickness among livestock; they complained of extensive crop damage. Foliage turned yellow, plants failed to mature and many crops were killed outright. There were reports of human illness, thought by some to be related."

Shell's plant manager from 1965 to 1983, J. Harvey Knaus, was cross-examined about this passage in the jury trial:

Q. "Mr Knaus, when you read *Silent Spring* were you aware that it referred specifically to the Rocky Mountain Arsenal before you got the book?"

A. "No."

Q. "So when you got to page forty-two and saw that she was zeroing right in on the Rocky Mountain Arsenal, did that come as a jolt to you?"

A. "By the time I had gotten there, I had an understanding of what the book was about."

Shell knew what was happening at the Rocky Mountain Arsenal but did nothing about it. Most of the pollution came from freshwater lakes used to cool reactors producing two potent pesticides, aldrin and dieldrin. Chemical by-products from the reactors leaked into the cooling water continually recirculated from the lakes. Other highly toxic wastes leached into the ground from evaporation basins used as open chemical sewers.

The damage caused by these processes was obvious. In June 1954, a neighbouring farmer reported widespread crop damage on his farm. A year later, the University of Colorado concluded that the Arsenal's unlined basins were funnelling vast amounts of chemical pollutants directly into the groundwater. By then, Shell knew it had a major problem on its hands. It was the company's policy to collect all duck and animal carcasses in order to bury them before scheduled visits by inspectors from the Colorado Department of Fish and Game. One former employee said that on a single day he collected over eighty-five dead birds and paralysed jackrabbits around the lakes. In 1961 Dr. Ted Walker, a member of the University of Colorado team, published a study of the Arsenal. It noted: "its waste disposal practices have seriously contaminated the underlying free groundwater aquifer in a large area that extends northwest from the waste basins." The report concluded: "Approximately six-and-a-half square miles of aquifer now contains groundwater that generally is toxic to plants, impotable to humans and apparently injurious to livestock." By 1967, in the words of the president of the Shell Chemical Company, Jack St. Clair, it was common knowledge that the lakes "were a sore on the landscape."[2]

In May 1970 the US army, the owner of the site, which had been pressing Shell for more than a decade to stop its pollution, delivered a written warning. The oil company, it said, would be liable for 85 percent of the costs of clean-up. The reaction of Shell's plant manager, J. Harvey Knaus, was recorded by the official who handed over the letter: "This is really a bomb. I thought I had seen some big problems but this beats them all. We have felt there would be something coming on this sooner or later, but we were hoping we would be able to hold out longer. We have been concerned about the contamination problem for some time. But only the government could underwrite such a plan as this. Paragraph C, at the bottom of page two [requiring the payment of claims due to groundwater contamination] would probably kill us."[3]

IN COURT

Despite the ultimatum, Shell continued to use the leaking open-air evaporation basins for its toxic wastes for a further eight years. The reason was simple: the returns were excellent. Shell generated profits from Rocky Mountain of between $12 million and $24 million a year. These damaging facts emerged during the four-month trial to determine whether Shell or its insurers would have to pay the $2 billion reclamation bill. In its opening statement, Shell said that it had acted throughout in accordance with its lease, which required it to dispose of hazardous wastes at the Arsenal. It had not known that pollution at the site would cause wider harm to the environment. The company claimed that it was a casualty of changing public attitudes which had resulted in unforeseen federal legislation. It also claimed that it was a victim of its insurers, who had charged huge premiums in the past but failed to inspect the site, and were now seeking to avoid having to meet their obligation to compensate the company.

The case for the insurers was put by Barry Bunshoft, senior partner in Hancock, Rothert and Bunshoft, a Californian law firm coordinating the defence for Lloyd's. He told the court that Shell knew precisely what it was doing when it polluted the Arsenal for nearly thirty years. Far from being accidental or sudden, it was a deliberate policy. The company knew, from the moment it took over, that its hazardous wastes were fouling ponds where ducks were dying in their thousands and that its wastes were leaking from chemical basins into aquifers miles from the Arsenal, poisoning crops. In his closing argument to the jury, Bunshoft developed the theme that the case was not just about insurance law: "I asked all the Shell witnesses whether they felt they had a moral responsibility for turning the Rocky Mountain Arsenal into the most polluted place on earth. Not one Shell witness said he thought he had a moral responsibility. Not one Shell witness said he was sorry for what he had done. Not one Shell witness said he wished he could do it all over again, so this time he would do it right. . . When it comes to judging the thirty-year history of the pollution of the Rocky Mountain Arsenal, the conduct of the Shell Oil Company was morally bankrupt."

After this peroration, the jury deliberated for six days. On 18 December 1988, it delivered a verdict against Shell in each of the thirty-one years for which the company had sought coverage. The jury voted eleven to one for the defending insurers on policies dating from 1952 to 1959, and eleven to none, with one abstention, on policies between 1960 and 1982. It was a significant victory for Lloyd's and its co-insurers; potential claimants in other jurisdictions were closely watching the verdict. Four years later, on 22 January 1993, the lower court verdict was partially upheld by California's Court of Appeal. In a 104-page judgment, it ruled that Shell could not collect on 800 comprehensive general liability policies issued after 1969 when insurers introduced a clause limiting cover for pollution. But on the crucial question of whether Shell had knowingly polluted the Rocky Mountain site, the Appeal Court found that the lower court had been misdirected and that the issue should be retried. The issue, said Judge Ming Chen, was not whether Shell should have known that it was contaminating the site, but whether it had actually "expected and intended" the pollution. So after a decade's hard slogging and legal bills of $100 million, the Rocky Mountain case is still undecided.

At this point it is necessary to turn back to the beginning of the pollution saga. Lloyd's was particularly vulnerable because it had underwritten thousands of loosely worded general liability policies for Fortune 500 companies across the United States during the 1950s and 1960s. These policies did not mention, let alone exclude, environmental damage, however caused. Ironically, an attempt to introduce a specific exclusion clause for non-accidental pollution was made by a few London underwriters in the 1950s, but their fears were ignored. As a result, most of the policies were written on a basis which enabled policy-holders to claim on long-extinct policies and even to argue that deliberate acts of pollution were covered. Lloyd's syndicates had also written huge amounts of reinsurance for primary insurers of US general liability policies.

After 1970 Lloyd's, along with other American insurers, began to scent trouble, and liability policies were rewritten with an exclusion clause designed to prevent claims for environmental damage apart from "sudden and accidental" incidents. The intention may have been clear, but the American courts were not accommodating, frequently redefining plain language to extend coverage to policy-holders. A federal judge, Joseph Sadofski, went so far as to enunciate the novel legal concept that "public interest overrides contractual language."[4] In many other cases, the attraction of the deep pockets of the insurers was to prove irresistible. As Tom Wolfe noted in *The Bonfire of the Vanities*, an American inner-city jury is simply a means of redistributing wealth.

The first major claim to hit Lloyd's came in the summer of 1978 when residents of Love Canal, a blue-collar housing development near Niagara Falls, New York State, noticed that, following a heavy rainstorm, large foaming pools of a coloured chemical liquid had formed in some of their gardens. The third base of the local school's baseball pitch disappeared into a rusted chemical drum buried just below the surface. Children and dogs burned their feet playing in nearby fields. Within days, the first of some 300 families was being evacuated, leading President Carter to declare a federal emergency. State health officials found that the Love Canal families had been living on top of a bubbling quagmire of chemicals; pollution levels were up to 5,000 times higher than safety standards. Altogether eighty-two chemical substances, eleven of them carcinogenic, were identified by the Environmental Protection Agency (EPA) as being present. Extensive medical testing subsequently established that the residents had a higher than average level of cancer, liver disease, miscarriages, and retarded children.

The cause of Love Canal's blight was soon established. In 1942 the site had been bought by Hooker Chemical and Plastics, a subsidiary of Occidental Petroleum, for use as a landfill for toxic wastes from its chemical manufacturing plant in Niagara Falls, New York State. During the next decade, Hooker dumped some 21,800 tons of chemicals into the canal. In 1953, it sold the sixteen-acre site, about eight miles from the city centre, to the Niagara Falls school board for a nominal $1. A condition of the sale was that no building might be constructed directly on the canal—in reality little more than a large ditch. The school board, which undertook responsibility for any chemical leakage, proceeded to build a grammar school, and sold the remaining land for private housing. As the years went by, the sale restrictions were ignored; the landfill site became a playground for the neighbourhood's children; the menace of the industrial legacy left by Hooker was forgotten.[5]

The scandal of Love Canal provoked an anguished debate throughout the United States. It was quickly realized that this was by no means an isolated case. For Lloyd's, it was an ominous warning of a torrent of pollution claims to come. Across the country, thousands of forgotten toxic waste dumps were leaching their contents into the environment. "We've been burying these things like ticking time-bombs. They'll all leak out in a hundred to a hundred thousand years," warned a regional director of the EPA. In the early 1970s, Congress had passed legislation to control the disposal of toxic wastes, but there was a gaping hole in both the Federal Toxic Substances Act and the Resource Conservation and Recovery Act—they did not cover disused sites.

DRACONIAN POWERS

Public outrage over Love Canal and belief that corporate polluters must be punished spurred approval of new legislation. Few in Congress appreciated its scope or consequences; no-one foresaw the legal roller-coaster that it would unleash. The Comprehensive Environmental Response, Compensation and Liability Act (CERCLA) has three principal weapons. The first permits the government to carry out reclamation work and then recover the cost from those responsible for the pollution. The second enables it to issue administrative orders requiring corporate polluters to conduct immediate remedial work in cases of "imminent and substantial endangerment to the public health or welfare of the environment." Failure to comply results in fines of $25,000 a day and treble damages. Lastly, the government has the right to apply to the federal courts for orders requiring those responsible for polluted sites to take remedial action.

There are virtually no defences against these powers. Unless it can invoke "Act of War," "Act of God," or "Act of Third Party," the corporate polluter has no option but to pay. "You clean it up or we will at your expense" is a powerful weapon, particularly as federal clean-up charges can be double or triple those of a private operator. As a result, the vast majority of environmental clean-up actions are settled by consent; the polluting company carries out the remedial work under government supervision. The legislation was strengthened in October 1986, when President Reagan signed the Superfund Amendments and Reauthorization Act (SARA). Section 21 requires the EPA to select remedial action that is "protective of human health, that is cost effective and that utilizes permanent solutions and alternative treatment technologies or resource recovery technologies to the maximum extent possible."

Such all-embracing powers have led corporate polluters to take to the courts in the hope of limiting their share of the costs of reclamation. The saga of the court-ordered clean-up of Picillo Farm, a hazardous waste site near Coventry, Rhode Island, is not untypical. Five years after several chemical drums at the site caught fire in 1977, an emergency clean-up was ordered by the EPA. The EPA proceeded to sue twenty-seven companies which had dumped waste on the site. Negotiations about who was to pay went on for four years, while legal proceedings were started by several of the companies in an attempt to shift the burden. The clean-up of Picillo Farm has so far cost $10 million, but that does not include huge legal and other transaction costs. Altogether thirty-seven law firms have been hired by sixty-two companies, or "potentially responsible parties" (PRPs) as they are known under the legislation. Meanwhile the PRPs have sued 164 insurance companies seeking reimbursement of their costs.

Another example of environmental regulation gone mad is a court-ordered clean-up of a landfill site near Utica, New York. More than 600 defendants, representing nearly 400 corporate entities including an Elks club, a gym, a doughnut shop, a sausage factory, two nursing homes, a dog kennel owner, and forty-four local authorities, have been dragged into the litigation. As one commentator noted: "Superfund has degenerated into an elaborate and costly game in which each player's behaviour is driven by the constant need to prepare for litigation against the other players, and where the ultimate goal is not cleaning up hazardous waste sites, but, instead shifting the costs of cleaning up to the other players."[6]

Multiply Picillo Farm and Utica a thousand times, and you have a legal, financial, and social nightmare. The EPA, the organization responsible for implementing the act, has so far identified 1,245 sites as urgently needing to be cleaned up. These have been placed on its national priority list, which is growing at a rate of about a hundred a year. But that is only a fraction of the number that may eventually require reclamation. The US Office of Technology estimates that 10,000 sites will have to be dealt with. The Government Accounting Office takes an even more pessimistic view, suggesting that there may be more than 400,000 hazardous waste sites needing action. With an average site taking about fifteen years to clean up at a cost of $30-$50 million, the potential bill is staggering.[7]

The legal bonanza is unprecedented. The *New York Times* reported that in one clean-up action the lawyers were spending $80,000 a year on Federal Express deliveries of papers to keep 400 companies and law firms abreast of developments.[8]

The cost of cleaning up corporate America is unquantified and probably unquantifiable, but actuarial estimates of $500-$1,000 billion dwarf official estimates.[9] When CERCLA was enacted a decade ago, the federal government set up a $1.6 billion trust known as Superfund, charged with carrying out remedial work as well as identifying and billing those companies responsible for the pollution. In 1985, Congress was asked to approve a new Superfund budget of $8.5 billion for the next five years. An additional $5.1 billion was approved in 1990 to see the programme through to 1994. Yet by 1 April 1993, only 155 of the 1,250 sites on the EPA's national priority list had been cleaned up; most of the $15 billion so far authorized has been spent on litigation. A decade ago, only 2,000 lawyers in the United States specialized in environmental law; today more than 20,000 make a comfortable living.[10] Partly because of the huge legal bills and other transaction costs, the price of reclamation has been consistently underestimated. The Chemical Manufacturers' Association predicted in 1980 that clean-up costs would be approximately $1 million per site. By 1989 the EPA had raised this to $19 million; its latest guess is $31 million. The Office of Technology and Assessment estimates reclamation and legal charges at $50 million per site.[11]

The average clean-up costs hide large differences. Purifying contaminated groundwater requires expensive filtration techniques—the cost of pumping water to the surface for replacement is at least $30-$40 million per site. The EPA takes a purist approach, which it pursues irrespective of cost. An example is an eleven-acre site in Missouri which had been used to store highly toxic PCBs used as insulating fluids by makers of electrical transmission equipment. Barrels of the chemicals had been removed from the site many years earlier, but residues were still present in the buildings, the soil, and the bed of a small stream. The cheapest way to deal with the problem would have been to isolate the site at an estimated cost of $71,000. This would, however, have left a one-in-ten-thousand chance of accidental contamination by trespassers or cattle, so the EPA ordered that the site be made completely safe by the removal of all contaminated soil and materials and incinerating them off site, at a cost of $13.6 million.

Leaking underground storage tanks are less costly to deal with, but the EPA estimates that of the five million storage tanks in the country containing hazardous substances, as many as a third may be leaking. Texaco, the US oil company, is suing Lloyd's and others in the London market for reimbursement of the costs of cleaning up more than 1,200 petrol stations. At an average of $250,000 per tank, that claim alone amounts to $300 million. The last major group of pollution claims arises from municipal and private landfills. More than 200 have been placed by the EPA on its priority list, with clean-up costs averaging $30 million per site.

A by-product of the pollution crisis is a new breed of experts—insurance archaeologists who spend their lives digging out old liability policies. The London market recently received a claim for pollution of the water table by creosote, caused by railway sleepers laid down in the 1880s. The Insurance Archeology Group (IAG) boasts that through "meticulous detective work" it has helped locate previously unknown policies worth over $4 billion. "Hundreds of millions of dollars in insurance assets lie in cardboard boxes and paper shopping bags on the floors of storerooms and warehouses," says IAG's President, Sheila Mulrennan. From her company's offices on Madison Avenue in New York go teams of investigators who help Fortune 500 companies trace policies dating back to the early 1940s. Lloyd's, she says, is particularly vulnerable, because prior to 1960 it was the leading general liability insurer in North America, and its policies often had no aggregate or time limits. Ms Mulrennan believes it is useless for British insurers to complain about the American legal system or hope that their liabilities will disappear. "To me it seems as though they're sticking their heads in their hands," she says. "The day of reckoning will come."[12]

How much of the burden of cleaning up corporate America will fall on Lloyd's is unknown. A University of Tennessee study, published in December 1991, suggested that the number of sites needing clean-up will exceed

3,000, and the total cost will be between $106 billion and $302 billion. The US Office of Technology and Assessment calculates that it will cost $500 billion to reclaim the worst affected sites. A study by the actuarial company Tillinghast, Nelson and Warren for a congressional committee on Policy Research and Insurance, in September 1990, set out three possible outcomes. In the low scenario, gross clean-up costs are estimated at $60 billion; the medium and high scenarios are $200 billion and $750 billion respectively. Tillinghast then adjusted these gross figures for various legal outcomes. In the best scenario, in which the insurers would be required to pay only 10 percent of the claims, the projected final bill together with legal costs would amount to $41 billion. In the middle scenario, with insurers having to pay half the claims, the total is $215 billion. The worst outcome, with insurers paying 90 percent of the claims, amounts to $1,065 billion. Unless these estimates are wild exaggerations, they point to the fact that the cost of cleaning up America, if implemented in full, will bankrupt many, if not all, casualty insurers around the world. The US Insurance Information Institute, for example, calculated the assets of all US property-casualty insurance companies at the end of 1990 at only $135 billion. For Lloyd's, the potential scale of pollution losses is no less serious. The total value of its premium trust funds stands at just over £12 billion. Members' funds held at Lloyd's are just under £5 billion, and the central guarantee fund is £1 billion. So the total assets on which Lloyd's can call are about £20 billion, against potential total losses which are at present incalculable.

A WARNING

Given these uncertainties it is not surprising that the Rowland Task Force, which was appointed by Lloyd's council in 1991 to peer into the future, felt obliged to sound a clear warning. Noting that continuing prior year losses on the scale of 1987 and 1988 would be very damaging, it said: "Should court decisions go against the industry as a whole, Lloyd's needs to have only a modest share of the problem for it to face very serious losses. . . An approach to managing these problems must cater for the enormous range of possible outcomes. Credible scenarios range from the manageable (consistent with trading out) to those which clearly threaten the survival of the market."

Lloyd's may be particularly vulnerable, but it says that it has done more to reserve for pollution than its competitors, which have yet to face up to their problems. Whether or not that claim is correct—and it is highly debatable—the London market is not alone in fearing the future incidence of pollution claims. The director of Superfund Enforcement for the Pennsylvania Department of Environmental Resources, Donald Brown, believes the current rate of claims is unsustainable: "The untold Superfund story may be that we have created problems so damn expensive that all the money in the world may not clean them up." A Brookings Institution study by Robert Litan concurs: "The cost to the property-casualty industry for hazardous waste clear-up could extend into hundreds of billions of dollars, enough to wipe out virtually all commercial liability insurers." Gary Westerberg, a partner in Lord, Bissell and Brook of Chicago, told a London insurance seminar: "Today the financial burdens associated with these claims are serious. In future they may prove disastrous—to industry, its insurers, or both."[13]

Who goes bust depends on the outcome of hundreds of cases wending their way slowly and expensively through the US court system. So far, most of the billions of dollars expended by Lloyd's and other liability insurers have gone on legal costs. A study in 1992 found that 88 percent of insurers' outlays on pollution claims were bills from lawyers.[14] The extraordinary lengths to which plaintiffs are prepared to go was shown in a recent successful action brought by Central Illinois Public Service Co (CIPS) against its main insurer, American Empire, and forty other insurance companies. The utility had operated a coal gasification plant from 1912 to 1938 before selling the land on which it was built, in 1961. Nearly a quarter of a century later, coal tar residues were found to have seriously polluted the surrounding groundwater. The utility was required to spend more than $6 million on removing 20,000 cubic feet of contaminated soil. To improve its chances of countering its insurer's claim that it knew that the plant was polluting the groundwater, CIPS hired a market research firm to take demographic samples of the areas from which the jury was being drawn in Cook County. It used the results to construct several "mock" juries to hear arguments put forward by its attorneys. The jurors' responses were video-taped, allowing the utility's attorneys to judge which themes were likely to be the most effective in influencing the actual trial. The cost of such an exercise—$50,000—was a bagatelle according to the lawyers.[15]

The issues at the heart of the pollution litigation are so complex, and so bitterly fought, that they are unlikely to be resolved for many years. To a layman they appear to be a horrendously expensive exercise in nit-picking semantics, but with so much at stake neither side is willing to settle. As one policy-holder attorney told the *New York Times*: "The volume of dollars on the table is so staggeringly high that no one can figure out how to compromise." Under the standard comprehensive liability policy issued before 1985, the insurer agreed to compensate the assured for any property damage arising from "an occurrence." Property damage is generally defined as "physical injury to property of others," and an occurrence as an accident which results in damage during the policy period which is neither "expected nor intended" from the standpoint of the assured. It sounds simple enough, but the battles being fought over these policy wordings are set to occupy the American courts for a generation. The legal roller-coaster has been made worse because the US Supreme Court has repeatedly turned down requests that it should intervene. Questions of contract interpretation are subject to state law. Differing state jurisdictions have made, and continue to make, opposing rulings. Insurers and policy-holders are therefore engaged in separate hugely expensive struggles in up to fifty different judicial forums.[16]

Four main arguments have so far dominated the litigation. The first is whether a government-ordered clean-up of a polluted site is covered by a general liability policy. The companies claim that money spent on reclamation meets the property damage test imposed by such policies. The insurers, on the other hand, say that "response costs" are a matter of restitution rather than liability. Initially, the insurers appeared to be having the better of this argument; two federal courts, the Fourth and the Eighth Circuit Court of Appeals found in their favour. But a peculiarity of the US court system is that such rulings are not binding on state courts. And most of the state supreme courts which have considered this question, notably California, Illinois, Iowa, Massachusetts, Minnesota, North Carolina, and Washington DC, have ruled in favour of policy-holders.

The second issue is whether pollution of the assured's own premises and the groundwater underlying it is excluded from coverage. Virtually all general liability policies carry such an exclusion clause which might seem difficult to dispute. However a number of states, notably New Jersey, have found for policy-holders on the grounds that the cleaning up of pollution is designed to protect others, and that groundwater is third-party property. The defendants' contra-argument, that there has to be physical injury to third-party property, and that groundwater cannot be defined as such, has succeeded in some jurisdictions. But overall the balance of judicial opinion is swinging against the insurers.

The third issue centres on the interpretation of the pollution exclusion clause which was added to liability policies from 1973. A typical wording

Richard Rogers' startling design of glass and steel – the £165 million new Lloyd's building. A centre for insurance or a tourist theme park? Its future is uncertain. *Courtesy Lloyd's of London*

The quill pen is still in use to record shipwrecks in the ceremonial loss book.

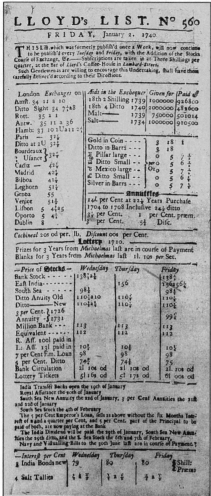

Lloyd's List. A daily source of shipping intelligence and news for three centuries.

A view of the Room – the modern Lloyd's at work.

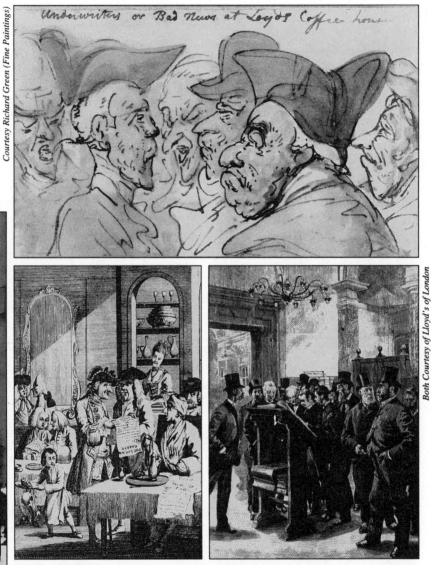

Courtesy Richard Green (Fine Paintings)

Both Courtesy of Lloyd's of London

CARTOONS: Taking the bad news on the chin. Underwriters live on their nerves.

A costly catastrophe – devastation caused by Hurricane Betsy. It plunged Lloyd's into three years of losses in the mid-1960s.

Piper Alpha – the worst human tragedy ever experienced by the offshore oil industry. The few who escaped did so by diving hundreds of feet into the sea. 'It was stay and get toasted or jump and chance it,' said one survivor.

Clearing up after Hurricane Hugo which wrecked hundreds of miles of coastline and thousands of buildings. The final bill was $5 billion.

The catalyst – the Hooker chemical plant in Niagara Falls, New York, whose dumped wastes turned Love Canal into a toxic quagmire.

There is no-one more dangerous than the man with nothing left to lose. Some ruined Names took to the streets to embarrass Lloyd's.

'The most polluted site on earth' – the Rocky Mountain Arsenal outside Denver, Colorado, where Shell produced a powerful range of insecticides. The clean-up bill came to nearly $2 billion.

Ian Hay Davison, the market's outspoken first chief executive. When he resigned in 1986, he said he had been dismayed to find more than the odd rotten apple at Lloyd's. The rot had spread to the barrel.

Sir Peter Miller, chairman of Lloyd's from 1984 to 1987, who, according to *Lloyd's List*, 'presided over ruin in the making'.

Murray Lawrence, chairman of Lloyd's from 1988 to 1990, whose years in office coincided with the market losing more than £5 billion.

David Rowland, the first paid chairman of Lloyd's in three centuries. A broker's broker.

Peter Middleton, former monk, diplomat, and bank executive, taking his first press conference after his appointment as Lloyd's chief executive in September 1992.

David Coleridge, chairman of Lloyd's from 1991 to 1992: 'He conceals his ability behind a tired teddy-bear outlook.'

'So pure he makes Snow White look smutty.' The accolade given to Sir David Walker by Lloyd's. To its relief, he dispelled the wilder accusations of fraud and corruption in the market.

Tony Andrews/The Financial Times

Ashley Ashwood/The Financial Times

The biggest loser of them all. Stephen Merrett, deputy chairman of Lloyd's, was humbled when members' agents deserted his syndicates and forced him to quit underwriting.

excludes coverage of "bodily injury or property damage arising out of the discharge, dispersal, release or escape of smoke, vapours, soot, fumes, acids, alkalis, toxic chemicals, liquids or gases, waste materials or other irritants, contaminants or pollutants into or upon land, the atmosphere or any watercourse or body of water; but this exclusion does not apply if such discharge, dispersal, release or escape is sudden and accidental."

This last qualification has provoked interminable argument. Insurers contend that the meaning and intent of the clause is plain—to exclude all claims unless the pollution was both sudden and accidental. Policy-holders, on the other hand, argue that the clause is ambiguous and thus does not exclude pollution, even where the act itself, or the damage caused by it, has been gradual. The insurers have generally won this debate, though there have been important exceptions, with some courts straining the English language to redefine "sudden" as "unexpected," and "accidental" as "unintended." In 1990, the Wisconsin Supreme Court decided in Land Reclamation v. Bituminous Casualty Corp. that the pollution exclusion clause was unclear, and therefore coverage should be interpreted in favour of the insured. This provoked David Coleridge, shortly to become chairman of Lloyd's, to complain publicly: "It is difficult, for example, for those of us who lack the benefits of legal training to understand how an insurance policy covering 'sudden and accidental' emission of what proved to be substances causing pollution can be applied to deliberate discharges and to discharges taking place over several months or even years."[17] An equally bitter comment came from George Bernstein of the American Insurance Association in evidence to a US congressional committee: "The courts in seeking a deep pocket may be able, by standing the English language on its head, to rewrite past and existing policies to impose liability on insurers where none was contracted for and where no premium for the judicially created coverage was collected." But if that happened, he warned, it would be counter-productive—insurers would simply withdraw from covering pollution in future.

The fourth issue is whether the pollution falls within the policy wording's definition of "an occurrence." The insurers claim that if the damage caused by the company was "expected or intended," there is no coverage under a general liability policy. The policy-holders argue that, provided there was no deliberate intention to inflict harm, the pollution was accidental and is therefore covered by their policies. This issue of "fortuity" has so far proved to be the defendants' strongest card.

DIAMOND SHAMROCK

An important legal victory on "fortuity" came in April 1992, when the New Jersey Appeal Court ruled that Lloyd's and more than a hundred other insurers were not liable for a $25 million government-ordered clean-up of a chemical plant in Newark. In 1951 Diamond Shamrock, now a subsidiary of Occidental Petroleum, had taken over a plant producing DDT and a potent group of defoliants called phenoxy herbicides, later used in the Vietnam War under the name Agent Orange. Subsequent tests on animals disclosed that a chemical by-product created in the manufacture of Agent Orange was one of the most toxic compounds ever synthesized, causing cancers, birth defects and miscarriages, even when absorbed in very small amounts.[18]

From the start of production, Diamond's plant workers began suffering from a skin complaint called chloracne. Though the company was not at first sure what was causing the disease, it was advised to reduce air contamination and to insist on higher standards of cleanliness. These suggestions were ignored, and the incidents of chloracne, marked by a painful form of acne around the eyes and ears, increased. According to one worker, Chester Myko, highly toxic chemical residues solidified on the plant floor into a slippery, oily film which hampered normal working. Every other week or so, the floor was washed down with sulphuric acid, and the waste water was allowed to flow into trenches which led from the building into the river. A manufacturing process worker who was employed in the plant until 1969 told of numerous leaks in the autoclave room from pipes, and from drums where Agent Orange was stored.

Evidence of Diamond Shamrock's carelessness was widespread. Several plant workers testified that the company's waste disposal policy amounted to "dumping everything" into the Passaic River. So much was dumped at times that a mid-river "mountain" of DDT was created. Diamond's employees were ordered to wade into the water at low tide and cut up the deposits so that they would not be seen by passing boats. Pollutants were also regularly vented into the atmosphere. A former Diamond employee said that a greyish cloud of smoke would belch out of a scrubber at the top of one of the process buildings, and residue from it would settle on cars in the parking lots, causing the paint to pit as if it had been exposed to acid. In September 1959, Diamond's plant manager learnt that a German chemical manufacturer had identified the probable cause of his workers' sickness as dioxin, a highly toxic by-product of the process of manufacturing Agent

Orange. The company was advised that decreasing the reaction temperatures in the autoclave would reduce the levels of dioxin produced—advice that was rejected because it would diminish production efficiency.

After this shaming recital, the Appeal Court's judgment was inevitable: "The only conclusion to be drawn is that Diamond's management was wholly indifferent to the consequences flowing from its decision. Profits came first." In upholding the decision of the lower court, the three judges accepted that Diamond had knowingly and routinely discharged contaminants for eighteen years. "Whatever else may be said, the continuous release of dioxins from the plant was not 'unforeseen' and the resulting damage was not 'unexpected'. . . We recognize that we should not judge Diamond's conduct from the vantage point of twenty-twenty hindsight. The critical fact remains, however, that Diamond knew it was dealing with a toxic substance. . . We cannot ignore reality by accepting the blithe assurance of Diamond that it did not intend to injure others. The evidence abounds the other way."

The Diamond Shamrock and Rocky Mountain cases demonstrate that Lloyd's can successfully defend pollution claims where there is clear evidence that the company "expected or intended" the pollution that resulted from its negligence. But the costs are horrendous. Hundreds of thousands of documents have to be reviewed and presented with expert evidence at trial. The $100 million cost of the Shell case, still unfinished after a decade, is an indication of the extent of legal warfare involved. Moreover, most cases will not be as straightforward as Rocky Mountain. Take, for example, a company which delivers its hazardous waste to a transport firm which in turn takes it to a licensed dump site which later is discovered to leak. The chance of an insurer successfully defending such a claim from any of the parties—generator, transporter or operator—would probably depend on whether the court would uphold the pollution exclusion clause.

An ominous reverse for the London market came in December 1992, in a closely watched case brought by the Outboard Marine Corporation against its insurers. The company operated a die-casting plant near Waukegan Harbor, which used hydraulic fluid containing PCBs. A faulty waste disposal process led to severe contamination of Lake Michigan for over more than fifteen years up to 1972. Despite this lengthy period, the Illinois Supreme Court ruled by a majority that even those policies containing an exclusion clause against gradual pollution must respond to the company's claims. A dissenting opinion by Chief Justice Miller, however, noted: "I fail to see how occurrences continuing for more than a decade may be considered 'sudden' under any reasonable reading of that word." The court also struck down two other defences advanced by the insurers: that the costs of cleaning up Lake Michigan were not damages as defined by the policy, and that the company should have known the scale of the pollution that its products were causing. In fact, the court ruled the claim could be barred only if the polluter actually knew, not should have known, that its discharges would cause damage.[19]

It was a triple blow for Lloyd's. According to Randolph Fields, a policy-holder attorney: "The impact of this decision upon the London market is dramatic. Illinois is the first major US jurisdiction to have addressed all three of the principal insurer defences together and found for the insured." Mr Fields added that until recently he had found the prospect of a default by Lloyd's too remote to contemplate seriously: "Now I am not so certain. I can foresee a scenario where a Lloyd's meltdown is caused by increasing demands being placed upon the central fund resulting from the defaults of members of open years facing cash calls."[20]

Barry Bunshoft, the Californian lawyer co-ordinating Lloyd's fight against pollution claims, is cautious about the future course of litigation. "The impact on the London market in the interim period, while the outcome of the major coverage litigation is in doubt, is enormous," he told a London insurance seminar in 1992. "In the first place, the reserve potential which each syndicate must consider is staggering; in the second place, the IBNR (incurred but not reported claims) which each syndicate should carry is uncertain; and in the third place, the legal fees and attendant litigation costs which the London market must bear to defend itself are huge. I can only say that, based on results so far, the willingness of the London market to bear the legal fees to do what it takes to win—or to resolve the dispute by a favourable settlement—has a direct bearing on the outcome and on the future health of the London market."[21]

Lessons have, at least, been learnt from the asbestos litigation debacle, where the split between different groups of insurers resulted in court rulings that all policies covering all periods should be liable. To avoid a similarly damaging market split, an environmental group has been set up by Lloyd's, on which claims managers from the worst-affected syndicates are represented. It coordinates information from attorneys, loss adjusters and actuaries, and disseminates it to the market. Parallel to this group, a steering committee of lawyers representing the London market meets regularly to discuss tactics.

The true scale of the pollution crisis facing Lloyd's will possibly not be quantifiable for at least a decade. According to Eugene Anderson, senior partner at a New York law firm, Anderson, Kill, Olick and Oshinsky which represents policy-holders, there is a deliberate delaying tactic at work. "It is roughly three to five years before claims get resolved by the courts," he noted. "Then another three to five years between policy-holder and insurer. Then three to five years between insurer and reinsurer. It will be the year 2001 or 2010 before the bill comes due."[22]

Lloyd's undoubtedly hopes to use these legal delays to trade out of its troubles. Whether it can succeed is largely outside its control; the key decision will be taken in Washington. One closely watched initiative aimed at reforming Superfund is a $4-billion-a-year environmental trust fund, financed by a levy on all commercial and industrial premiums. This fund would handle all past instances of pollution, leaving Superfund to deal with future cases. The idea, put forward by Hank Greenberg of the American Insurance Group, has been welcomed warmly by insurers, but has had a distinctly cool response elsewhere.[23] A leading policy-holder attorney savaged the proposal as effectively allowing "the insurance industry to escape part or all of its massive contractual liability to private and public sector clean-ups." Congress, through the House of Representatives Banking and Finance Committee, has, however, begun to look at the solvency of American casualty insurers. Concerns are bound to grow as more and more companies go into liquidation. In 1992, more than 370 insurance and reinsurance companies worldwide ceased underwriting.[24]

An EPA think-tank report, *Resources for the Future*, has proposed that the US government should resolve the environment litigation crisis by dividing Superfund clean-up costs among insurance companies and policy-holders according to a fixed ratio. But given the huge sums involved, it is hard to see how such a formula could be agreed outside the courts. There is, however, growing recognition in Washington that Superfund is in urgent need of reform. This change of heart is likely to be reflected in Congress when the legislation comes up for reauthorization in 1995. A US Treasury paper has already advocated the abolition of retroactive liability and called for liability to be apportioned strictly according to responsibility.

Undoubtedly the best hope for Lloyd's and its increasingly impoverished Names is that the worst outcome of pollution—a loss of $1 trillion—is so huge that it would not only sweep away the London market but also bankrupt much of the US casualty insurance industry. "The effect of losses being actually settled at our level of reserving," said Stephen Merrett, chairman of the Merrett Group, "will be that a number of very important insurance companies in the US will prove hopelessly insolvent."[25] This prompts the belief at Lloyd's that sooner or later the Republican-dominated Congress will be forced to intervene. "The only real comfort in this whole saga," said Michael Wade, a member of the Rowland Task Force, "is that no US government is going to allow its insurance industry to go bust."

9

Spiral to Disaster

"For when they insure it is sweet to them to take the monies; but
when disaster comes it is otherwise and each man draws his
rump back and strives not to pay."
A Tuscan cloth merchant, Datini, writing to his wife in 1380

On 6 July 1988, just before ten o'clock at night, the high-pitched scream
of escaping high compression gas was heard on the Piper Alpha oil platform.
Thirty seconds later the rig, operating nearly a hundred miles out in the North
Sea, was destroyed by a gigantic explosion followed by a huge fireball. Of
the platform's complement of 226 workers, 165 died in the flames. The few
who escaped did so by diving hundreds of feet into the sea. "It was stay and
get toasted or jump and chance it," said one survivor.

It was the worst human tragedy ever experienced by the off-shore oil
industry. For Lloyd's, the main insurer of the Piper Alpha rig, it set off an
expensive train of events. There were four main investors in the platform:
Texaco, International Thomson, Union Texas Petroleum, and Occidental
Petroleum, the rig's operator. Each had its own insurance programme which
had been placed worldwide, but much of it had been reinsured at Lloyd's.

Within days of the explosion, rumours began sweeping the Room that
underwriters were seriously exposed, and that some of them with inadequate
reinsurance had been badly hit. The shock was all the greater because Lloyd's
had been relatively free from catastrophes for a generation. Not since

Hurricane Betsy swept in from the Caribbean, causing enormous damage to the east coast of America in September 1965, had the market been so severely affected.

A generation of complacency at Lloyd's was shattered by the explosion on Piper Alpha. Fifteen months later, on 15 September 1989, Hurricane Hugo spiralled out of the West Indies, hitting the South Carolina coast with 140 mph winds before dumping three days' continuous torrential rain on surrounding areas. Hundreds of miles of coastline were devastated and thousands of buildings wrecked. The final bill was $5 billion, much of it reinsured at Lloyd's. Two major disasters within eighteen months, though serious, might have been shrugged off, but they were only part of an unprecedented series of catastrophes which racked up more than $40 billion in insurance losses between 1987 and 1990. They included the Enchova oil platform fire, Hurricane Gilbert, the *Exxon Valdez* oil spill, the San Francisco earthquake, the Arco Baker fire, the Phillips petroleum explosion, the Australian earthquake, Typhoon Mireille in Japan, and three severe gales which struck Britain and northern Europe at the beginning of 1990.

Insurers all over the world were shaken, but for Lloyd's the consequence of this extraordinary cycle of natural disasters was particularly damaging. In the postwar years, it had developed into a specialist reinsurance market used by primary insurers to offload their high-level risks. Lloyd's role as a reinsurer dates back to the San Francisco earthquake of 1906 which destroyed 30,000 homes and killed more than 700 people. Shortly after the earthquake, Cuthbert Heath was approached by a large American insurance company, the Hartford, asking if he was prepared to insure it against a repeat catastrophe. The policy he devised was known as an "excess of loss." It was designed not to cover routine losses, but to provide protection in the event of a disaster causing losses above an agreed limit. A typical policy might provide cover of $5 million above a $1 million excess which had to be paid by the policy-holder.

From these modest beginnings the London reinsurance market grew. It met a crucial requirement of insurance—the need to spread risk. In essence the way the reinsurance market works is very simple. Just as a bookie lays off bets on the favourite with another bookmaker, so an underwriter lays off risks larger than he is prepared to run with a reinsurer. The market divides roughly into two: a primary insurer who deals directly with the broker placing the insurance, and a reinsurer who reinsures the primary insurer. By layering risks vertically according to value as well as spreading them horizontally among dozens of reinsurers, no single underwriter need expose himself or the Names he represents to intolerable losses in the event of a series of catastrophes. As the size of the risks grew—a North Sea oil platform is worth up to $2 billion—the spread of cover was extended even further with the development of a third tier of reinsurance, the retrocession market, which specializes in the reinsurance of reinsurers.

The theory of reinsurance may be simple, but the practice is complicated. Take the following example: A British insurance company insures two million household policies, each for £50,000. Its risk exposure is therefore £100 billion, for which it charges a premium of £250 million. The company is reluctant to carry a risk of this magnitude by itself so it lays off a large part, based on the crucial assumption that a single catastrophe would not exceed £250 million. It decides to retain the first 10 percent of this risk, and asks its broker to reinsure the remaining £225 million at a cost of £30 million. The original insurer thus keeps £220 million in premium to help pay attritional claims as well as the first £25 million claims from any catastrophe. The next level of the risk is passed to five reinsurers who each write £45 million for a premium of £5.4 million. The primary reinsurers, however, each keep only £10 million of the risk; the rest is reinsured. The next level is then passed to twenty-five secondary reinsurers who each write £7 million, though they retain only £1.5 million for a premium of £486,000. The highest level of the risk is retroceded to 125 retrocessionaires who each take £1.1 million for a premium of £43,740. At every level of the reinsurance chain, a broker gets a commission of 10 percent; the cost of accessing and servicing 155 reinsurers worldwide is thus about £5 million.[1]

As the size of risks underwritten in the London market grew, these complex reinsurance policies, with their numerous intricate layers, tended to become more and more intertwined. Underwriters, influenced by Lloyd's insistence on security, began to reinsure one another's excess of loss risks in what became known as the London Excess of Loss Market or LMX. An "excess of loss" policy reinsured by another excess of loss policy is known as XL on XL (an excess of loss policy on an excess of loss reinsurance). One result of this incestuous pattern of trading was that the tiers of insurance became hopelessly confused. Worse, this type of closed trading served to negate the basic principal of insurance by concentrating risk rather than diffusing it. And the higher up the spiral, the worse the effect.

"The lower tiers or levels of insurance," noted one report on the spiral, "can be likened to an inverted pyramid, with risk being spread in the classical reinsurance pattern, but the higher levels are akin to the top half of a diamond, with risk being concentrated."[2] This aggregation of risk was like an elaborate game of pass-the-parcel played for high stakes. Take the much simplified example of underwriter A who reinsures with underwriter B who reinsures with underwriter C who in turn lays off part or all of the risk with underwriters A and B. The fortunes of all three underwriters are so entangled that it does not take many more twists of the spiral for the nature of the original risk to become completely opaque. The ultimate reinsurer is so divorced from the primary cover that he has no idea of the extent of the risk being run.

HURRICANE BETSY

The development of the LMX market at Lloyd's was accelerated by the devastating losses due to Hurricane Betsy. Before 1965, it had been the practice for marine underwriters to purchase reinsurance that gave specific protection to an individual contract, say an oil rig. Betsy, however, caused such widespread damage that it led to claims across the whole book of business. With losses of nearly $10 billion in today's values, underwriters began to seek reinsurance which would protect their whole account. Lloyd's relaxation of its reinsurance rules undoubtedly encouraged the growth of the spiral market. In the mid-1970s, underwriters were discouraged from reinsuring more than 20 percent of their premium income with other insurers. By the end of the decade, this limit had been trebled to 60 percent, half of which had to be reinsured within Lloyd's. These changes were made to cope with the ever-increasing demands posed by huge single risks such as oil rigs, supertankers, and satellites. But with hindsight it is clear that the effect was deadly; it encouraged over-expansion, and concentrated risk within Lloyd's to a dangerous degree.

For almost a decade, these hazards were not recognized. So long as there is not a run of catastrophes, LMX syndicates can make large profits. And for a time in the 1980s they did, luring many Names to join them on the strength of their flashy performance in syndicate performance tables. The Gooda Walker non-marine syndicate 290, whose underwriter was Derek Walker, returned profits averaging 14 percent in the five years from 1984 to 1988. For a Name with a £20,000 stake on the syndicate, that meant average annual profits of nearly £3,000. But if the wind blows, the earth heaves and oil rigs explode, reinsurers need to monitor their total exposure carefully to avoid ruin. That task was made more difficult by the complexity of the reinsurance chain, which obscured the risk and effectively creamed off large amounts in broking commissions. By the time the top of the spiral was reached, a £1 million premium might have been skimmed by nearly two–thirds. The higher up the spiral, the smaller the premium, on the grounds that higher layers were less at risk. That was good business for brokers, who took their 10 percent commission every time they shunted an excess of loss policy from one LMX underwriter to another. But it was extremely hazardous for those underwriting risks at the very top. Piper Alpha, for example, ultimately cost Lloyd's a net $900 million but generated a staggering $15 billion in claims from 43,000 policies as the spiral unwound.

Once catastrophe losses started bouncing around the market, it was certain that some Names would be badly hurt. The spiral has been graphically described as a hurricane a mile wide swirling hundred-dollar bills.[3] A vicious cash squeeze, made worse by problems of double counting, was inevitable. In the past, underwriters had drawn some comfort, despite the risks they were running, from the fact that claims took a long time to be settled. Payments from Hurricane Alicia, dating back to 1983, were still being made a decade later. But this protection eroded in the late 1980s, when the spiral began to unwind much more rapidly as a result of an acceleration in claims handling.

None of these potential dangers, if they were perceived at all, were explained to the thousands of new Names who were recruited in the 1980s. Between 1982 and 1988, the market's capital base expanded by more than one-and-a-half times, far in excess of premium growth. By 1988, premium income was less than half the market's capacity. Much of this expansion came from LMX syndicates, which found it easy to attract new Names on the basis of their past profit records. The Feltrim syndicate 540 almost quadrupled in capacity, growing from £11 million in 1983 to £41 million in 1989. Gooda Walker's syndicate 290 went from just £6.2 million in 1982 to £69.4 million in seven years. It was a breathtaking pace which even in good times could not have been sustained. As it was, this hectic expansion of the highest risk syndicates sucked in large numbers of new Names who, when the LMX bubble burst, discovered they had been ruined.

The first public suggestion that spiral underwriters were riding for a fall was made at a specialist reinsurance conference held in London in May 1988, two months before the Piper Alpha disaster. A paper presented by John Emney, chief underwriter of a leading reinsurer, Charter Re, rehearsed the possibility of a catastrophe exhausting the protection of participants in the

LMX spiral because they had reinsured each other. A more direct warning was given by Richard Outhwaite. In his paper titled "The Catastrophe Time-Bomb," he did not mince his words: "I am not an adherent to conspiracy theory of history, as it is largely based on paranoia, but it does seem to me that there is an almost universal ostrich-like unwillingness to face facts."

Outhwaite, who was shortly to face his own underwriting trauma, pointed out the scale of the risks being run in the LMX market: "The maximum insured value of a platform on the North Sea is around $2 billion. At least 60 percent of that is insured in London and, looking through the list of marine companies and Lloyd's, I made an estimate of what each would maintain his retention was, should this platform be a total loss. On the most generous basis this would not exceed $100 million. There is no dispute that if there was such a total loss the London market would pay $1.2 billion net. Where will the other $1,100 million come from? It will come from the LMX market. In the event of a major windstorm where the initial loss to London could be much greater, the effects would be even more severe, but precisely the same thing would apply. If this is true, which it clearly is, why is this not recognized?"

The Lutine bell could hardly have been rung more loudly, but it was another two years before these warnings were heeded. Complacency, compounded by the unwillingness of the council of Lloyd's to regulate the wilder excesses of the LMX market, extorted a high price. The problem was the more serious because the normal disciplines of reinsurance were wholly lacking. Because it was known that Lloyd's would stand collectively behind any policy issued in its name, those placing reinsurance with even the most exposed syndicates were sure that they would be paid. It was widely known at Lloyd's that some LMX underwriters were taking huge risks, but that was regarded as someone else's problem.

The consequences of the bursting of the LMX bubble were every bit as serious as Outhwaite had predicted. In July 1992, Lloyd's announced a £2 billion loss, the worst in the market's history. The loss for the 1989 year of account was bad enough, higher even in inflation-adjusted terms than the darkest year of Hurricane Betsy when the average Name had to pay out the equivalent in today's money of £66,000. But the position was much worse now, for it quickly became apparent that the losses were damagingly skewed. Four thousand Names discovered that they had losses of hundreds of thousands of pounds; a few individuals faced demands for more than £1 million. Most of these ruined Names were on just five LMX syndicates which accounted for half the £1 billion spiral losses in 1989. Although nearly ninety syndicates were writing significant LMX business in 1988 and 1989, 95 percent of the losses were concentrated on just twelve syndicates in 1988. In 1989 the same pattern was repeated; nearly 80 percent of the losses were concentrated on fourteen syndicates.

LIME STREET

Many of the worst hit Names were those who had joined Kingsley underwriting agencies, subsequently renamed Lime Street members' agency. Founded in the mid-1970s by Robin Kingsley, a Lloyd's broker and member of the prestigious All England Lawn Tennis Club, the agency had grown rapidly as a result of a vigorous recruiting campaign lubricated by commission payments. Kingsley's underwriting strategy was to steer clear of the old-established marine syndicates, as he believed that they were seriously under-reserved. He preferred to place his Names on reinsurance syndicates specializing in the fast growing excess of loss market. He was a supporter of Derek Walker, the underwriter of Gooda Walker, and Patrick Fagan of Feltrim. Their LMX syndicates were hungry for capital and the new members' agent, with his energy, charm, and powers of persuasion, was in a position to supply it. Kingsley was also a patron of Walker's stop loss syndicate 387, whose business was to provide Names with excess of loss reinsurance on their underwriting. His involvement in this specialized market was unhealthily close, for his broking firm, Kingsley Carritt, was also a major seller of stop loss policies. These provided a "sleep easy" service to Names who could reinsure against catastrophic loss in any one underwriting year of account by taking out a policy which would cover a fixed amount, say £200,000, above an excess of 10 percent of his premium line. Thus a Name writing £250,000 would have to meet the first £25,000 of loss, but the next £200,000 of losses would be covered by his stop loss policy. The theory was that the results of such syndicates would reflect the fortunes of the market as a whole, but the practice proved very different; stop loss underwriters produced some of the biggest losses in the market. Worst affected was Derek Walker's syndicate 387 which has already racked up losses of 1,000 percent for its Names, three-quarters of whom had been introduced by Lime Street.[4]

Few of the investors recruited by Kingsley had any idea of these risks. The vast majority knew little about insurance, had never heard of the spiral, had no knowledge of the horrendous risks that were being run in their names and only a dim appreciation of the hazards of unlimited liability. The one thing they felt sure of was Lloyd's reputation for integrity. Buster Mottram, then Britain's leading tennis player, was relaxing in a bath in the changing rooms at Wimbledon after losing the men's doubles final in 1983 when he was first approached by a Kingsley agent. The spiel was a simple one. Did he know anything about Lloyd's? asked a fellow club member, who then told Buster in glowing terms about the advantages of joining. An introduction was effected and, persuaded by Kingsley's enthusiastic endorsement, both Buster and his father, Tony, signed on, a decision that was to land them with losses of more than £1 million. Buster looks back with bitterness on his decision. "I knew nothing about excess of loss insurance. I was never given any explanation by Kingsley, who said nothing about risk. The whole thing has been a nightmare. Sometimes I get letters from my agent threatening dire consequences if money is not forthcoming. In the same breath with the utmost consideration, the agency informs me that there will be nothing to worry about if I come to an accommodation with Lloyd's."[5] Two other British tennis players, Mark Cox and Virginia Wade, and Roger Taylor's wife, Frances, were also to rue the day they were persuaded to join Lime Street. Cox has already paid out £200,000 and faces losses of more than £2.5 million. "I couldn't meet these sort of figures if I lived for the next 300 years," he says. "All my savings have been eaten up. I'm just hoping that Lloyd's will be realistic about this situation." Cox believes that Lloyd's must shoulder its share of the blame for his predicament. "For them to allow a syndicate to operate with that amount of losses. . . Lloyd's is culpable and they have to accept some of the responsibility, otherwise we are living with no rules, no regulation, no morality."

The go-between who persuaded many of the tennis players to join Lloyd's was Freddie Della-Porta, a member of the three most prestigious London tennis clubs, Wimbledon, Queens, and Hurlingham. "I am trying to forget about Lloyd's," he says. "It's a nightmare, I don't want to get into the subject." Della-Porta says that he received no money in commissions for the introductions to the Kingsley agency, but that he had for many years taken a "financial and sporting interest in Lloyd's, and lost a lot of money like many others." He feels badly let down: "When I joined it was always assumed that an underwriter who took on a risk would reinsure anything apart from that which he felt he could safely carry."[6]

Another group to fall into Lime Street's net consisted of more than fifty Canadian dentists and lawyers living in Toronto and Hamilton in Ontario.

Each year, Kingsley would fly to North America on a recruiting drive. There he would find a local representative who would arrange regular meetings with prospective Names, at which the attractions of an investment at Lloyd's would be spelt out. Making your capital work twice, setting off losses against taxed income, and an unbroken seven-year record of profits, were just some of the advantages mentioned.

There was a nice line in reassuring patter for worried Names. When the Pan Am aeroplane exploded over Lockerbie in 1989, one anxious Canadian telephoned to inquire how it would affect the syndicate he was on. "Don't worry, it's merely a gin and tonic," said Kingsley. Names were constantly encouraged to increase their premium line—the stake they had at Lloyd's. "It was not a question of whether you wanted to increase your capacity but by how much," one of the Canadian dentists recalled. "He would say, rates are hardening, it's a fantastic time to take advantage, strike while the iron is hot."[7]

Though Kingsley, with his Rolls-Royce, his double-breasted suits and permanent sun tan, was frowned on by some of the more established members' agencies, his recruiting methods proved very successful. He believed in paying commissions to those who recruited Names for his syndicates. Not until the mid-1980s did Lloyd's insist that such introductory fees should be disclosed. By the end of the decade, Lime Street had more than 500 Names with nearly £200 million in assets staked in the market. Many of these new recruits, far from being wealthy, were people of modest resources, whose only real asset was their house which they used to secure a bank guarantee for the Lloyd's deposit.

When the LMX spiral collapsed these Names, who were usually on several spiral syndicates, found themselves in the unenviable position of having lost more money than anyone else in the market. The average losses of Lime Street Names for the years 1988 to 1990 were almost £2 million, far worse than any other members' agency.[8] Many were, as a result, hopelessly insolvent. Despite having asked to be put on conservatively run syndicates, they had ended up on some of the riskiest in the market. "We were completely misled," said one Name. "We were told that we would be put on low-risk syndicates until we had built up reserves and that if we had a loss on one syndicate, it would not be more than £10,000." An American Name from Austin, Texas wrote: "The principal reason I selected Kingsley to be my agent was that the company was independent and that it represented itself as specializing in low-risk, low-return syndicates. . . It is plain to me that they [Kingsley and some of his partners] misrepresented their own business philosophy to me." Despite the anger felt by Lime Street Names, it is only fair to note that more than fifty other members' agencies also put their Names on Feltrim and Gooda Walker syndicates, though none to the same concentrated degree.

The bitterness of ruined Names grew when creditors of the Lime Street members' agency discovered that Kingsley and three other directors, Patrick Corbett, Richard Gethin-Jones and Robert Hallam, had given themselves a total of £400,000 in bonuses shortly before the business was taken over by another Lloyd's agency in 1987. One Name asked the directors whether they would return the money in the light of the company's disastrous performance, but received no answer. In December 1991 the solicitors Norton Rose, acting on behalf of a group of Lime Street Names, wrote to the chairman of Lloyd's, David Coleridge, to complain: "Lime Street and their associated agencies seem to have unerringly homed in on the majority of the worst performing syndicates over the last decade." Many Names felt they had been used as cannon fodder. "None of us knew anything about the LMX market or spiral syndicates—they were never even mentioned," said Marie Louise Burrows, chairman of the Lime Street Action Group. She added bitterly: "I think Robin Kingsley is a third-rate spiv, though I think he was made a patsy by others in the market. I believe the responsibility of Lloyd's for this mess should not be underestimated. We have been ruined by their failure to regulate the market."

One Lime Street Name, an elderly widow who was taken to meet Kingsley after being advised by a friend that joining Lloyd's would be a good way of augmenting her slender financial resources, felt she had been completely bamboozled: "I was handed a sample seven years' results list (1977-83) at the meeting. I was very impressed; this showed excellent profits on a £300,000 premium share allocation of an annual average of nearly £29,000." The widow was then introduced by Kingsley's agent, Freddie Della-Porta, to Michael Royde of Allied Dunbar, who strongly urged her to join Lloyd's. On her agreement, he arranged a mortgage of £10,000 to cover the stop loss, estate duty plan, and initial membership fee for the first four years, and an endowment policy to cover the mortgage. Her only assets at the time were her house, then valued at £180,000, and a quarter share of an encumbered property in Hull, worth about £20,000. She now has nothing and is faced by the threat of eviction and bankruptcy, but is still reluctant to apply to the Lloyd's Names hardship committee. Michael Royde declines to talk about his role in introducing new Names.

For some, the experience of being a Lime Street Name was to prove even more tragic. Russell Bailey, an Ontario businessman, was persuaded by his dentist, on their local golf course, to join Lloyd's. Within a short time of becoming a Name, he was faced by losses of $50,000; within eighteen months they had grown to $800,000. Overwhelmed and depressed, he became a recluse. In the autumn of 1992, he committed suicide. His widow Margaret, who has to try to pay his losses from his dwindling estate, says: "We were obviously naive. But how could you question a body that has been trading for over 300 years. We thought it was as solid as the rock of Gibraltar."[9] Barely a month later, another Lime Street Name from Ontario also found himself unable to face the continuing demands from Lloyd's for money he did not have. Fred Yeo's wife found his body hanging in a barn. She said her husband had become increasingly depressed by the huge Lloyd's losses, which had coincided with his losing his civil service job.

Some months after the crash, when I met Robin Kingsley at Sudbrooke House, his mansion just off Ham Common, he was in a sombre mood. Many of his old friends had deserted him, acquaintances were shunning him, and he felt unable to play tennis at his beloved Wimbledon. "We had extremely good relations with our Names when times were good," he said sadly. "A great number of people who were one's friends are now no longer . . . there are other people who were extremely good acquaintances and when one meets them now, they turn the other way and avoid one." Did he feel responsible for what had happened? "I am devastated by the fact that so many of one's friends and relations and acquaintances and people I looked after are in such desperate financial straits. I accept that as chairman of the underwriting agency, I am responsible. I realize the frightful mess that I have led people into." Kingsley strongly denied, however, that Lime Street had engaged in a "hard sell" to recruit those who should not have gone near a risk market: "The people who found it hard to find Names levelled that accusation at us because they had to justify their own inadequacies." Most of the charges made against him were, he claimed, put about by his enemies in the market.

Kingsley, who claimed he was having to sell his house because of his own "appalling" financial situation, blamed Lime Street's misfortunes on Lloyd's failure to regulate the spiral market. "Many underwriters at Lloyd's who were in positions of power to regulate the market must have been aware of the terrific risks that were being run. To a large degree our Names, including myself, are the victims of the failure of regulation. It should have been possible to regulate the market and to warn off syndicates with a very high degree of exposure." Kingsley denied deliberately exposing Names to high-risk syndicates. "We were never warned that they were high risk. I feel badly let down by Derek Walker and Patrick Fagan. I often made it clear to them that they should remember, when they were writing risks, that they had the financial well-being of all our Names in their hands."

To the accusation that he had been reckless in exposing Lime Street Names to such a high concentration of spiral syndicates, he replied: "I think if a syndicate is worth backing, it's worth backing. If not you take your Names off." As for the £400,000 in bonuses that had been doled out to him and the three other Lime Street directors shortly before the crash, he replied: "I had no say in how much the amounts should be or to whom they would go. At a time before the figures were known to be as bad, one of the non-executive directors was given the task of deciding what the bonuses should be. The liquidators have looked into this very carefully and are clear that no impropriety took place."

When investors lose large sums of money it is inevitable that the professionals involved will be criticized. Robin Kingsley's vigorous recruitment methods, excessive optimism, commission payments, misjudgments of the calibre of underwriters, and over-concentration on high-risk syndicates are all open to criticism. But both he and members of his family, many of whom he had recruited on to the LMX syndicates, have shared the misfortunes of his Names. "If I could do a Lord Lucan, I would. It's a nightmare," he said.

BILL BROWN

Another Lloyd's professional blamed for the misfortunes of LMX Names was Bill Brown of Walsham Bros, the leading broker of excess of loss policies. A large, florid-faced man with a dominating personality, he had established an unusually close link with some spiral underwriters, handling nearly 80 percent of Patrick Fagan's reinsurance for the Feltrim syndicates and providing the bulk of his premiums. When the spiral bubble burst and the Feltrim syndicates were shown to be disastrously exposed to catastrophe losses, it was inevitable that questions would be asked about whether the huge number of policies sold benefited anyone except the broker. Shunting excess of loss policies around the market for a commission of 10 percent on each transaction was extremely lucrative, however hazardous it eventually proved for the underwriters. In 1989, Brown was paid a salary of £8.1 million which, together with several millions in dividends from Walsham Bros, made him by far the best paid man in Britain.[10] Though he shuns publicity, he is a larger-than-life character who naturally attracts gossip. His post-prandial exploits and financial insouciance are the stuff of market legend. One story tells how Brown and one of his brothers were strolling back to the office past a BMW showroom when his brother stopped and whistled in appreciation of the newest £50,000 model. "I'll get that for you," said Bill. "After all, you paid for lunch." On another occasion, lunching with a friend, he said he would have to miss coffee because he had to go and buy some jumpers. "Where are you going to—Gieves the thieves?" "Nah," responded Brown in his East End drawl. "I'm buying show jumpers." Apart from horses purchased for his two show-riding daughters, Emma Jane and Kelly, on whom he dotes, Brown's other weakness is cars with personalized number plates. In addition to a Rolls-Royce Corniche (BB7), a five litre Mercedes (BILLY) and a Porsche, he recently treated himself to a new Ferrari. Asked by a colleague, What kind? Brown replied: "A red one."[11]

Conspicuous consumption is bound to excite envy, but there is no evidence for the accusation made, under the protection of parliamentary privilege by Labour MPs such as Bob Cryer, that Brown's extraordinary wealth derives from the suborning of underwriters and the churning of the LMX market. He was not the only broker peddling such policies, nor was he the only one to realize that the LMX business was a goldmine. Many large publicly quoted broking companies such as Sedgwick and CE Heath also benefited from selling excess of loss policies to LMX underwriters. There were few expenses, and by merely walking a few yards between one set of underwriters and another it was possible to make a 10 percent commission on a policy worth hundreds of thousands of pounds. "I cannot understand," said Peter Nutting, a Lloyd's council member, "why anyone paid Brown so much to march from one side of the room to another. The underwriters must be idiots."[12]

No one could accuse Bill Brown of being stupid. When the spiral bubble burst, it was noted sourly by ruined Names that, though he had acted as broker for many of the LMX syndicates which lost more than 100 percent of their capital, he had avoided investing in them. Instead, Brown was a Name on the top performing LMX syndicates Chappell 575 and Cotesworth Berry 536, which between 1988 and 1990, thanks to astute reinsurance, returned profits averaging 20 percent. Nor were the Feltrim Names happy to

learn that some of these handsome profits may have come indirectly from
their pockets because Feltrim had reinsured many of the other spiral syndicates in the market. Cotesworth Berry, contrary to some reports, was not,
however, a net gainer.

The concentration of such huge losses on so few syndicates in 1989
was particularly damaging for Lloyd's, because it served to detonate the
explosive charge that the market was rigged in favour of insiders. The
allegation that Lloyd's was run for the benefit of professionals working in
the market, at the expense of external Names who provided the bulk of the
capital, contained sufficient truth to be extremely damaging. An Exmoor
hill farmer, Christopher Thomas-Everard, threatened by bankruptcy after
losing more than £1 million as a result of being placed on a string of LMX
syndicates by his members' agent, began to research the issue. A computer
buff, he quickly discovered that the professionals were over-represented
on the best syndicates and under-represented on the worst. Lloyd's working Names accounted for 12 percent of the capacity of the market and 19
percent of its membership, but very few had spiral or stop loss syndicate
losses. For example, more than 90 percent of the losses on the seven worst
affected LMX syndicates in 1989 had fallen on external Names because
the professionals had carefully avoided them. Devonshire had only 7
percent of working Names, Gooda Walker 6 percent, Feltrim 6 percent,
and Rose Thomson Young 4 percent. The working Names, on the other
hand, appeared to have an uncanny knack of getting access to the most
profitable syndicates. The best performing syndicate in 1989 was Bankside
45, which had 40 percent of its capacity taken by working Names who
enjoyed profits of £3,000 for every £10,000 of business underwritten. Of
the ten most profitable syndicates, working Names were over-represented
on six, while they were under-represented on all ten syndicates with the
worst records.

The explanation of this skewed record soon emerged. Some syndicates
with attractive profit records deliberately weighted their membership in
favour of working Names. Thomas-Everard wrote to his agent, Jardines, on
three occasions between 1985 and 1988, asking that his exposure to LMX
high-risk syndicates be limited, and requesting that he be placed on the
waiting list for a number of reliable syndicates that he had identified as
above-average performers. After five years, he came to the top of the queue
for one such syndicate, Mander, Thomas & Cooper, following the death of
an external Name. Though his application was initially accepted, he was told

two months later that the underwriter had made a mistake and that only working Names could join. This was not an isolated case. In March 1987 a letter from Cotesworth Berry, one of the most respected managing agencies, to a members' agent, H.G. Poland, made it clear that some Names were more equal than others: "I confirm that whereas we are not allowing any sub-agents to increase their capacity on syndicate 536, we are prepared to make exceptions for market Names and that therefore you are very welcome to increase your own share." The underwriter of syndicate 536, Tony Berry, denied that this amounted to preferential treatment, but confirmed that a few working Names had been accepted at a time when the syndicate wished to limit its financial capacity. "We did say at this stage that only working Names who could bring benefit to the syndicates, such as a broker placing business advantageous to the syndicate, should be able to join if they wanted to." Since 1987, syndicate 536 has made profits of nearly £6,500 for every £10,000 of premium capacity.

At the beginning of 1992 Labour MPs, prompted by Tory backbenchers who had lost large sums of money at Lloyd's, put down a series of early day motions alleging that external Names had been deliberately dumped on loss-making spiral syndicates. With almost daily headlines in the papers and backbench MPs on the rampage, Lloyd's felt obliged to respond. It briefed financial journalists that one of the reasons why the LMX syndicates had such a high proportion of external Names was that they had expanded their capacity at a time when their results were attractive and large numbers of new Names were joining Lloyd's. It also noted that in the three years to 1988 the average annual returns of both external and working Names were almost identical, at 2.3 percent and 2.5 percent respectively. The disgraced former chairman of Lloyd's, Sir Peter Green, put the blame on Names for their "lemming rush" to join Lloyd's in the 1980s. "There were certain people who you could try and explain it to them what was going on and at rota committees we took enormous trouble, but they were all so starry eyed and just waiting for the cheques to roll in. I don't think half the time they listened to what they were being told."[13]

THE WALKER COMMITTEE

Such a response could never convince ruined Names that insiders had played fair. In a bid to put an end to the spate of damaging publicity the chairman of Lloyd's, David Coleridge, telephoned Sir David Walker, former head of the Securities and Investment Board and Deputy Governor of the Bank of England: "We're in a terrible hole," he said. "I know that," replied Sir David, who was an independent member of Lloyd's council.[14] The upshot was that he was asked to head an inquiry into the operation of the LMX market—in particular whether insiders had benefited at the expense of external Names. Sir David laid down two conditions: he should have a free hand in choosing who would help him, and he should be free to publish his report. A small team was assembled: John Lock, chairman of Mercantile and General, Britain's largest commercial reinsurer, Leslie Lucas, chief executive of Norwich Winterthur Reinsurance, Sir William Clark MP, chairman of the Conservative backbench finance committee, and Peter Mynors, a senior partner at Coopers & Lybrand Deloitte.

After a commendably short inquiry, the Walker committee published its report in June 1992. It concluded that there was no evidence for the wilder allegations made by some of the Names' action groups, that their losses were the result of conspiracy, churning, fraud and improper underwriting. Many company insurers, it noted, had been similarly hit by spiral losses. However, the fine print brought scant comfort to Lloyd's. The committee viewed "standards of professionalism, care and diligence on the part of a number of members' agents and managing agents and active underwriters as falling materially below best practice." It further noted that "the approach to fiduciary responsibilities, in the case of several members' agents was lax, with an unattractive appearance of preferencing of brokers and of members' agents themselves in some cases." And it highlighted "certain aspects of regulatory policies, at any rate with hindsight, as insufficient to identify shortcomings in performance and concentrations of exposures in a timely way." As to the performance of some managing agents, it said that there were "seriously flawed underwriting judgments." In short, no one emerged with credit, least of all the Lloyd's authorities, whose "arrangements for monitoring syndicate exposures indirectly through premium income were insufficient in respect of LMX business, especially in the light of the strong growth of capacity and the sharp reduction in premium rates."

On the thorny question of whether the market was rigged in favour of insiders, the report found that working Names were at an advantage "though not, in general and in most years, on an immodest scale given the inevitably superior market knowledge available to many working in the market as against outsiders." But at what point does immodesty become shameless? The report noted: "While the earlier advantaging of insiders that arose through baby syndicates had substantially disappeared by the mid-1980s, it is clear that working Names have generally, though not always, obtained better returns than external Names, that working Names were proportionately under-represented on the ten worst LMX syndicates subject to loss reviews and that, overall, the directors of members' agents had better returns than their Names, particularly in 1989." When the report's dry prose is translated into money terms, the insiders' "modest advantage" becomes clearer. In the eight years to 1990, assuming a standard premium line of £400,000, a member of Lloyd's council would have had a profit of £72,400 from his syndicates, an underwriter £64,000, and a director of a managing or members' agent £40,800. The average loss of an external member, by contrast, was £11,200. An external Name in the USA, Canada or Mexico would have fared even worse, losing an average of £35,200.[15]

All markets are to some extent a conspiracy of insiders against outsiders, but this wide gap in performance raised more searching questions than the Walker committee answered. If Names believe that the odds are loaded against them, they will rightly cry foul and steer clear. Nor is the problem of market professionals benefiting at the expense of external Names a new phenomenon. Three decades previously, the Cromer report, commissioned by Lloyd's in the wake of the losses caused by Hurricane Betsy, noted: "We feel it would be a mistake to disregard the degree of bitterness felt by some outside Names drawing heavily on their personal capital to meet underwriting losses while seemingly the earning power of underwriting agents and brokers is less affected."

Other recommendations made by the Walker committee were sharper. The report said that in future Lloyd's should publish annually information about how insiders and outsiders had fared, and that members' and managing agents should be required to inform Names of the degree of risk of their underwriting. Perhaps most important, it urged that Lloyd's should change from its traditional stance of a passive regulator to a much more active role. In particular, the market authorities should monitor Names' exposure much more closely and introduce a new system of risk weighting of syndicates that would limit any Name's exposure to high-risk business. "I was amazed and ashamed that I should have been on the council of Lloyd's which so signally failed to monitor risk," Sir David said shortly after his report was published. "It is clear now that there was a gaping hole in the system."[16] Hailed by the Lloyd's chairman as "so pure he makes Snow White look smutty," Sir David succeeded in silencing the most serious accusations of corruption in the market. But for ruined Names his report was scant comfort. "It constitutes a damning indictment of the behaviour and competence of the underwriters, managing agents and members' agents," noted the Lloyd's Names Associations' Working Party. As for the outside commentators, they were no more polite. *The Sunday Times* concluded: "The professionals of Lloyd's are not fit to regulate a flea circus, never mind a multi-billion market."

LOSS REVIEWS

The unravelling of the spiral saga continued with the publication of the official inquiries into the most heavily loss-making syndicates, which Lloyd's had commissioned in an attempt to stop Names rushing to the courts. The first to report was the Gooda Walker review committee, headed by Kieran Poynter, a partner in Price Waterhouse, which published a damning 1,500-page indictment of poor underwriting judgment allied to defective management controls. The basic reason for the losses of the four Gooda syndicates was "the underwriters' failure to recognize the aggregating potential of the spiral business accepted and their willingness to run a high degree of risk for high profit." The report pointed out that some participants in the spiral market appreciated the almost infinitely accumulative nature of the business they wrote, and purchased substantial vertical reinsurance protection. "The underwriters of the Gooda syndicates did not take this course and only partially protected their spiral aggregates' exposures."

The failure to buy adequate reinsurance led directly to the Gooda syndicate's huge losses, which could eventually reach £1 billion. It was the highest of risk business, yet many of the external Names whose underwriting affairs were managed by the Gooda Walker members' agency were reassured by Tony Gooda's favourite comment to new Names: "We won't make you a fortune, but we won't lose you one either." When Dr Brodie Lewis, a retired blood transfusion specialist from Aberdeen, was introduced to Gooda in 1984, he was handed an introductory prospectus which professed to set out the underwriting philosophy: "We adopt a conservative policy in our underwriting with our aim being a steady return from a wide spread of business." In fact, the syndicates were neither conservative in their underwriting practices nor did they write widely spread risks.

Another Gooda Name, Mrs. Fernanda Herford, the wife of a London accountant, was told by Tony Gooda that her investment was "so safe you could mortgage the cat."[17] The Poynter loss review report pointed out that all the Gooda syndicates were exceptionally hazardous, with underwriters willing to carry huge risks in the hopes of large profits. It also noted that the syndicates shared a high concentration of liabilities, made worse by the practice of incestuously reinsuring each other's risks: "There was thus a high probability they would all be affected by the same loss events." By the end of 1993, average losses of the 250 Names who had joined Lloyd's directly through the Gooda Walker member's agency amounted to more than £500,000. The loss review committee could only conclude that the common management and ownership of the members' and managing agency "may have inhibited the ability of the members' agency to take an objective view of the underwriting activities of the managed syndicates." In plain English, Names were shovelled on to Gooda syndicates regardless of risk because the financial interests of the members' and managing agency were closely aligned.

Some months later an even more damning report was published by GW Run-off, the company appointed to manage the syndicates after the Gooda Walker Group went into voluntary liquidation. Its author, Ken Randall, former head of regulation at Lloyd's, alleged that many Names were sucked into the syndicates by illusory profit figures that were artificially inflated by the use of time and distance policies. Such policies are widely used by long-tail syndicates as a means of discounting their reserves against future claims. The policy-holder pays a premium which is invested by the reinsurer. The proceeds are repaid at an agreed future date to meet claims as they arise. In effect, it is a way of spreading losses over many years as an alternative to discounting reserves. But, according to Randall, the time and distance policies purchased by Gooda Walker via Pinnacle, a Bermuda-based reinsurer, were used to inflate the profits of the Gooda syndicates. "Virtually all of Syndicate 164's profits for the 1980, 1983 and 1984 years of account resulted from the benefit taken from T&D policies," said the report. Similarly it revealed that "all of Syndicate 290's profits for the 1981, 1983, 1985 and 1987 years of account" were a result of manipulation. In 1981, according to Randall, a loss of 15 percent of premium income on syndicate 290 was transformed into a profit of 38 percent by the use of time and distance policies. It was on the basis of such illusory profit figures that membership of the syndicate swelled by more than ten times during the 1980s. Three months after the Randall report was published, it was referred to the Serious Fraud Office which after mulling over its contents for nearly a year, decided not to take the matter any further. None of this was any comfort to the more than 4,500 Names on Gooda Walker syndicates whose losses of £900 million between 1987 and 1990 amounted to a sixth of the market's total deficit. If the pain had been evenly spread, that would have been £200,000 per Name, but some of the worst hit faced losses of more than £1 million.

TONY GOODA

Behind the formal prose of these reports lay a story of spectacular boom and bust. Tony Gooda was the son of a successful Lloyd's underwriter, W.G. (Bill) Gooda, who founded an agency in the postwar years. Derek Walker, who eventually became the agency's star underwriter, joined as a fifteen-year-old office junior straight from school. His quick wit and way with figures led to his becoming a protege of the founder, and he established a reputation as a reinsurer of aviation business. Throughout the 1970s business boomed, and several new syndicates were launched by the partnership of the old-hand underwriter with his Marks and Spencer suits and polyester ties, and the public-school-educated Tony Gooda who managed the agency and brought in clients. In 1981 there was a serious hiccup. Walker was accused of being involved in a series of fraudulent reinsurance transactions and stood trial with the broker Christopher Moran, at the Old Bailey. He was acquitted and awarded costs. Immediately after the trial, the then chairman of Lloyd's, Peter Green, warned Tony Gooda that if Walker came back as his under-writer, the market authorities would "throw the book" at the agency. Gooda ignored this warning, and soon Gooda Walker was heading for rapid expansion, thanks to Derek Walker's seeming ability to conjure large profits from the rapidly growing spiral market. The capital base of the group's seven syndicates grew more than five times, from £48 million in 1983 to £270 million in 1988. The number of Names on Walker's flagship syndicate 290 trebled to more than 3,000, as year after year it appeared at the top half of the league tables published by Chatset, the independent market analyst. In 1986, the syndicate was the seventh most profitable of more than a hundred non-marine syndicates, returning a profit to Names of 23 percent. With success came the rewards. In one year in the late 1980s, Walker received almost £300,000 from the company of which he was now managing director as well as star underwriter. He owned a Porsche, a Mercedes, and a single-engined Cessna light aircraft which he used for day trips to the Isle of Wight and the Continent. "They lived the good life," said a former manager. "They entertained royally. There were cars for senior people and senior people's wives."[18]

Looking back at the wreckage, Walker is at pains to stress that he and his family have been as badly hit as anyone, facing cash calls of more than £1 million. "I put my money where my mouth is. What people don't seem to realize is that we have been wiped out too. One always knew there was a risk in the spiral, but one didn't expect all the layers to blow. No one imagined it going so horribly wrong." He points out that Names were warned of the risks they were running. In syndicate 290's annual report for 1984, he wrote: "We believe it is our duty to remind our Names of the nature of the class of business that we underwrite and we must apologize if we have to constantly point out the higher risk nature of this syndicate."

Walker is philosophical about his fate, attributing the huge losses facing him and his Names to bad luck and the string of catastrophes beginning with Hurricane Hugo. Why had he gambled with Names' money? "I don't use the word gamble, but if you are in insurance you are a risk taker. I always warned Names it was high risk. I never encouraged anyone to join Lloyd's. I had forty-seven years in the market, I did quite well. I made big money and I lost big money."[19]

Tony Gooda was equally fatalistic when I met him: "It's a risk business," he said. "I always knew it could happen and that we could be wiped out. I never sought to encourage anyone to join Lloyd's—they all knocked at our door. But at the end of the day we just didn't have enough reinsurance. I was always of the opinion that underwriters should have a very free hand. Derek [Walker] was and is a very clever underwriter and an acknowledged expert in reinsurance." Gooda is, however, unhappy at Lloyd's taking the management of the agency out of his hands after the LMX losses began to emerge: "If Lloyd's hadn't withdrawn our franchise, then Names wouldn't have been so badly affected. We could have done a very much better job in rescuing Names than the run-off company."[20]

GOODA NAMES

Gooda's ruined Names feel less dispassionate. Dr. Brodie Lewis, who has already paid out more than £300,000 in losses and is now beset by further demands for £525,000, is threatened with the loss of his house and has had to apply to the Lloyd's Names hardship committee. "For the first time in my whole life, I have found that I have been dealing with dishonourable people," he says bitterly. Around Coneyhurst in West Sussex, where Tony Gooda lives in a seventeenth-century farmhouse with his invalid wife who has multiple sclerosis, he is a virtual outcast. Many of the ruined Names were neighbours and golfing partners at the West Sussex Golf Club. "Anthony was part of our circle of friends," said one Name. "He is an extremely likeable man, someone we have known for years. When the question of becoming a Name arose, we trusted him implicitly because he is, well, one of us. To this day, I cannot say one discreditable thing about him, except he has lost all our money."[21] Others feel less charitable. Gooda has been bombarded with hostile letters and phone calls. One ruined Name told *The Financial Times*: "My wife saw Tony Gooda in Budgen's supermarket. She said: 'You dirty sod, why don't you commit suicide?' " The news that Gooda has been forced to apply to the Lloyd's hardship committee in respect of his own personal losses of more than £1 million has not assuaged the anger of those he has ruined. His sister, Valerie Baker, who faces losses of more than £1 million and stands with her husband to lose their only livelihood, a small sheep farm, is among the critics. Asked on a *Panorama* television programme whether she thought her brother was an honest man, she replied: "I have to say it is questionable."

One of the 250 Names whose affairs were managed by the Gooda Walker members' agency is Norbert Mallet, who is having to sell his fifteenth-century four-bedroomed farmhouse as the losses incurred by himself and his wife grow to more than £500,000. "The numbers now are just academic," he says. "We can't pay. The thing is that if you're drowning, it doesn't matter if you're drowning in the Atlantic or a pond—you're still drowning." Mr. Mallet, a former broker who built up his own reinsurance business, cannot be said to have joined Lloyd's with his head in the clouds. "I knew it was long-term," he says, "but there was a lot I was not told. When I was in the business, I used to work out what would happen if everything went down, and cover it. Some of these jokers didn't and I want to know why. The system was wide open to abuse."

Richard Platts became a Name at Lloyd's in 1986 on retiring from his post as senior lecturer in economics at Queen's University in Belfast. His grandfather had been a Name as had other members of his family, so when a friend suggested that he should join as a way of boosting his retirement income, he agreed. His first members' agent was almost immediately bought out by Nelson, Hurst and Marsh who placed him on several high-risk LMX syndicates including Gooda Walker. "At the outset I knew nothing about insurance," he explained. "I placed my trust in him [the agent] and with it the future of my family. As must be the case with all Names, I trusted the expert who knew the market, the underwriters, and the real risks to which he subjected his Names."[22]

Platts began with a premium limit of £400,000 and was rewarded with a modest profit in his initial underwriting year. Encouraged, he steadily increased his limit to £850,000 which, he was assured, would provide a greater spread and more safety. But soon came the first hint of trouble with the Piper Alpha disaster in 1988. Platts shifted to another small agent, K.C. Webb, which in turn was taken over by Gardner Mountain in 1990. At this point he was warned that he was excessively exposed to high-risk spiral syndicates. Gardner Mountain took him off several of the worst for the 1990 year of account, but by then it was too late. Platts' losses already amount to more than £1 million, and though he is involved in several of the litigating groups he sees no hope of recovery. "I am completely finished financially," he says. "I keep getting statements and demands that I can't possibly meet. They [Lloyd's] have already drawn down my deposit of about £190,000 in shares. There's nothing left. My losses will be four or five times my assets. The figures are so overwhelming that even if I won all the law suits, I would probably be bust." Platts, whose wife is also facing serious losses from spiral syndicates, is angry about the quality of the advice he received from his first three members' agents. "They were competent at taking people out to lunch but that's as far as it went," he says. "A total lack of proper regulation allowed these incompetent agents to flourish and they in turn failed to supervise the managing agents."

Clive Francis, a former RAF fighter pilot who owes Lloyd's nearly £3 million on spiral and other syndicates, is no less bitter. "I am getting a reputation as a very slow payer," he says. His is a story of rags to riches to rags. Twenty-five years ago, Francis left the airforce as a squadron-leader, with a £1,500 gratuity which he used to buy a small flat. Within a decade he was a property millionaire. He was then persuaded by a dinner party guest who, he later discovered, was working on commission, to join Lloyd's. He began underwriting through Fielding's, a well-known members' agent, and was placed on what he was assured were a number of conservatively run syndicates. "A guest at my dinner table saw that we lived well. I was hooked by snobbery and greed," he says, recalling that he once owned two aeroplanes. "Now I own a bicycle." He has been forced by Lloyd's to sell his London house and move into rented accommodation. He says the hardship committee has allowed him a grand total of £8,000 a year, including his RAF pension, to live on. Francis, who is actively involved in a number of the action groups which are suing members' and managing agents, blames his losses on the perverted culture of a market in which conflicts of interest and incompetence were rife. "To think that my fortune is now in the hands of those fools," he says ruefully.[23]

PATRICK FAGAN

Many other spiral underwriters lost large sums of money, but Patrick Fagan of Feltrim has the dubious distinction of having written some of the worst risks in the market. In 1986 Fagan, a former WMD underwriter, became the active underwriter for Feltrim, the combined members' and managing agency which picked up the pieces of Peter Cameron-Webb's and Peter Dixon's empire which had failed in the spectacular circumstances described earlier.

Despite these antecedents, Fagan's syndicates specializing in LMX risks proved extremely popular with members' agents across the market. Syndicate 540, which had 985 Names writing a total of £27.3 million in 1987, nearly doubled in strength in 1989 to 1,672 Names writing £41.1 million. There was, as the loss review report was later to point out, "widespread approval of and enthusiasm about the Excess of Loss market and confidence in the skills of Fagan and his team."

Not everyone was quite as enthusiastic. In the autumn of 1986, when Feltrim was seeking registration from Lloyd's as an approved managing agent, it ran into problems in securing errors and omissions insurance without which it would not be able to trade. One of those whom Fagan approached to secure the vital cover was Stephen Merrett, chairman of the Merrett Group, who had been the lead E&O underwriter for the WMD Group, an underwriting agency started by Cameron-Webb. He refused, bluntly telling Fagan: "I am sorry but I just do not feel that you have a board that I am prepared to support."[24] Other E&O underwriters took the same line. Fagan turned to Bill Brown of Walsham Bros who managed, albeit with difficulty, to place Feltrim's E&O insurance, after which Lloyd's approved its registration.

It appears that these events helped to persuade Feltrim to place a large part of its business with Walsham Bros, amounting in 1987 to 61 percent of inward premiums and 74 percent of reinsurance premiums. When Patrick Fagan was asked by the loss review committee whether he accepted that "market reciprocity" had played a part in his relationship with Bill Brown, he replied: "He managed to place our errors and omissions for us, without which we would not have been there anyhow. We owed him a certain allegiance for that. You do not turn and kick a chap in the teeth when he has got you afloat so to speak. One tended to treat him with a certain amount of caution because he is a very forceful character. But he had done us enormous favours in getting that errors and omissions done."

For the Names concerned, there were no favours. By the time the Feltrim loss review committee, headed by Sir Patrick Neill, reported in September 1992, the Names on syndicate 540 had suffered a "totally unacceptable" loss of £73,700 for each £10,000 of premium, and the Names on the smaller non-marine syndicate 847 had lost £45,400. The three-volume report concluded that Feltrim executives had entirely failed to appreciate how the LMX market would respond in the event of a major catastrophe. In the event, the underwriter had neglected to keep track of his aggregate exposure, and had been badly under-reinsured on the top layers of his underwriting. "I do not think any of us appreciated the way the spiral would work and how incestuous it had actually become," said Fagan.

The Feltrim committee's conclusions were mirrored in other loss review reports. The report on Rose Thomson Young's syndicate 255, whose Names lost more than 500 percent over two years, concluded there was no evidence to support the claim that there was a conspiracy in which one group of syndicates had enriched itself at the expense of other, less competent, underwriters. "Some underwriters," the report noted dryly, "were more successful than others." It also found no evidence that LMX contracts were fraudulent or had been deliberately churned by brokers in order to earn commission. The committee noted that the mistake of most LMX underwriters was to think that the higher the layer covered by an excess of loss policy, the less likely it was to be hit. In practice, once a loss the size of Piper Alpha occurred, the intervening layers of the spiral were rapidly eroded.

Nick Gratwick, a thirty-six-year-old insurance broker who has been driven to the verge of bankruptcy by his losses on Rose Thomson Young syndicates, was in a militant mood when I met him at Lloyd's extraordinary general meeting on 27 July 1992. "Why should I mortgage my future for that bastard down there," he said pointing at the chairman. "I am going down to the County Court next week to declare personal bankruptcy. If they want my future, they can whistle for it."

Gratwick joined Lloyd's in 1985, aged twenty-seven, and was immediately put on a number of high-risk excess of loss syndicates. "I remem-

ber standing in the old Lloyd's building before a polished table at which the
six men of the Rota committee sat," he said. "There were chandeliers, high
ceilings and carpets. It was very impressive. I remember thinking, 'This is
it, I've made it.' I felt so privileged at being invited to join that I didn't ask
basic questions. I would have asked for more details if I was buying a
second-hand car." Gratwick, who now faces losses of more than a quarter of
a million pounds, has had to sell his insurance business and a small farm left
to him by his father. "I ran out of money last year," he says. "I'm down to a
rented room and a motor-bike. I was somebody who was very careful with
money. I never had a champagne lifestyle. I thought I'd paid it into a nice
safe business at Lloyd's. I trusted them."[25]

A common criticism expressed in many of the LMX loss reports was
the failure of managing agents to exercise adequate supervision over syndicate underwriters. A director of Cuthbert Heath, whose 1084 marine syndicate lost nearly 150 percent in 1989, said that he did not feel it was part of
his job to question the way the syndicate was being run: "I am not at all
satisfied that it was incumbent upon me or my fellow directors to ask chapter
and verse of a man in his mid-forties who, as I have suggested to you despite
what people may think to the contrary, was a very able and experienced
underwriter."

An industry news letter, *The Digest of Lloyd's News*, was less easily
satisfied: "Few agents understood the logic of the LMX market," it noted,
"and few appreciated the need for aggregates to be kept and monitored." The
Association of Lloyd's Members was also critical: "The authorities emerge
from these inquiries in a poor light. Those ultimately responsible must be
the Working Members of successive Councils of Lloyd's . . . they appear to
have been remarkably unaware of the way in which the Room was being
used as a casino, with extraordinary odds being accepted on Names' behalf;
or, if they did know about it, their failure to take swift remedial action was
an act of inexcusable neglect."

By any standards Lloyd's failed in its duty to protect Names by
neglecting to control the wilder excesses of the spiral. Several members of
the council must have known the risks that were being run by new Names
with only limited capital. The nicknames such as "the Nodding Donkey" and
"Time-bomb" given to certain notorious spiral underwriters suggest that
many at Lloyd's had a shrewd idea of what was going on. Sir David Walker's
statement, quoted earlier in this chapter, that he was "amazed and ashamed"
to have been a member of the council of Lloyd's which so signally failed to

protect Names, is a sobering admission. Many others had a far greater responsibility than Sir David for what happened, though few have acknowledged this. It is noteworthy that leading underwriters on the council steered well clear of the worst-hit spiral syndicates and refused to put a single Name on them. They knew how risky they were, but they either felt unable to act or preferred to keep quiet. David Coleridge, then chairman of Lloyd's, was not understating the matter when he told a general meeting of Names in June 1992 that recent events were "one of the darker chapters in the long history of our society."

10

Open Years

"We are being asked to pay losses on policies written before we were born, to set up reserves to pay claims which will arise after we are dead, surely there is no doubt as to the reasonable answer to the question: 'Should I pay or not?'"
Tom Benyon, Society of Names

For three centuries Lloyd's traded on the basis of a financial system dependent on trust, under which past liabilities which had been incurred but not yet paid were reinsured by succeeding generations of Names. The devastating claims for asbestos and pollution in the 1980s undermined this trust; the debacle of the spiral losses finally destroyed it. Lloyd's system of trading involves a three-year accounting period at the end of which a syndicate's financial position is finalized by means of an internal reinsurance. This transfers the liability for all claims arising from policies written in prior years on to the syndicate's successor year in return for a premium. The profits, or losses, for the closed year are then paid out to, or recouped from, Names.

For a long time this system worked well enough, despite an inevitable element of rough justice. For motor and other syndicates specializing in short-term risks, there were few problems. By the end of three years virtually all the claims were known and had been carefully assessed, and the majority had been paid. The premium for the reinsurance to close (RITC) paid to the successor year syndicate was therefore relatively small. But for long-tail syndicates, where claims for latent disease might arise on long extinct policies, the reinsurance premium was large, and it also involved a considerable element of guesswork. The estimate made by the underwriter of the extent of the incurred but not reported claims, known as IBNR, was crucial. If the reinsurance premium was too small, the Names on the subsequent years of account would be at a disadvantage, because the eventual claims would be greater than the amount paid. If, however, the risks were exaggerated, the Names on the current year would have paid too much.

In the end it depended on the judgment of the active underwriter; the size of the reinsurance to close was the most crucial decision he had to make each year; its outcome often determined whether his syndicate would make a profit or a loss. Though the decision was subject to audit, and to the market's regulations for reserving particular classes of business, the temptation in hard times for underwriters to skimp and produce a favourable result was undeniable. Moreover as Lloyd's, in yet another of its accounting peculiarities, did not until 1985 insist on "a true and fair" audit, the basis on which underwriters reserved throughout the 1970s and early 1980s was extremely flexible. Few Names, however, understood the risks they were running by joining long-tail syndicates.

One underwriter who appreciated the danger was Robert Kiln. He resigned from the committee of Lloyd's in 1981, after warning that the market was fundamentally under-reserved. He is blunt about the RITC: "It is quite absurd to pretend that any realistic figure, let alone a 'true and fair figure', can be put on the premiums for a reinsurance to close at the end of thirty-six months on most syndicate accounts. It is sheer guesswork and if any actuary, underwriter or accountant were asked to guarantee that any RITC they are recommending to Names will fall within say a 20 percent margin either way they could not do so." Kiln rubs in just how self-serving some underwriters' judgments had been: "Many Names who joined Lloyd's in the 1980s have suffered unfair and enormous losses due to the gross inadequacy of the reinsurance to close made over the past forty years and which were well known about in the early 1980s."[1] This comment, by a respected Lloyd's insider, goes to the heart of the litigation that is plaguing the society. Names who had been persuaded to join grossly under-reserved syndicates understandably felt that they had been victims of fraud when the bubble burst.

In the early 1980s few of those working at Lloyd's, and even fewer external Names, had any idea of the financial time-bomb that was ticking away. Most were convinced by the spiel of members' agents pointing out the attractions, at a time of high personal taxation, of syndicates with large reserves on which capital gains could be made. Before 1980 it was unusual for a syndicate to remain unclosed. Occasionally, if an underwriter died or defaulted leaving his Names exposed, a year might have to be left open, but generally such a syndicate was taken over by another syndicate which undertook the run-off almost as a market duty.

The avalanche of asbestos, pollution and spiral claims put paid to such gentlemanly behaviour. For the first time, Names saddled with open years began to appreciate how tight a noose had been closed around their financial neck. To their horror, they discovered that if an underwriter decided to leave a year open because the scale of potential claims was unknowable and/or so large that he could not arrive at a fair reinsurance to close, their exposure to past claims was unlimited. For Names on syndicates exposed to asbestos and pollution claims dating back half a century or more, it was a life sentence with no remission. Apart from seeking to buy an individual commercial reinsurance policy in the market at a very high cost, often as much as 2,000 percent of their original premium, there was no escape. Not even death wiped out a Name's continuing liability—his estate, unless protected by a special reinsurance, could not be wound up until all his outstanding underwriting debts had been paid. And that could not be determined until the open year was closed, which might take a quarter of a century or more.

Just how serious an open year could be was shown by the case of Forbes 274/300, a small marine syndicate which ceased trading in 1970, leaving its fifty Names to cope with future claims on old policies. By 1981, claims on the policies it had underwritten over half a century of trading had reduced to a trickle, so another syndicate, Brooks and Dooley 89, agreed to reinsure its run-off. It was a costly mistake. On discovering that Forbes had a large exposure to asbestos and pollution, the syndicate was forced to leave its 1982 year open. A decade later its 740 Names, a third of whom are now dead, are still trapped on the 1982 open year, having paid out 75 percent of their average line of £20,000, with many more losses to come. The managing agents estimate that, without a central rescue, it could be as much as another quarter of a century before the syndicate is closed. By then the vast majority of its Names will have died, leaving their executors to wrestle with the mess.[2]

The troubles of Brooks and Dooley were a forerunner of what lay ahead. The first of the problem syndicates were those most heavily exposed to asbestos claims, such as Don Tayler's non-marine syndicate 90, which had written a large book of general liability policies in the USA in the 1950s and was forced to leave its 1982 year open. Then came the syndicates affected by stop loss, spiral, pollution, and professional indemnity claims. As the losses spread other syndicates, faced by a rapidly declining capital base, were forced to leave years open; in many cases they had no choice, as there was no successor year syndicate into which they could reinsure and no other syndicate was rash enough to accept the run-off.

By 1988, the rot had spread so far that fifty-seven syndicates had left open ninety-seven years of account. When the 1989 year closed, the numbers, swelled by the spiral debacle, had grown to 103 syndicates and 162 open years with a capacity of nearly £3 billion, a quarter of the market. By the time of the 1990 account, the numbers of open years had doubled again to 317, and virtually all Names found themselves trapped on at least one of their syndicates. The administrative burdens of these run-offs, quite apart from their potential future insurance losses, were dismayingly large. Alan Pollard, the chairman of the main specialist run-off company, Syndicate Underwriting Management, predicted that the administration costs alone of running off all the main open year syndicates would be £1.2 billion.

At the beginning of 1993 Chatset, the independent Lloyd's analyst, plunged the market into even deeper gloom by estimating that the costs of closing all the open years would eventually amount to an astronomical £5 billion, equivalent to more than half the market's current capacity. Even assuming that some of the claims might not have to be paid for many years, the discounted figure to bring the reserves up to scratch was put at £2 billion.[3]

A BLOODY FORECAST

The scale of under-reserving disclosed by Chatset was so large that the majority of Names appeared to be heading straight for bankruptcy. Syndicate 90 was estimated to have further losses of 1,000 percent of line, in addition to its current losses of more than 250 percent which, for Names writing an average line of £40,000, was the equivalent of £500,000. Colin Mackinnon's syndicate 134, which specialized in providing personal stop loss policies to Names on other syndicates, was estimated to be facing deficits on each of its three open years of between 800 and 1,200 percent.

These detailed forecasts were too bloody to be ignored. The market appeared to be threatened by an imminent meltdown of both confidence and capital. This provoked leading underwriters to denounce Chatset's forecast in extravagant terms. "Grossly misleading," "irresponsible," "entirely specious'—the epithets volleyed around the Room. John Wetherell, underwriter of non-marine 190, told *The Times* angrily: "I believe speculation about syndicates, reserving and potential deterioration is . . . totally misleading." Richard Youell, underwriter of syndicate 932, expected to lose between 300 and 400 percent, said: "I have very deep doubts about Chatset's ability to read underwriting accounts. This is not the first time they have come out with dotty figures."[4]

Unfortunately for Lloyd's, Chatset's credibility at this juncture was rather greater than that of its critics. At the beginning of 1991, it had warned that the 1989 year would lose more than £1 billion. This was denounced by Lloyd's as "alarmist," but the loss turned out, eighteen months later, to be almost precisely double that figure. Chatset's equally conservative estimate of a further loss in 1990 of more than £1.5 billion (just over half the final figure), again in the teeth of Lloyd's expressions of scorn, had convinced most outside Names that its "doom-mongering" was soundly based.

The extraordinary saga of Peter Cameron-Webb's syndicates, which collapsed in 1982, lent credence to the view of the pessimists. After years of wringing its hands, the council eventually agreed, in 1987, to a complex settlement which acknowledged that PCW Names had been victims of fraud. The syndicates' liabilities were estimated to be £135 million, of which the Names were asked to contribute £40 million and the brokers and accountants £55 million. Lloyd's put in £40 million, and agreed that the central fund would set aside an additional £100 million to cover any unforeseen future deterioration.

Far from being adequate, these provisions proved to be hopelessly optimistic as it emerged that PCW was heavily exposed to asbestos and pollution claims. The warning of former Lloyd's chairman Sir Peter Miller, that its affairs were so tangled that they would not be cleared up within his lifetime, was shown to be all too accurate. Lioncover, the special rescue vehicle set up by Lloyd's to run off PCW, has already called for further sums amounting to £150 million, which have had to be charged against the central fund to which all Names are obliged to contribute. Chatset now estimates that Lloyd's total bill for this one group of syndicates may eventually run as high as £750 million. It notes gloomily: "Added together this means that every Name can look forward to an annual sum of at least £2,000 collected through the central fund for at least the next twenty-five years. Put another way, anyone considering joining Lloyd's should set aside an amount of

£20,000 as 'dead money' to pay his PCW losses."[5] At the beginning of 1995, Chatset forecast that the scale of under-reserving for the market as a whole had doubled to £10 billion. Even discounted over twenty years, this was a nightmarish prospect.

The immediate reaction of Lloyd's to the open year problem was to wish it away. In December 1989 the council passed bye-law 17, aimed at making life awkward for underwriters who wanted to leave a year open. It required a number of administratively burdensome and expensive provisions to be made, including actuarial assessment, before any year could be left unclosed. This response failed to work; within two years the number of open years had doubled. By 1993, more than 90 percent of Lloyd's active membership of roughly 20,000 had at least one run-off year. In addition, 12,000 Names who had stopped underwriting, mostly because they had run out of money, were trapped and unable to quit the market because of their open-ended exposure to old year claims, unlimited in time and amount.

Rodney Pickles, a Lancashire businessman, joined Lloyd's with seven friends in 1979. At the time it seemed a good idea. Today, faced by accelerating losses on five syndicates with open years, he has ceased underwriting but cannot escape the demands for more and more money that come in the post. "Through these open years, Lloyd's has a captive membership," he says. "If they found an answer to the open years, there would be a mass exodus." Pickles has no doubts where the blame for his predicament lies: "My firm belief is that Names have been ripped off. If they [the underwriters and managing agents] had been modest with their commission charges and profits, Lloyd's could have weathered the storm." He says he has had enough: "I have paid them £96,000 this year. They are now asking for more money."[6]

Julian Tennant, a relative of Lord Glenconner, has been forced to sell his Grade II listed eighteenth-century house, Plush Manor, set in grounds of more than seven acres, and move into a rented cottage in a neighbouring Dorset village. "Our faith in Lloyd's has been totally destroyed," he told a public meeting of Names at the Albert Hall in May 1993. "It's bad enough to be forced to move out of your house into a small cottage but it's even worse to learn that Mr. Brockbank's [underwriter of marine syndicate 861] salary was £430,000 last year. That is obscene. It is the greed of the people at Lloyd's who have destroyed the confidence of the Names."

As confidence evaporated, the risk of the whole market collapsing became all too real. With old year losses running at an average of £450 million annually, the capital base of the market was haemorrhaging away.

Since 1990 fewer than 400 new Names, nearly all professionals, have joined the market, whereas more than 6,000 ceased active underwriting in the same period. By 1994, it was estimated, more than half the membership would have lost all the funds that they had deposited with Lloyd's to secure their underwriting. For those who continued to underwrite, the nightmarish prospect opened up of being held responsible for the losses of those who had ceased to trade and could no longer pay. If the market's capital base were to collapse, all syndicates would have to be left open, and the costs of a total run-off would be borne by an ever-diminishing band of Names. This was the Armageddon which made a nonsense of the principle, drummed into every new recruit to the market, that Names were sole traders and were responsible only for their own losses. A meltdown would engulf everyone.

Lloyd's response to the growing crisis was to set up Centrewrite, a reinsurance company designed to provide an exit route for Names with open years. It was charged with offering commercial reinsurance quotations to all open year syndicates in order to free them from their prior year claims. Quotations were also to be offered to individual Names if the syndicates' underwriters refused the collective deal. Centrewrite's progress turned out to be disappointingly slow, and its quotations were very expensive. A year after it was set up, it had issued only one quote, to the small Langton syndicate 12 in respect of its 1984 open year. The reinsurance terms of 140 percent, equivalent to more than four times the syndicate's reserves carried forward, were so high that few Names accepted. By the end of 1992, a few more quotations had dribbled out; Warrilow's 553 syndicate's 1984 open year was quoted at 330 percent, a figure which, like Langton's, was higher than independent estimates. The longer Centrewrite laboured, the more evident it was that Chatset's "dotty" forecast, that £5 billion was needed to dig Lloyd's out of its asbestos and pollution black hole, might not be far off the mark.

The next stab at finding an answer to the open year problem was made by a leading broker, David Rowland, chairman of Sedgwick, who was appointed in November 1990 to head a Lloyd's task force. Rowland's report, published more than a year later, concluded that the best hope for badly wounded Names was to trade through their losses. Instead of discouraging underwriters from leaving years open, it said that Names' interests were best served by accepting that it was impossible to come to any realistic estimate of the eventual costs of asbestos and pollution claims. Despite these "huge uncertainties," the Task Force recommended somewhat perversely that Centrewrite should accelerate its efforts in order to offer a reinsurance quotation to every open year syndicate within three years.

The Task Force's advice to Names to trade through their troubles was more of a prayer than a solution. If old year losses continued to run at roughly £500 million a year, it was inevitable that thousands of Names in addition to those immediately hit by the spiral would sooner or later be ruined. Even on the optimistic assumption that Lloyd's made an extraordinary return of 10 percent each year from 1993 onwards, the average old year losses of the 10,000 Names most heavily exposed to long-tail claims would be about £50,000 a year, almost double any profits they might hope to receive from their average line of £300,000. "What will happen," warned one aggrieved Name, "is that those with an above average exposure on open years will be steadily eliminated over the next few years. There will thus be a consequential requirement for Lloyd's to impose an annual levy to strengthen the central fund in order to cover the outstanding liabilities of failed members. In effect there will be a gradual *de facto* mutualization of old year losses. At the same time Lloyd's will experience a steadily declining membership and a shrinking capital base."[7]

A NIGHTMARE SCENARIO

The prospect of a drastic decline in the number of Names, leading to a meltdown of the whole market, concentrated minds. In November 1990, James Sinclair, managing director of Willis Faber, one of the largest members' agencies, had written a blunt letter to the head of Lloyd's Regulatory Services forecasting just that: "The sad answer our unhappy Names have concluded is the way the society is carrying on you cannot have any confidence in Lloyd's—Policies, Regulatory Control or Agents. . . Culminating with the bad underwriting years 1988/89 plus the realization Lloyd's contracts can and do fail, I guess Names will herd out of the market as confidence plummets. Lloyd's will have a very high price to pay for the clottish underwriting policy of a few of our greedy underwriters. And it will all happen in the next twenty-four months."

Sinclair's prediction proved all too accurate. Even those traditionalists on the council most opposed to a central rescue or any hint of mutualization began to appreciate that simply "burning off" badly wounded Names was not a viable long-term solution. There was widespread agreement on the need for a more effective central mechanism to handle the running off of prior year claims. It made no sense, for example, that Centrewrite was obliged to provide commercial reinsurance quotes for unquantified and unquantifiable claims that might not have to be paid for a quarter of a century. The uncertainties were so great that its premiums were bound to be heavily inflated. Whatever estimate was made for a run-off reinsurance, it risked being wrong by several orders of magnitude. No less absurd was the fact that many badly affected Names found themselves having to fund large syndicate reserves in case litigation which they themselves were bringing succeeded. Double counting of losses was rife within Lloyd's, because most errors and omissions insurance, which was the target of Names' litigation, had been placed within the market. So with Name suing Name, often one and the same person, and losses mounting, there was every reason to attempt a central solution. Lastly, it made little sense to have fifty different managing agents spending more than £100 million a year in running off individual syndicate years. The specialized tasks of managing claims, litigation, and reinsurance recoveries cried out for centralization.

In the autumn of 1992 David Springbett, a former broker, put forward the framework for a rescue plan in a confidential paper titled *Operation Springclean*. Pointing out that it was unacceptable that thousands of Names should be faced by liabilities unlimited in both time and amount, he recommended that open year syndicates should transfer their prior year claims, together with all their reserves, to a new central body. The reserves of each syndicate would have to be comparable, which might mean some Names having to find large sums. In addition, Names would have to agree to pay a provisional levy equivalent to 200 percent of the transferred reserves of the syndicate. The central body would be entitled to demand all or part of this levy, depending on the number of claims over the next four years, but at the end of this period the Name would face no further liability.[8]

Over the next few months, variations on this proposal were refined. In November 1992 Lloyd's new chief executive, Peter Middleton, set up a committee composed of external and professional Names charged with coming up with a solution to the open year crisis. Led by Christopher Stockwell, chairman of the Lloyd's Names Associations' Working Party, it included Robin Jackson, the chairman of Centrewrite, and John Charman, underwriter of marine syndicate 488. The panel's report, submitted to the council at the beginning of March 1993, did not mince its words. The market, it warned, was facing "a critical challenge because of the near wholesale alienation of its traditional source of capital." Without significant restructuring of the current liabilities falling on Names, almost half of the membership would have lost all their funds deposited at Lloyd's, and the deficit would then have to be met by the remaining membership. Estimated total losses over the next few years, it noted, were likely to be greater than Names' assets at Lloyd's. "Considerable replenishment of deposits," it warned, "will be required if the Society is to have any capacity going forward with which to underwrite." The report's conclusion was blunt: "The basic choice facing the Society, therefore, is one of an orderly and planned settlement with consequent goodwill and publicity benefits, or a settlement by default."[9]

The warning of disaster could hardly have been starker. The panel's solution was clear-cut. All old years should be divided into two groups, "soft" and "hard." The "soft" group would consist of syndicates which could be closed relatively easily by conventional means, and this process should be carried out by Centrewrite without delay. The "hard" group, those syndicates affected by latent disease and pollution claims, should be reinsured into a limited company which would require a common level of reserving before they would be allowed to cede their liabilities. There would be three stages: the first would involve setting up the corporate vehicle and handing over to it responsibility for handling claims; this would enable it to assess a recommended level of reserves for each syndicate. Finally, after reserves had been agreed on a fair basis, syndicates would have their old year claims reinsured by the new limited company which would take charge of their reserves.

There were a number of arguments in favour of this approach; perhaps the most forceful was that it delayed dealing with what appeared to be an insoluble problem. As the panel's report pointed out, the nightmare of long-tail claims was common to many reinsurers, but only Lloyd's reserved on a basis which threatened immediate bankruptcy for its Names: "It seems highly unlikely that any of Lloyd's major international competitors would feel it necessary to recognize a potential liability decades before it becomes payable. Furthermore for those competitors with old year liabilities, reserves are strengthened when necessary from current profits. The major difference affecting Lloyd's is not therefore a function of the policies written but rather of the structure of the capital base."

The report hinted at a more veiled motive for handing over the problem of old years to a new body with only limited liability: "The panel believes that such a structure would be desirable from the viewpoint of limiting the tendency of the US Courts to regard Lloyd's as an acceptable and unlimited source of funds." A few pages later, the report recommended that, though the "phoenix" strategy of US insurance companies plagued by long-tail claims seeking the protection of Chapter 11 was not available to Lloyd's, "alternative ways of achieving the result should be explored." The message could hardly have been plainer. If the worst came to the worst, Lloyd's should at least have the option of walking away from its old year problems.

NEWCO

It was a measure of the crisis facing Lloyd's that this radical solution was endorsed by the council. The market's first ever business plan, published a month later in April 1993, accepted that new capital would be attracted to the market only if the problems of asbestos and pollution claims were separated from the rest of the market. It proposed to do this by the setting up of a limited liability company, NewCo, into which all old year claims prior to 1986 would be channelled together with syndicate reserves. The aim of NewCo, which was retitled Equitas in September 1994, was far-reaching. "With this restructuring the market will have put in place the strongest practical ring fence against the impact of old year liabilities." Syndicates trading on would be protected from all claims on old year policies. To give further assurance to providers of new capital, the business plan promised that neither central fund contributions nor a special levy would be raised without consulting the membership. However it acknowledged: "In time it is possible that NewCo may require additional capital. The Council will be able to use the resources of the central fund, its ability to levy capital and future profits and its ability to borrow funds to recapitalize NewCo."[10]

At first blush this sounded straightforward, but behind the measured prose lay undoubtedly the greatest gamble Lloyd's has ever taken. If Equitas (NewCo) is to succeed, the tide of ever-increasing pollution and asbestos claims will have to be contained. The scale of the latent disease and long-tail claims facing the market is unknowable and is likely to be only marginally less uncertain in the next few years. Everything depends on the decisions of the US courts and Congress over the next decade. The potential exposure of the whole American insurance industry to environmental claims is so large that the numbers make little sense. According to testimony given to the Congress sub-committee on Policy Research and Insurance, the range of possible outcomes is between $40 billion and $1,000 billion. As Lloyd's task force pointed out in January 1992: "Assessing the range of Lloyd's possible exposure to pollution claims is subject to huge uncertainties. Should court decisions go against the industry as a whole, Lloyd's needs to have only a modest share of the problem for it to face very serious losses."[11]

Lloyd's plans to free its beleaguered Names from this devastating uncertainty, but a price will have to be paid. If Equitas (NewCo) insists on a safety-first policy of reserving against all possible future claims, then the calls on Names on open year syndicates will be so large that thousands will be bankrupt. If, as is more likely, Equitas tempers its demands to what it believes Names can afford, this is bound to impinge on the credibility of the "ring fence." At some point, probably in the next decade, Lloyd's may have to decide whether to pay its multi-billion pollution and asbestos liabilities or walk away from its debts. The latter is still regarded by many market professionals as unthinkable. The advantage of the business plan is that it defers such awkward decisions until a time when, it is hoped, the market will have returned to profit.

The consequence if Lloyd's fails in its gamble to solve the open year problem was underlined by Lloyd's chairman, David Rowland, in his introduction to the plan. It was not, he stressed, a consultative document but rather a programme for action: "The alternative is bleak. Should membership and market not unite behind this plan then Lloyd's may have no future. In those circumstances all members should realize that they remain individually responsible for the insurance risks underwritten on their behalf."

11

Sue First, Pay Later

"Self-regulation as practised at Lloyd's is fair, responsive, economic and effective—it is a delicate mechanism but it works well."
Lloyd's background briefing

'What we have been dealing with here is a unique combination of greed, criminality, and incompetence."
Daily Telegraph

As the losses at Lloyd's escalated, the 30 percent of Names on whom 70 percent of the losses had fallen were faced by a choice: pay up or fight. Many determined to sue, a decision taken at a series of meetings which brought together worried farmers, angry businessmen, depressed small traders and belligerent landed gentry. They had little in common except their membership of Lloyd's and a conviction that they had been cheated. Most of them had little understanding of how the market operated, knew nothing about spiral risks, and were bewildered that they could have lost so much money. As one disillusioned Name put it: "What has been destroyed is trust. People joined Lloyd's confident in its reputation for 'Utmost Good Faith'. No one in his right mind entrusts his whole future as we have done to perfect strangers. To be a member of Lloyd's was a distinction—something of which one could be proud. No longer."[1]

Deserted by their members' agents and cold-shouldered by the council, which blamed the losses on a freak series of natural catastrophes, the Names had to look to their own resources for help. The vacuum left by cries of outrage was soon filled by action committees. "If we don't pay up, we are thrown out; so why aren't those who have defrauded us thrown out?" asked one irate small trader. Quite apart from the Names' passionate belief that they had been deceived, the arguments in favour of litigation were compelling. The outcome of the Sasse and PCW cases showed that those who sued had a chance of recovering part of their losses; those who did not, but merely whined to the media, would be ignored. The arithmetic was also persuasive. Most of the troubled syndicates had lost at least 100 percent, in some cases more than 1,000 percent, of Names' premium; in contrast, an individual rarely had to pay more than 10 percent to fund a legal action. For a Name writing £40,000 on a syndicate, a legal fee of £4,000 was a bagatelle compared with losses which might amount to £400,000. Even with these relatively small subscriptions, the biggest syndicate action groups were able to amass a war chest of several million pounds. The law might be a lottery, but the risks of the Commercial Court were certainly no worse than those of underwriting.

The £116 million settlement won by the thousand-strong Outhwaite Action Group against the Outhwaite managing agency and several dozen members' agencies in February 1992 reinforced the argument for litigation. It showed that members' agencies could be held liable for the failings of a managing agent, a point later confirmed by Mr. Justice Saville in October 1993. It also demolished the notion that the business of underwriting was so arcane that it was not subject to normal commercial tests of competence and prudence. To the shock of the Lloyd's professionals, the inbred culture of the market simply did not stand up to prolonged cross-examination in the Commercial Court. Above all, the Outhwaite trial showed that if Names combined they were a force to be feared.

Within a year of the trial, more than 15,000 Names had either filed writs or were actively contemplating legal action. The litigation had three objectives: to obtain compensation for past and projected future losses, to stop Lloyd's drawing down on deposits, and to prevent banks from honouring letters of credit given as collateral to support a member's underwriting. With Names refusing to pay, the council was forced to send thousands of threatening letters in an attempt to recoup money owed to syndicates and ultimately to policy-holders. As writs flew around the market, the prospect of a decade of litigation loomed. The Commercial Court came under pressure to recruit additional judges; the largest firms of City lawyers, charging £300 an hour, rubbed their hands in anticipation of a bonanza.

The Names' writs were issued against managing and members' agents, and in some cases against brokers and auditors. As few of the defendants had large assets, the real target was the agents' professional indemnity insurers, because they controlled the only pot of money sufficient to meet multi-million-pound claims for damages. But as most of their E&O policies had been placed within the market, this meant that Names were often suing one another—indeed, in some cases, themselves—a reflection on the incestuous knot into which Lloyd's had allowed itself to be tied. With the E&O insurers desperately playing for time, the ruined Names' bid for compensation looked set to run and run. A torrent of litigation in Britain, the United States and Canada gave the impression of a market at war with itself. Lloyd's failure to establish a binding arbitration procedure made unravelling the mess almost impossible.

TAKING TO THE COURTS

The first legal actions were brought by Names on long-tail syndicates, seeking to recoup huge losses from asbestos and pollution. They maintained that the underwriter should not have written unlimited reinsurances in an area unfamiliar to him with the potential for producing huge losses. That was the allegation made against Outhwaite; similar claims were to be levelled against Stephen Merrett, the underwriter of syndicate 418. More than 800 Names on long-tail syndicates such as Pulbrook 334 and 90, where reinsurance protecting old years of account had failed as a result of alleged non-disclosure, also issued writs against their members' and managing agents and brokers. The number of litigants swelled rapidly, as more long-tail syndicates were forced to leave years open. Over 4,000 Names on Wellington 406 and 448, Poland 105 and 108, Merrett 421, Secretan 367, Janson Green 932, and Lambert 604 formed action groups to investigate their losses. Many Names who had been recruited in the 1980s believed they had not been properly informed by their managing and members' agents about the long-tail risks they were inheriting. Often the complaints centred on the closing of earlier years of account at a time when the liabilities for asbestos and pollution were so uncertain that a fair reinsurance to close could not have been fixed.

The second group of litigants consisted of members of spiral syndicates whose underwriters had racked up staggeringly large losses. The 5,000 Names on the Gooda Walker, Feltrim, Devonshire, Rose Thomson Young, Cuthbert Heath, Bromley, and King syndicates were among the biggest losers in the market. Feltrim and Gooda Walker Names alone were claiming damages of more than £1 billion. The losses of those with multiple exposure to spiral syndicates often exceeded £500,000; some went much higher. The average loss of the 500 Names on the worst hit members' agency, Lime Street, was estimated at more than £2 million.[2] The series of loss review reports commissioned by Lloyd's established that many spiral underwriters had failed to calculate their potential maximum losses in the event of a series of catastrophes, let alone secure adequate reinsurance. All this provided a solid basis for legal action. But Names were faced by the problem that the agents' insurance cover was in most cases inadequate to meet the vast sums they had lost. Even if they won in court, there was no guarantee that they would recoup more than a fraction of their losses.

The third group of litigants was more varied. A straightforward case of negligence was brought by nearly 500 Names on Aragorn syndicate 384 against its underwriter, Graham Potter. He wrote a large line of 30.5 percent of a loss-making Warrilow retrocession contract, but admitted that his intention had been to write only 2.7 percent. At the doors of the court in November 1993 the case was settled, with E&O insurers paying Names 83 percent of the £2 million claimed. Some 600 Names on non-marine syndicate 553 fared less well in the settlement of their complaints against the Warrilow members' agency and some forty other members' agents. They received only £4 million, a fraction of their estimated £80 million losses due, they alleged, to under-reserving, over-writing, and poor record keeping.

Amid the growing vortex of litigation there were desperate attempts by Names to prevent Lloyd's running down deposits to pay cash calls and solvency deficiencies. On joining Lloyd's every Name is required to hand over a deposit which varies from 20 to 40 percent of the amount of premium he is planning to underwrite. A Name writing £500,000 on an ordinary "bespoke" portfolio of syndicates will have to deposit £150,000 and undertake that if losses are incurred he will make good any deficiency. Lloyd's is obliged to make a solvency return each year to the Department of Trade in respect of every individual trading in the market; a Name must have sufficient funds deposited with Lloyd's to cover his net losses over a three-year period. If an individual's actual and projected losses are larger than his deposit, a notional "earmarking" is made against the central fund. Where losses remain unpaid, Lloyd's seeks to recover the money by drawing down on the Name's deposit. It was this process which a group of 800 severely hit Names, advised by solicitor Michael Freeman, sought to prevent on the grounds that most of their losses were invalid because the underwriting had been improper, if not fraudulent. The bid to secure an injunction restraining Lloyd's failed when Mr. Justice Saville ruled that members' agents were entitled to draw down on deposits where cash calls remained unpaid. In his judgment on 16 April 1992, he said that the plaintiffs had failed to show that spiral underwriting was "so extraordinary that it fell outside the scope of the sort of underwriting business which the Names had authorized the agents to conduct on their behalf." He added: "Those joining Lloyd's as Names must appreciate that the system can only work if the business of underwriting is conducted by professionals who must be left to judge, among other things, and of course in good faith, what funds are required from time to time for the underwriting business. Were this not so and Names were entitled to withhold funding until personally satisfied that the money was needed, then in view, again among other things, of the numbers of Names involved, claims could not be settled promptly, nor could the attendant expenses of the underwriting business be met and, in short, Lloyd's could not exist as a market."[3] Shortly afterwards a separate action by the Gooda Walker action group, which sought an injunction restraining Lloyd's from drawing down on Names' deposits until an application for a judicial review was heard, was also rejected. The Names lost a further important legal joust in December 1993, when Judge Saville dismissed a series of preliminary points advanced by the Writs Response Group on behalf of two Names who were refusing to pay their losses. The claim that Lloyd's had acted anti-competitively in breach of both British and European law was not upheld. This decision was in part reversed by the Court of Appeal in November 1994.

American Names were similarly unsuccessful in attempts to prevent Lloyd's running down their deposits to pay unpaid losses. The largest case, filed in 1991 on behalf of 120 American Names by Proskauer Rose Goetz and Mendelsohn in the US District Court in New York, alleged violation of federal securities laws and anti-racketeering legislation. The action was dismissed by Judge Morris Lasker, who ruled that the proper legal forum for the dispute was the English courts. The judge noted that the international character of Lloyd's and the adequacy of legal remedies available to American Names in the UK were important factors in his decision. "Plaintiffs went to England to become members of a distinctively British entity, invested in syndicates operating out of London, and entered numerous contracts, all of which stated plainly that Lloyd's affairs and plaintiffs' investments would be administered in England and subject exclusively to British law." A final setback for the Names came when the US Supreme Court declined to hear their appeal, thus sustaining the earlier ruling that Lloyd's could not be sued in the US courts for securities fraud.[4]

A group of seventy Canadian Names was also frustrated in its attempt to stop Lloyd's cashing letters of credit guaranteed by Canadian banks. The Names—doctors, dentists, lawyers and other professionals from Hamilton and Toronto—sought to have their contracts with Lloyd's declared null and void by a court in Ontario. The suit alleged that "had they known of the fraudulent misrepresentations and fraudulent practices, they would not have become members of Lloyd's." But the court ruled that the action would have to be brought in the British courts in accordance with the agreements that the Names had signed.[5] Following this judgment, Lloyd's also won a case in London against five Canadian banks which were refusing to honour letters of credit lodged as security, on the grounds that Lloyd's had acted fraudulently. Mr. Justice Saville ruled that as the banks were not directly claiming fraud but merely repeating their clients' allegations, the defence failed and he gave judgment for the £2 million claimed.[6]

Despite these setbacks, the American and the Canadian Names are still determined to defend their dwindling assets in the British courts. "Who amongst us would have joined if we had been told, 'Lloyd's has no duty of care to you'?" said Jacki Levin, one of the leading Canadian Names. "Who would have joined if we had been told that an avalanche of asbestos and pollution claims was coming that we were going to have to be responsible for? Who would have joined if they had told us that we would be underwriting on a spiral which had no insurable risk at its base which was a churning of policies around the market, a fraudulent practice which Lloyd's knew to be going on? None of us."[7]

Along with the Canadians and Americans, a growing number of British Names were refusing to acknowledge, let alone pay, their losses. In April 1992 Lloyd's issued nearly 200 writs, followed some months later by a further 3,000 letters threatening a writ if solvency deficiencies remained unpaid. Those who received writs were a disparate group. They consisted initially of the Names whose losses were so large that they had every incentive to fight until their cases for negligence against the members' and managing agents were resolved. By the autumn of 1993, more than 6,000 Names, a fifth of the entire market, received warnings that they had solvency deficiencies which must be cleared within twenty-eight days; otherwise the recipient faced a writ for civil debt.

HIGH STAKES

The stakes were rising on both sides. For Lloyd's, the need to pass solvency each year, and to ensure that valid claims were met, made it essential to increase the pressure on recalcitrant Names. But the council was faced by the difficulty of distinguishing between those who were able to pay but wouldn't—the won't pays—and those who wished to pay but couldn't—the can't pays. To pursue thousands of insolvent Names through the courts was as unappealing as it was futile. But the council could not just sit back and wait for the Names to pay up. By September 1993, the amount earmarked from the central fund to make good solvency deficiencies had reached dangerous proportions, having risen fivefold in two years to £1,136 million.[8] The fact that the earmarking was larger than the entire central fund was an indication of how close the abyss was. The previous year, Lloyd's had imposed a levy on Names which raised £500 million. But a further special levy was not considered possible by the council because of its effect on confidence.

The stakes were no less frightening for the 6,100 Names threatened with a writ. About half were facing bankruptcy and the loss of their family home. The alternative of applying to the members' hardship committee, chaired by Dr Mary Archer, was hardly more appealing. The committee required ruined Names to make over all their remaining assets to Lloyd's, in return for which they would be allowed to retain a "modest" roof (worth about £150,000) over their heads and an annual net income, after tax, national insurance and mortgage payments, of about £11,600 for a single person and £17,600 for a married couple. What stuck in the craw was that ruined Names were required to acknowledge their debt to Lloyd's as a condition of accepting the "hardship" offer, even where fraud had been alleged. They also had to commit themselves to handing over any proceeds that they might eventually recover by litigation. No less disliked was the requirement of full disclosure of a spouse's assets, which were taken into account in any offer. The terms of hardship were significantly relaxed in October 1992, when it was accepted that it was counter-productive to insist that Names could never be freed from their debts to Lloyd's, whereas a bankrupt can obtain a discharge after three years. "We take very great care that the terms we offer are better than bankruptcy," says Dr Archer. The claim that hardship was preferable for the majority of ruined Names was true, but that made it no more palatable. To have to appeal for help to the very people who had brought about their ruin was more than some Names could bear. The provisions of "hardship," even when they were later relaxed to give finality, were never to prove popular. After four years and more than 1,500 applications, fewer than two hundred Names had accepted their hardship offers by the beginning of 1994.

Angered by evidence that their losses were the result of negligence, if not fraud, one group of Names decided that their best option was to challenge Lloyd's head-on by refusing to pay a penny. "Sue first, pay later" was their slogan. With two fellow Names, Richard Platts, a retired economics lecturer from Queen's University, Belfast, consulted a London firm of solicitors, Lawrence Graham. This led to a defence being constructed by barristers William Gage and Adrian Brunner, using European anti-trust law as a way of circumventing Lloyd's immunity from suit under the 1982 act. In October 1992, a hundred-page complaint was lodged with the European Commission, alleging that Lloyd's had breached Articles 85 and 86 of the Treaty of Rome. It claimed that Lloyd's had failed to regulate the market and to provide adequate information to investors. This initiative coincided with the formation of the Writs Response Group which, despite fratricidal splits in the months ahead, was to play a leading role in representing several hundred of the most financially desperate Names.

The six-month moratorium on legal action announced by the market's new chief executive, Peter Middleton, on taking up his post in the autumn of 1992, was the first sign that Lloyd's was having second thoughts. By the time the moratorium expired in the spring of 1993, the council had decided there was little point in taking thousands of Names to court. In the following nine months fewer than a dozen new writs were issued, and the attempt to secure a summary hearing of the 200 writs that had been issued was dropped. Instead, Lloyd's decided on a targeted approach, doing deals where possible with ruined Names and, where it was not possible, selecting a few specimen cases for full-scale trial.

OAKELEY VAUGHAN

More than thirty groups, meanwhile, were busy pursuing their legal actions. One of the more notorious cases involved Names underwriting through the

Oakeley Vaughan members' agency. They alleged that Lloyd's had failed to warn them that a secret official inquiry had concluded that their affairs were being woefully mismanaged. The facts of the case are, even by Lloyd's standards, bizarre. The chairman of the Oakeley Vaughan Group, Charles St. George, was one of the market's most colourful characters. More at home on the racecourse than in Lime Street, he attracted some well known Names to his syndicates, among them the boxer Henry Cooper, the promoter Jarvis Astaire, and a clutch of world-class jockeys including Lester Piggott, Joe Mercer, and the amateur rider Sir William Pigott-Brown.

St. George, known to his friends as "the blue bear," was born in Malta to a Maltese mother and a German father, and spent a peripatetic childhood in Italy and Ireland. By the time he became a captain in the Coldstream Guards, his surname had changed from Zimmerman Barbaro Sa Giorgio to something with a snappier ring to it. With his house in Belgravia and a retinue of servants, he lived life to the full and gave every appearance of commercial success. Whatever St. George's merits as a businessman—and he admitted that he knew little about insurance—he was a shrewd judge of horse flesh. With his old friend Tim Sasse, whose troubles with New York properties bursting into flames are recounted in an earlier chapter, he owned a share in the classic racehorse Rheingold, which won the Prix de l'Arc de Triomphe.

In the mid-1970s, St. George bought the Oakeley Vaughan agency from the widow of Sir Charles Oakeley, a baronet best known for his wrestling. It comprised a Lloyd's broking company and a members' agency. Though St. George acted as chairman, he was content to leave the day-to-day running of the business to James, his son by his first wife, Mary le Bas. His brother, Edward St. George, who was chairman of the port authority of Freeport in the Bahamas, was also a director. The Oakeley Vaughan syndicates were fashionable and fun—with luck a Name would get invited to a box at Ascot, where there would be pretty models and lots of champagne. The syndicates were notably less successful at underwriting, being heavily exposed to US public liability suits.

As an earlier historian of the market has noted, one of the pleasures of writing about Lloyd's is that the same cast comes round again and again, like a stage army.[9] At this point a familiar character returns to the story—Christopher Moran, the thrusting young broker who became the first person for more than a century to be expelled from Lloyd's by vote of a special meeting. Shortly after his acquittal at the Old Bailey on fraud charges in 1981, Moran demanded an interview with the chairman of Lloyd's, Peter Green, and the deputy chairman, Alex Higgins. He handed over evidence suggesting that Oakeley Vaughan had been massively over-writing on aviation syndicate 862. By accepting risks greater than the Names' premium limits, it exposed Names to heavy losses if the business went wrong. Oakeley Vaughan had sought to disguise the over-writing by underdeclaring the amount of premiums to the Lloyd's Policy Signing Office. This was done by a subterfuge known as "netting," in which premiums net of expenses and brokerage were declared, rather than gross premiums as required by the regulations. The evidence produced by Moran consisted of slips, an insurance schedule, and premium advice forms, which he had obtained from a former manager of Oakeley Vaughan's reinsurance department, whom he had employed after he had been disciplined by his former employer for getting drunk once too often. Moran's motives are not entirely clear, but there was no love lost between him and the St. Georges.

Faced by Moran crying foul, Lloyd's had no alternative but to set up an inquiry which it announced in a formal three-line press release. On 6 March 1981, Oakeley Vaughan wrote to its Names in bland terms approved by Lloyd's, stating that such an inquiry was "not unusual . . . and was purely of a technical nature." However, further damaging information continued to emerge about Oakeley Vaughan's business practices. At the beginning of April, the chairman of Lloyd's Aviation Underwriters' Association, E.O. Walklin, provided evidence of other instances of false accounting. At the same time Nigel Holland, a senior partner of the accountants Ernst & Whinney and a member of the inquiry team, noted that information about the agency's reinsurance to close for the 1977 year of account had been deliberately kept from the syndicates' auditors.[11]

At the end of May 1981, the chairman of the inquiry, Henry Chester, a leading underwriter, reported its findings to the chairman of Lloyd's. They were damning. Barry Bowen, the underwriter of syndicate 862, was found to have been a party to false accounting on several occasions, to have concealed evidence from auditors, and to have deliberately misled the Lloyd's Policy Signing Office. Two other directors of Oakeley Vaughan, James St. George and Michael Whitelock, were said to have failed in their duties of supervision, and the chairman, Charles St. George, was criticized for poor judgment. The inquiry found that syndicate 862 was owed £129,250 by the company's brokerage arm. Debit notes had been issued and then mysteriously cancelled. In brief, the inquiry concluded that the management of Oakeley Vaughan was incompetent.

The Names knew little or nothing of this because Lloyd's refused to publish even a summary of the findings. Nor were they told about a follow-up inquiry into Oakeley Vaughan's affairs by Lloyd's audit department, which concluded that the agency's profits had been inflated by false accounting and that it was insolvent. A third inquiry into Oakeley Vaughan's tangled affairs, by accountants Ernst & Whinney, promised to get at the root of what had been going on, but this was ended after a meeting between the Lloyd's chairman, Sir Peter Green, and Charles's brother, Edward St. George.

IN THE DARK

These details emerged six years later as a result of the Names' litigation. The only information given to Names at the time was in a formal notice posted at Lloyd's on 29 September 1981, stating that three directors of Oakeley Vaughan: Bowen, Whitelock and James St. George, had been found guilty of discreditable conduct and were suspended from the market for two years. Charles St. George was reprimanded, and the notice of his penalty was to have been posted in the Room, but after another quiet meeting with the chairman, Sir Peter Green, the notice was withdrawn and a private reprimand was substituted. The only direct communication that Names received was a letter from Oakeley Vaughan advising them that Barry Bowen had resigned, and that a new underwriter had been appointed who would "continue the established success of the syndicates." In fact all the syndicates were in deep trouble as a result of over-trading. Six years later, in 1988, the Oakeley Vaughan Group went into liquidation owing £2.5 million, and the run-off of its remaining business was taken over by a new agency called CCGH. For the next four years, the run-off agency tried to get access to documents held by Oakeley Vaughan in order to trace the causes of its extraordinary misfortunes. On 11 November 1992, CCGH finally obtained a High Court order allowing it to see the documents which were stored in a warehouse at Codham Hall Farm, near Romford. That night the warehouse mysteriously caught fire, and all the computer records were destroyed.

Oakeley Vaughan Names were by this time facing serious losses; the average deficit per Name was more than £200,000. Why, the Names complained, had the Chester report not been published? Why had Oakeley Vaughan been allowed to carry on underwriting? Why had Lloyd's failed in its duty to warn them about what was going on? Lloyd's response to the Names' writ was to deny that it owed such a specific duty of care. That might

have been the legal position, but when the newly elected chairman of
Lloyd's, David Coleridge, was asked at the 1991 general meeting whether
the council owed a duty of care towards Names, he replied: "The answer . .
. is of course, yes. The council does have a duty of care. It has a duty of care
to see that the society is properly regulated."

It might have seemed a straightforward issue, but the meandering
course of the litigation over the next decade was to prove otherwise. In April
1987, the Oakeley Vaughan Names served points of claim alleging that
Lloyd's failure to warn them of what was going on was an abuse of trust. A
year later, the High Court ruled that the Names were entitled to see the
Chester report. Three years later, the trial finally opened in the High Court
in April 1991. The lawyers had barely cleared their throats before Mr. Justice
Gatehouse accepted Lloyd's submission that the question of whether it owed
a duty of care should be tried as a preliminary issue. This decision was
reversed by the Court of Appeal, which snubbed Lloyd's counsel when he
invited it to reconsider. The invitation, said the Appeal Court huffily, was
"inappropriate and unprecedented." Nothing daunted, Lloyd's petitioned the
House of Lords direct for leave to appeal. The Lords granted the petition,
and ruled in favour of Lloyd's. The case returned, somewhat dog-eared, to
Mr. Justice Gatehouse for hearing on the preliminary issue. In July 1992, he
ruled that while Lloyd's had duties to regulate the market and to act fairly,
it owed no specific duty of care to Names. The Oakeley Vaughan Names
initially decided to appeal this judgment. But after seven years and the
expenditure of more than £1 million, Lady Patricia Ashmore, the lead
plaintiff, and thirty-nine other Names finally decided they had had enough
and on 21 February 1994, they threw in the towel. They are, however,
continuing to sue their members' and managing agents.

THE MERRETT ACTION

The Oakeley Vaughan case was unusual in that it was an action by Names
against Lloyd's itself. Other Names were prevented from taking similar
action because, under the 1982 Lloyd's Act, the council of Lloyd's and its
officers enjoyed immunity. Most Names' actions were directed against
members' and managing agents, and in some instances also against brokers
and auditors. An example was the writs issued by more than 2,000 Names
against agents and auditors involved with syndicates 418 and 421 managed
by the Merrett Group. The former was a long-established marine syndicate,

a leader in the market for over half a century. Its active underwriter, Stephen Merrett, was one of the most powerful men in the market, and heir to a leading Lloyd's dynasty. His acknowledged expertise in many areas of underwriting had helped Syndicate 418 into a dominant position covering a wide area of marine and non-marine risks. The syndicate expanded rapidly in the mid-1980s until at its peak it had more than 4,000 Names. The balloon burst when it was forced by mounting losses on long-tail claims to leave open its 1985 year. It now faces losses estimated by Chatset at 300 to 400 percent. Syndicate 421, a non-marine offshoot of the larger marine syndicate, began trading in 1979, specializing in excess of loss and North American casualty business. Like its larger sister syndicate, it was severely hit by unlimited run-off policies, and was forced to leave its 1983 year open. Its losses are expected to exceed 2,000 percent.

The legal actions against the two syndicates were separate but based on the same underlying set of circumstances. Both had written large lines on run-off policies for older syndicates heavily exposed to asbestos and pollution claims. The Names complained that the underwriters had taken on unlimited reinsurances in an area with which they were unfamiliar, which had the potential to produce huge losses. "I am led, with regret, to the opinion that MUAM (Merrett Underwriting Agency Management Ltd) displayed recklessness in accepting the inwards run-off contracts without at the same time ensuring sufficient precautions had been taken to protect Names from a potentially disastrous monetary loss," wrote Thompson Reinsurance Researches, the specialist adviser hired by the Syndicate 418 Names Association to investigate its grievances. The second complaint was that syndicate 418 had closed the 1982, 1983 and 1984 years of account improperly, at a time when it was impossible to fix a fair reinsurance to close. This had a material effect on the 2,000 Names who had joined the syndicate between 1982 and 1985. These new Names thus found themselves trapped on a syndicate heavily exposed to old-year losses, for which inadequate reserves had been made. The role of the auditors in approving the syndicate's accounts despite the inadequacy of the reserves also prompted a writ. "We are quite unable to understand how Ernst & Whinney felt able to state their opinion, without material qualification, that the syndicate accounts gave a true and fair view of the syndicate's affairs," noted the Names' counsel, Anthony Boswood QC.

A scathing analysis of the quality of Merrett's underwriting emerged in the loss review report on syndicate 421 chaired by Roger Whewell, senior insurance partner of KPMG Peat Marwick, published in July 1993.[12] Seven of the unlimited run-off contracts for syndicates 417/8 and 421 produced heavy losses. But one particular contract with Fireman's Fund, which accounted for nearly 40 percent of the syndicate's losses in the 1983 open year of account, was singled out for attention. The story goes back to 1974 when Ralph Rokeby-Johnson, the underwriter of Sturge's leading non-marine syndicate 210, purchased a run-off policy from Fireman's Fund, a leading American insurer, which protected his 1969 and prior years of account. Rokeby-Johnson recognized the danger of asbestos, for shortly afterwards he told a fellow underwriter that the old-year risks were so serious that Lloyd's was threatened with bankruptcy. Asbestosis, he warned, was "going to change the wealth of nations."[13]

By 1981, with asbestos and pollution claims growing by the day, Fireman's Fund realized what a lemon it had taken on, and brought pressure to bear on the broker C.T. Bowring, which had originally persuaded it to write the policy, to take it off their hands. It indicated that it would cease to do business with the broker unless its problems with the policy were alleviated. Bowring approached Stephen Merrett who took personal charge of what appeared to be a highly politicized and expensive game of pass-the-parcel. That, at least, is the account given by Merrett's deputy, John Emney, who told the loss review committee that the Sturge contract was "very peculiar," and that if the decision had been left to him, he would not have gone near it. "It was more an exercise to get Bowrings out of the shit than to place a risk—if you will excuse my French," he explained. This version of events was disputed by Merrett in his evidence: "We were aware that Fireman's Fund were putting heavy pressure on Bowrings, with whom they had had a very long relationship, to do something to ease the problems that the Sturge contract had created for the Fireman's Fund. But, in no sense, to my knowledge, was it argued overtly that we should write this account for the sake of Bowrings. I would state quite categorically that I gave John [Emney] no understanding, to the best of my recollection, and certainly no instruction, that he should write that contract."

Whatever the reason for Merrett's taking over the Fireman's Fund policy, it proved alarmingly expensive for his Names, who shared 50 percent of the risk. By April 1985, Merrett acknowledged his mistake in a letter to Names: "The contracts were outside the traditional scope of our business and it is quite simply the fact that, in hindsight, they represent poor underwriting judgment." The next stage of the saga came on 9 February 1989, when Merrett reached agreement with Fireman's Fund on revised terms which limited the policy's impact. The game of pass-the-parcel thus took one more turn, but by then the syndicate's Names were facing huge losses. By 31 December 1990 the loss on the contract had reached £7 million, and each Name had lost nearly six times his original £10,000 stake. At a meeting to explain what had gone wrong, Stephen Merrett said: "Unfortunately it was an exercise which was invalidated by subsequent developments." The loss review committee concluded dryly: "The risks assumed resulted in syndicate 421 having a substantial exposure to potential adverse developments on old years of account in respect of much older and larger syndicates, an effective concentration of risk into a new and small syndicate."

As the legal actions proliferated, attempts were made to co-ordinate the activities of the various action groups. Millions of pounds were being spent by nearly forty different groups on similar, if not identical, legal actions. Cooperation obviously made sense. A body representing all the litigating groups, the Lloyd's Names Associations' Working Party (LNAWP), was formed at the beginning of 1992 in an attempt to negotiate an overall settlement. But cooperation was not easy, given the differing interests involved. The syndicate groups not only had separate causes of action, they were often in a race for the same limited insurance cover. The action groups which won "the dash for cash" and got to court first might well scoop the E&O pot, leaving later successful litigants with nothing. The deepest and most unbridgeable split, however, was not between action groups, but between individual Names. Those continuing to underwrite at Lloyd's naturally had a different view of the litigation from those who had resigned. The former believed that their only hope was to trade out of their difficulties; they still had a stake in the market and, though many were badly hit, were reluctant to pursue any course of action which threatened its prosperity. The latter, most of whom had been ruined and were facing the threat of bankruptcy, were understandably less concerned about its future. Having lost everything, their only hope was to shame Lloyd's into mutual-izing their losses which meant that in practice other, less badly affected, Names would have to pay. The lack of a common purpose was a fundamental problem for Names in their attempt to secure compensation. It was not difficult for the council to divide and rule by splitting the militant ruined minority from the moderate still trading majority. The painful search for a settlement of the litigation crisis is a story of that process.

12

The Gathering Storm

"Remember this face; I hope you have nightmares over it;
you have ruined me."
A bankrupt Name to the chairman of Lloyd's

"The degree of incompetence to which many Names have
been exposed beggars belief."
Trevor Bradley, managing director of the Knightstone Group

Three thousand names crammed on to the trading floor for Lloyd's annual meeting in June 1991 to hear the size of the market's first overall deficit for twenty-one years. Shocked by the loss of £510 million, the Names were even more dismayed by forecasts of further serious losses in the years ahead. Reflecting the strain he was under, a tear trickled down the ample cheeks of the chairman, David Coleridge, as he was thanked at the end of three hours of angry questioning. Even before the market's bad news had been officially declared, 20 percent of Names had resigned. From a peak of 32,400, membership was heading for a precipitous fall. A poll conducted by Market Opinion Research International (MORI) found that disaffection among Names was growing; more than half said they would consider resigning if profitability were not quickly restored. Alarm among market professionals was acute. James Sinclair, managing director of Willis Faber's members' agency, predicted that unless quick action was taken, Lloyd's capital base would vanish. He was critical of the fact that earlier action had not been taken to defuse the complaints of the worst hit Names: "It's madness," he said. "Lloyd's could have shut this whole thing down for not much more than a windstorm loss."[1]

The golden years were over, but few foresaw the scale of the losses that lay just ahead. Chatset, the independent analyst, which had consistently taken a pessimistic view of the market's prospects, predicted at the beginning of 1991 that the 1988 account year would just about break even and the 1989 year would record a loss of £850 million. A year later, it estimated that the market would lose more than £3 billion in three years. The forecasts were denounced by Lloyd's as "without foundation," but in the event they underestimated the magnitude of the loss. Lloyd's own estimate, issued in a press release on 30 January 1992, that the 1990 loss would be less than £400 million and 1991 would return to profit, proved hopelessly wrong. The chairman of the Lloyd's Underwriting Agents' Association, Paul Archard, proved no more accurate in his prediction published in September 1992: "I am confident that the 1991 and 1992 accounts will have returned to profit."[2] This apparent attempt to gloss over the dire state of the market was attacked by John Rew, editor of Chatset. Criticizing Lloyd's "appallingly low standards of accounting and practice," Rew said that Names had every right to be horrified at back-of-the-envelope forecasts aimed at persuading them to part with more and more money.[3]

The new Lloyd's chairman set out three initiatives to cope with the gathering storm. The first was the strengthening of the hardship committee, set up two years previously to help Names faced by overwhelming losses. Chaired by Dr Mary Archer, wife of the millionaire novelist, who had herself faced some rough times, the committee was to be beefed up to meet the expected flood of new applicants. The second initiative was the setting up by Lloyd's of its own insurance company, Centrewrite, designed to help members of open year syndicates by offering commercial reinsurance quotations to free them from their liabilities. Names desperately wanted an agreed exit route and a degree of certainty about their underwriting. The result, as described earlier, was disappointing. A further attempt to reassure the market was made with the announcement that syndicate losses above 100 percent would be subject to automatic review. If the aim was to head off a flood of legal actions from Names with heavy losses, Lloyd's was to be disappointed. The negligence revealed in the loss review reports on Gooda

Walker, Feltrim, Rose Thomson Young, and other spiral syndicates strengthened the resolve of Names to take their grievances to the courts.

The most important new initiative announced by the chairman was the setting up of a task force advised by McKinsey, the management consultants, to review the market's trading structure. Chaired by David Rowland, chairman of Sedgwick, its members were widely drawn: four underwriters: David Mann, Stephen Merrett, Andrew Beazley and Elvin Patrick; a broker, Michael Wade; two managing agents: Robert Hiscox and John Gordon; Andrew Duguid from the corporation of Lloyd's, and four outsiders: Ron Artus, a director of the Prudential, Matthew Patient, an accountant and nominated member of Lloyd's council, John Kay, professor of Economics at the London Business School, and Antony Haynes, former chairman of the Association of Lloyd's Members. They were given just over a year to complete their inquiry. It was obvious that, with its capital base rapidly eroding, Lloyd's could not hope to survive unchanged. The need to staunch and isolate the continuing losses on the open years, to seek new forms of capital, and to make drastic reductions in the market's costs, dictated the pace of reform.

THE TAX REVERSE

If Lloyd's believed its desperate struggle to survive would be met with public sympathy, it was quickly disillusioned. An attempt had been made to secure a concession in the 1991 Budget which would have allowed Names to carry losses back three years, thus allowing tax paid on successful underwriting in the past to be reclaimed. The chancellor, Norman Lamont, expressed a willingness to help; the Inland Revenue acknowledged that similar concessions were being given to hard-hit companies; the Treasury briefed friendly journalists; even the opposition initially made sympathetic noises. Paul Boateng, MP for Brent South, speaking for Labour on the committee stage of the Finance Bill, argued that the case for relief should be taken seriously: "Lloyd's is more than just a place in which the seriously rich dabble in the insurance market," he said. "It is dangerous to regard Lloyd's in that way. There is a tendency by some sections of the media and the public to do that. Such a response is not found in my party."[4]

Within days, Labour's Treasury spokesman was obliged to sing a more traditional left-wing tune as the media weighed into the attack. The *Independent* set the tone for a classic media blitzkrieg: "Members of Lloyd's insurance market should not be bailed out by the Government," said its editorial; the *Daily Express* joined in: "It is not a lifeline Ministers should be thinking of for Lloyd's but a bargepole'; *The Financial Times* gave the *coup de grace*: "There is no case for having the taxpayer shoulder a bigger share of the losses of Names. The Chancellor should not give way to such blatant special pleading from one of parliament's most powerful lobbies." After this barrage the concession, denounced by opposition MPs as "a retrospective charter for freeloaders," was politically dead. The chairman of Lloyd's was left to lament: "Once all that press hoo-ha started there was no way the government could do it. It had become a political football. . . That's really what screwed it."

The formation of a new group of disaffected Names was another sign of trouble. The Society of Names (SON), chaired by Tom Benyon, a former Conservative MP, aimed to represent those Names facing the heaviest losses. The latter felt they had been abandoned by the Association of Lloyd's Members (ALM), the majority of whose members had not been seriously affected, and whose chairman, Mark Farrer, had caused offence by appearing to scorn the worst hit. "We must look to the future. We must make sure Lloyd's works," Farrer told a Names' meeting in the autumn of 1991, adding that the only place for those seeking vengeance for their losses was "the psychiatric farm."[5] Into this vacuum of the dispossessed stepped Benyon, who had himself been hit by serious spiral losses. Pointing out that most of the losses had fallen on fewer than a third of the members, he said that the problems of the Feltrim, Outhwaite, Oakeley Vaughan, Spicer and White, Poland, Pulbrook, and Warrilow syndicates were only the visible tip of a dung-heap: "We intend to shine a torch into the mists of Lloyd's. The bad practices of managing agents who line their own nests at the expense of Names must be exposed."[6]

Prodded on by Benyon, dissatisfied Names from a wide range of syndicate action groups across the market held their first meeting in the spring of 1991. The task of coordination devolved to a new representative body, the Lloyd's Names Associations' Working Party (LNAWP). Its membership consisted of all thirty action groups, but inevitably it was dominated by the Gooda Walker and Feltrim chairmen, who headed the most powerful and best financed action committees. The Super Group, as it became known, was initially led by Peter Nutting, chairman of the Outhwaite Names Association, but tensions soon emerged when the more militant chairmen made clear that, as a member of the council, he was too much part of the Lloyd's establishment for their taste.

The disagreements came to the fore at one of the early meetings, on 21 May 1992, which developed into a shouting match. Nutting had infuriated some of those present by declining to disclose proposals being discussed by the council to settle the litigation. Alfred Doll-Steinberg, the mercurial chairman of the Gooda Walker action committee, declared the meeting to be a waste of time and walked out: "I don't see how you can sit here and wear two hats," he told Nutting as he headed for the door. Though his chief tormentor had left, it was clear that Nutting did not have the confidence of a number of the more militant Names present. "If the council do not start negotiating on a sensible basis, then we will break the market," warned Claud Gurney, an accountant who liked to describe himself as "a bankrupt economist of the Chicago school." Shortly afterwards Nutting also stalked out of the meeting, saying it was clear that his views had little in common with those present. This blood-letting only partially eased the situation. At the next meeting of the Super Group, the new chairman, Christopher Stockwell, a reproduction furniture businessman, exchanged heated words with Gurney, whose idea of tactics was to threaten to smash Lloyd's. "What has got up the noses of this group is the way you are attempting to steamroller us," Stockwell shouted.

The growing militancy of Names spelt trouble. Much damaging publicity and years of litigation by the disaffected and the ruined stretched ahead. Benyon, an energetic publicist, was not an opponent to trifle with. An attempt by Lloyd's to counter his advice to "sue first and pay later" ended expensively in a libel writ when David Coleridge incautiously gave vent to his growing irritation. "It's a total waste of time," said the Lloyd's chairman, "I think Benyon's a busted flush—he's trying to make money out of the misery of a certain number of people saying, you come to me and you pay me some money and I'll try to arrange for you to sue."[7] These rash comments cost Lloyd's £25,000 plus costs; apologies are never cheap when lawyers are involved. David Coleridge was equally off-base when he predicted that the result of the Outhwaite case would put a stop to the threat of litigation: "If Outhwaite wins that case and he is found not to have been negligent . . . then all these things will drop into the sink."[8] Such comments were as out of touch as another of the chairman's early diktats reported by *The Times*: "Most of the people who are bitching and whining are doing it because they don't like losing. I understand that. It's human nature to only want to win. No one has been swindled and it has nothing to do with unlimited liability. It's simply pure losses."[9]

David Coleridge is a cleverer man than he pretends or these comments suggest. But his belief, when he became chairman, that Lloyd's would soon return to profit, indicates that he had no idea of the scale of the crisis facing the market. As late as June 1992, he was predicting that the overall 1991 result "may be better than break-even."[10] Part of the problem was that he had spent his whole life at Lloyd's. The son of a wealthy cotton broker, he joined straight from Eton after being turned down for national service in the Green Jackets because of flat feet. After an initial spell at a small broker, Glanvill Enthoven, he joined Sturge and amassed a fortune, estimated at more than £10 million, before becoming its chairman in 1978. At the beginning of 1991, *Business Insurance* quoted him as saying that he had made "huge amounts" of money from Lloyd's. Great wealth brings independence of mind and inner confidence. Coleridge is a man of laid-back charm; only his wary eyes suggest a steely ambition. His long-time partner at Sturge, Ralph Rokeby-Johnson, for many years the company's leading underwriter, says: "He conceals his ability behind a tired teddy-bear outlook."[11]

That ability was to be severely tested over the coming months. The pressure from ruined Names was unrelenting. At one meeting an irate Name went up to Coleridge and spat: "Remember this face; I hope you have nightmares over it; you have ruined me."[12] As the problems grew more and more acute, the chairman won round many of his critics by his willingness to listen, his determination to reform the market and, above all, by his good temper. Characteristically, he put an end to the libel action with Tom Benyon by inviting him to lunch. Even those who were immune to the chairman's Old Etonian charm recognized that the blame for the crisis could not fairly be laid at his door. The losses he had to announce had been hatched under previous regimes; the responsibility for the market's horrendous mess lay elsewhere. As *Lloyd's List* was to point out: "It was his predecessors Murray Lawrence and Sir Peter Miller who presided over ruin in the making." David Coleridge never publicly attributed blame, but he did once venture to comment: "In retrospect it started during Murray Lawrence's time. I feel sorry for him in a way. If the LMX spiral was to have been regulated, it should have happened when it started to go wrong in 1986-87. Or before, when Miller was there. But then at that time any interference was resented."[13]

THE TASK FORCE

The Task Force's report, published on 15 January 1992, singled out the failure of market regulation as a main cause of the crisis. Analysing the competitive strengths and weaknesses of Lloyd's, it detailed the way capacity and costs had been allowed to expand out of control. From 1985 to 1988, the amount of money available for underwriting had increased by 70 percent, far in excess of the amount of good business. The number of Names, meanwhile, had increased by more than a third. The result was an unsustainable growth in the market's capital base, driving down rates at a time when administrative costs were rising and premiums were in sharp decline. Insurance is a cyclical business. When times are good and underwriters are awash with capital, they are so eager to write even poorish risks that rates decline until the discipline of losses administers its own corrective. By the late 1980s, the market, despite being hungry for premiums, was writing less than half its capacity. As a recipe for running a business into the ground, it could not have been bettered.

The Task Force had been asked to look into the future and come up with long-term proposals for reform. But so grave were the continuing losses and the erosion of confidence among Names that it felt it must address Lloyd's immediate problems. It identified four key areas for change: the problem of open years; the requirement to shore up the capital base by the introduction of corporate capital; the need to cut costs and to change the way the market was administered; and, lastly, the importance of restoring Names' confidence by modifying the principle of unlimited liability.

To the most crucial problem—old year losses from pollution and asbestos—the Task Force had no answer. Its recommendation that Names should attempt to trade out of their liabilities appeared to be based more on hope than on analysis. In the four years from 1985 to 1988, the cumulative old year losses, the consequence of decades of under-reserving, had amounted to more than £1.6 billion, and the report was forced to admit that if this level continued it would be "very damaging." As the report was unable to make any reliable estimate of the scale of future claims from either asbestos or pollution, it could only recommend the acceptance of open years as a way of life, and the setting up of a "centre of excellence" to deal with the ensuing reserving problems. Centrewrite, meanwhile, was to be encouraged to offer individual quotes to Names who wished to leave the market, rather than continue to seek to close entire syndicates.[14]

The report emphasized the need for a strategy of growth. It argued that to maintain its ability to set terms and lead business, Lloyd's had to be able to offer sufficient capacity to clients. To achieve a real increase in capacity over the next five years, it recommended the introduction of corporate capital with limited liability, though it believed—wrongly as it turned out—that this would require a new Lloyd's Act.

The Task Force's view that the executive functions of the market should be split from regulation led to its recommending the setting up of two new bodies: a market board which would dictate the trading strategy, and a regulatory council chaired by a nominated member. These recommendations proved controversial and were opposed by the council of Lloyd's. David Coleridge dismissed the proposals as "codswallop and absolute hot air;" the chief executive, Alan Lord, said the governance reforms were "retrogressive and unworkable," and he would resign rather than implement them.[15] An external member of the Task Force, John Kay, formerly professor of Economics at the London Business School, commented acidly: "I can't think of any business structure where the regulatory and executive functions are combined. You wouldn't ask the chief executive of British Telecom to be director general of Oftel." A full-blown public confrontation, the last thing Lloyd's needed, was averted only when the chairman and council backed down and decided that the Task Force's proposals should be reviewed by a new working group headed by Sir Jeremy Morse. "I don't mind changing my mind," said David Coleridge. "I don't find it embarrassing—I don't find I have lost face."[16]

The last initiative recommended by the Task Force was the introduction of a high-level stop loss scheme financed by a levy on Names. Capping all losses over a four-year period starting in 1993, at a level equal to 80 percent of their premium limits, it offered some comfort to those able to continue underwriting. A Name writing £350,000 of premium would have any losses above £280,000 met centrally. But the report offered nothing to those Names already devastated by spiral, pollution and asbestos losses. For the 2,000 Names who were effectively bankrupt and in no position to continue trading, the news that there was to be no central rescue was deeply dismaying. Though the Task Force did not put it in quite such bald terms, it had concluded that the losses of the worst hit were so concentrated that it made neither commercial nor political sense to bail them out.

A "RIGGED" MARKET

This tough approach touched off a furious reaction. Feeling that they had nothing to lose, the ruined Names turned to Parliament and the media to broadcast their complaints that Lloyd's was a rigged market run for the benefit of insiders. The result was a blizzard of damaging publicity whose intensity appeared to catch the council by surprise. The *Evening Standard* headlined an inflammatory feature: "Is it time to put Lloyd's into liquidation?" and argued that "the one-time gentleman's club now has the morals of a Lebanese casino." The *Independent* attacked the market's poor performance and conflicts of interests under the heading "Rot Throughout the Orchard." There were many other attacks. The market was finding to its cost that it had few friends, and that in those it had ruined it had some determined and influential enemies.

In particular, Lloyd's found to its dismay that its traditionally cosy relationship with the Conservative Party had turned sour just when it was most needed. An attempt to influence parliamentary opinion misfired when action groups arranged their own pre-emptive counter-briefing. The Names' discontents were put to an all-party group of MPs by the then chairman of the Gooda Walker action group, Alfred Doll-Steinberg. He was accompanied by Christopher Thomas-Everard, an Exmoor hill farmer and computer expert who stood to lose his farm because of spiral losses, and who provided a wealth of supporting evidence for his allegation that the market had been rigged in favour of the professionals.

When the Lloyd's chairman, David Coleridge, arrived to meet the Tory backbench Finance and Trade and Industry committees two weeks later, on 11 February 1992, he therefore found a hostile audience armed with a sheaf of well-directed questions: Why were the worst-hit syndicates composed predominantly of external or retired working Names? Why had Lloyd's encouraged the recruitment of thousands of small traders whose only asset was a bank guarantee of £100,000 secured against the value of their house? Why were underwriters of poorly performing syndicates getting salaries of £300,000 when Names on their syndicates were having to pay out huge losses? Lastly: Was there not a structural rottenness over the conflicts of interest of the regulators within Lloyd's which could only be met by outside regulation under the Financial Services Act?

David Coleridge was ill prepared for such an onslaught. *The Financial Times* quoted one of those present as saying that he "practically had apoplexy" when confronted by the questions. Forced on the defensive, he kept on repeating: "There are a lot of people who can't tell a loss from a scandal."[17] Few of the MPs present were impressed. Spencer Baptiste, MP for Elmet, said afterwards: "We have seen Mr. Coleridge on two occasions and found him to be very unconvincing." Another MP was quoted as saying that the Lloyd's chairman's "lack of certainty or positiveness in addressing the questions [left] a considerable feeling of unease."[18]

News of this confrontation might not have seen the light of day if two Tory MPs who had lost heavily at Lloyd's had not leaked details to the opposition. Brian Sedgemore, Labour MP for Hackney South, a former rugby prop-forward who is proud of his reputation as a bruising backbench trouble-maker, was sitting in the library of the House of Commons when he was approached with an account of the meeting.[19] An hour later, copies of the confidential briefing document and questions which had so embarrassed the Lloyd's chairman were sent anonymously to another prominent parliamentary "bovver boy," Dennis Skinner, MP for Bolsover. Within hours, "the bruiser" and "the beast" had submitted three early day motions attacking Lloyd's. This is a parliamentary device whereby an MP may make a statement in the guise of a motion and be protected by parliamentary privilege from a libel action. As soon as the motions, with their allegations of insider trading, were published, they touched off a wave of press, radio and television coverage. Labour's front bench spokesman on the City, Marjorie Mowlam, who had also been sent a set of the documents, wrote to the trade secretary demanding an official inquiry into the charge that Lloyd's was a rigged market.

That same day, 13 February, a group of Tory MPs led by Paul Marland, MP for Gloucester West, accompanied by the chairmen of three action groups, went to see the minister for trade, John Redwood. This provoked a further burst of headlines. "Tories declare war on Lloyd's," said the *Independent* on its front page, with a sub-heading: "MPs leak claims that insiders are creaming off best business." The minister pointed out that he did not have direct control over Lloyd's, and that he had yet to see evidence to persuade him that its exemption from the Financial Services Act had been an error. Political pressure, though, was building up. The message that Lloyd's had to be seen to be dealing fairly with external Names was driven home by the chairman of the all-party Trade and Industry committee, Kenneth Warren. In a letter to the chairman of Lloyd's expressing concern about the relationship between Names and their agents, he wrote: "I would like to be assured that a responsibility is placed on those who handle the commitments [of Names]. I would have expected that they would be required to be transparent so that all who have a right to see what is going on can do so." Mr. Warren was not satisfied by the reply he received a week later, that Lloyd's did not hold centrally the information requested.

He professed himself "deeply concerned," and said that the chairman's response did not convey "the breadth and depth of urgency which the problems of the Names demands."[20]

After a week of bruising front-page stories, the *Independent on Sunday* drove home the message that things were getting out of control. "Lloyd's Grinding to a Halt," it declared in its 16 February edition, justifying this headline with a quote from the vice-chairman of the Tory Trade committee, Richard Page, MP for Herefordshire West: "Unless Lloyd's positively gets its act together, I can see the whole thing grinding to a halt and becoming unworkable. Every day that goes by, the situation is getting more and more desperate." The daily *Independent*, picking up the baton, claimed that David Coleridge was ready to resign. Even *The Financial Times* joined in the hunt with a front-page story suggesting that Lloyd's had had to go cap in hand to the Bank of England for a loan to ease an acute cash flow crisis. A few days later, after furious protests from Lloyd's, the paper staged a partial retreat and published an amended account saying that "leading market figures" had opened preliminary talks with the Bank and ministers about Lloyd's future.

Just how tense relations were becoming between Lloyd's and its critics was evident at a meeting on Lime Street the following week. The chairman, David Coleridge, had invited a group of more than twenty MPs and peers to be briefed on the market. Flanked by senior market executives including Paul Archard, chairman of the Lloyd's Underwriting Agents' Association, and David Rowland, chairman of the Task Force report, Coleridge was once again subjected to a grilling. Paul Marland, MP for Gloucestershire West and a heavy spiral loser, got up at the start of the meeting to ask the Lloyd's chairman pointedly: "In which of your three capacities are you appearing? As the chairman of Lloyd's, as the man responsible for regulation of the market, or as the chairman of Sturge Holdings from which you earn over £800,000 a year?" Coleridge's stiff response that his Sturge salary was £75,000 and that he drew no salary as chairman of Lloyd's drew a further taunt from Marland: "But what about your other income?" Coleridge shrugged his shoulders and replied: "I do have a considerable private income." Another heavy loser, Earl Alexander of Tunis, son of the Field Marshal, asked: "Has Lloyd's any sense of duty to its members?" The discordant note shocked some of the parliamentary group. "I have never ever witnessed such gratuitous rudeness and bad behaviour," said Tam Dalyell, the one Labour MP to attend the meeting.[21]

THE WALKER INQUIRY

The confrontation had one positive outcome: it convinced David Coleridge that the allegations would not be put to rest without an independent inquiry. Sir David Walker, a nominated member of the council and a former head of the Securities and Investment Board, was asked to investigate the spiral losses and report whether the market had been rigged against external Names. Lloyd's also released its records of syndicate membership, which allowed outsiders to reach a more informed judgment. The statistics were suggestive rather than conclusive. Working Names were under-represented on the biggest loss-making syndicates in 1989 and over-represented on the most profitable, but they also exceeded their average representation of 12 percent on a few heavy loss-making syndicates. For example, working Names comprised 42 percent of a non-marine syndicate which racked up losses of £7,495 for every £10,000 of premium in 1989. The *Financial Times'* conclusion was that insiders, with their superior knowledge of the market, had steered clear of the worst performing spiral syndicates rather than that outsiders had been dumped on them. This was a fine judgment; it was not shared by many ruined Names.[22]

The appointment of an independent inquiry only temporarily halted the spate of damaging stories. The Labour MP for Neath, Peter Hain, put down another early day motion on 12 May 1992, calling on the government to hold a public inquiry into financial mismanagement and corruption at Lloyd's. The real point of the motion was its claim that two dozen Tory MPs faced bankruptcy as a result of their Lloyd's losses, and therefore the government's majority was at risk because MPs are not allowed to serve if insolvent. This spurious allegation was too good a story for the media to ignore and was reported on most front pages, despite being dismissed by one of the so-called "bankrupt" MPs, Sir Nicholas Bonsor, as "scurrilous mischief-making cloaked in parliamentary privilege."[23] Most of the MPs named were not seriously affected by their losses, and the handful who were knew that so long as they cooperated with the hardship committee they would not be made bankrupt. Nothing abashed, the Labour MP for Neath continued to harry Lloyd's in a series of early day motions claiming that members of the council were running syndicates that had acute conflicts of interest because they had "benefited massively from the LMX reinsurance system which has caused such punitive losses for thousands of outside names in the London insurance market." The motions named David Coleridge, Murray Lawrence, Bryan

Kellett, Richard Hazell and Stephen Merrett as among leading underwriters who had made "reinsurance gains worth £500 million" in the 1989 year of account. A Lloyd's spokesman wearily dismissed the charge as "yet another example of the abuse of parliamentary privilege by Mr. Hain to make unsubstantiated allegations in an area which he clearly does not understand."[24]

The parliamentary baiting continued with an early day motion tabled by Paul Marland, MP for Gloucestershire West, which alleged that professionals at Lloyd's had "favoured themselves and their close relations [by] placing their own business on highly profitable and safe syndicates ahead of outside Names." The motion referred to five leading Lloyd's professionals, and noted that none was a member of the worst affected catastrophe reinsurance syndicates on which they had placed their Names. No sooner had the motion been tabled than it had to be withdrawn after protests that it was factually inaccurate. This gaffe provided a cue for a vitriolic riposte from David Coleridge's journalist son Nicholas, editorial director of Conde Nast. Writing in the *Evening Standard* on 29 May 1992, he pointed out that Marland had only himself to blame for his Lloyd's losses, having insisted on transferring in the 1980s from conservatively run syndicates to much higher-risk ones. Rather than pay his debts like a man, Marland had devoted "his days in the House of Commons to abusing my good-natured, hard-working father... I find it outrageous that he's entitled to make defamatory allegations in the House that get reported in the newspapers and then, a few hours later, withdraw the motion." The filial attack ended with a condescending quote solicited by the son from his papa: "Paul Marland," said the Lloyd's chairman. "Well, I can't help feeling sorry for him really. He's made some awfully odd decisions, poor chap, but I suppose if you become used to getting a large cheque every year, and then you're asked for some of it back, it must be distressing."[25]

RESCUE HOPES

The tactics in the bitter war of words between the ruined Names and Lloyd's were unedifying, but they produced results. The Names knew that the louder they shouted foul and the more they embarrassed the professionals in the market, the less likely they were to be ignored. The chairman and council, on the other hand, were engaged in a balancing act. They were averse to mutualizing losses, and were only too well aware that the majority of Names would be bitterly opposed to paying large sums to bail out others less fortunate. But they also knew that confidence in the market would not be restored until the complaints of those who had been ruined were addressed. The distressed Names were suddenly and unexpectedly tossed a straw to clutch when, at a private lunch at Lloyd's at the beginning of April 1992, the chairman said he believed something would have to be done for those suffering the biggest losses.[26]

What David Coleridge had in mind was none too clear, but he appeared to accept that the way the worst losses had hit a minority of Names was intolerable. The first public hint that a central rescue was being considered came five days later, when the chairman told a conference of risk managers that the question of whether Lloyd's could help "the walking wounded" was on his desk. At the beginning of May, Coleridge told *Lloyd's List*: "I am anxious not to raise expectations too high, but we hope to do something."[27] The council's deputy chairman, Dick Hazell, was put in charge of a working group advised by the merchant bank S.G. Warburg, charged with coming up with a viable rescue scheme. It was no easy task; the losses of the past two years alone amounted to more than £2.5 billion. It was fanciful to believe that brokers, underwriting agents, or anyone else, would come up with such huge sums.

Despite these problems, hopes remained high that a scheme of some sort would emerge. Three options were investigated in detail: the capping of losses over 250 percent on individual syndicates, a portfolio approach under which an individual's net underwriting losses at the end of four years could be limited, and lastly, a loan scheme to allow Names suffering solvency problems to trade through. Mark Farrer, the chairman of the Association of Lloyd's Members (ALM), hinted publicly that the front runner was a levy of 1 percent of Names' premium limits which could cap losses on the 1988-1990 years of account at 50 percent of overall premium limits.[28]

It was not to be. The hopes of the ruined Names were dashed for a second time on 18 June 1992, when Lloyd's announced that it had ruled out a central rescue on the grounds of impracticability. The market's chief executive, Alan Lord, said the scale of the 1989 losses was so large that neither the funds available nor the uses they could legally be put to would secure a satisfactory solution. The decision touched off a predictably angry response. Tom Benyon, chairman of the Society of Names, warned that Lloyd's now "faced death by a thousand writs." Christopher Stockwell, chairman of the Lloyd's Names Associations' Working Party, said: "It's a tragedy. They have missed a major opportunity and face mounting chaos."[29]

These views found an echo among independent commentators. "If Lloyd's is to have a future," warned the *Daily Telegraph*, "then those who have escaped will have to bail out those who face ruin. The solvent members will not like the prospect, but the can't-pays and the won't-pays have the nuclear weapons of litigation in their hands; legal fees alone are quite capable of destroying Lloyd's and its solvent members." Even *Lloyd's List*, published by Lloyd's of London Press, regretted that hopes of a market rescue had been raised only to be dashed. In an implied criticism of the chairman, it said: "Particularly regrettably, these were hopes that had been fanned by Lloyd's itself in recent weeks with its public statements that it was looking for a way of helping bail out the so-called 'walking wounded.'"[30]

The rejection of a bail-out was an acknowledgement that the sums could not be made to add up. The losses in the 1988-1991 years were so concentrated on two to three thousand distressed Names that a rescue fund of more than £2 billion would have been needed. Just restricting losses on the 1989 year to 50 percent of underwriting limits would have cost £700 million, around £35,000 for each of the other 20,000 Names. Even if they could have been persuaded that this was a price worth paying to avoid strife, it would have done little to strengthen the market's capacity, because many of the Names with the heaviest losses had already been forced to cease trading. In an attempt to sweeten the pill of rejection, Lloyd's announced that the hardship committee's rules would be relaxed to make them less onerous, and that an additional fund would be set up with contributions from brokers and agents to help Names in particularly difficult circumstances.

Despite these concessions, it was clear that Lloyd's had decided that its priority was the market's future. The immediate problem was solvency. Chatset, the independent analyst, was forecasting that such was the scale of the losses that capacity would decline by more than half by 1995. The threat of an ever-decreasing number of Names having to face larger and larger losses because of the need to meet the claims of those who had gone bust—the dreaded meltdown scenario—could not be ruled out. "Lloyd's needs some sort of lifebelt thrown to it to keep it trading," claimed Chatset's co-editor, Charles Sturge.[31]

With its own survival at stake, Lloyd's turned its back on the problems of individual distressed Names. The die was cast when, at the beginning of June 1992, the council announced that it had decided to increase the size of the central fund to £1 billion by means of a special levy of 5 percent of allocated capacity over three years, equivalent to about £20,000 per Name.

Doubling the size of the central fund, whose primary purpose was to ensure that no valid claim remained unpaid, was a determined response to those who had said that Lloyd's would have to go to the Bank of England for a loan. But it effectively ruled out any central rescue, for it was impossible in the short term to impose a second levy on the membership. Lloyd's had evidently decided to play it tough. Coinciding with the publication of the annual accounts, the chairman said he was confident that the market would be able "to shape its own destiny [despite] the recrimination and hostility" of its critics.

The critics were not just the militants. The chairman of the moderate Association of Lloyd's Members, Mark Farrer, launched a stinging attack in his annual report published in June 1992. "Many Names," he said, "now face horrendous financial problems as a result of a decade of commercial indiscipline in the Lloyd's market." There was, he noted, "a harmful and destructive perception that Lloyd's is a great deal better at enforcing its regulations against Names who may have lost everything than enforcing proper standards of trading in the market." In a bleak warning on the market's prospects, Farrer added that Names' willingness to support Lloyd's in meaningful numbers was "uncomfortably close to the reasonable limit of endurance at the present time."

The strains were evident at the annual meeting on 23 June 1992 attended by more than 5,000 worried Names, with fifty Australian Names in Sydney listening via a landline. Sitting beside me were an elderly couple, both members of Gooda Walker syndicates. "We've now been asked for £500,000 which we haven't got," said the anxious-looking wife. "We just have one shop and we are so worried we will lose it." At that moment the Lutine bell was rung once—the traditional signal of disaster, now used only on ceremonial occasions. Minutes later David Coleridge, surrounded by members of the council, strode on to the floor. "We meet today in the midst of one of the darker chapters in the long history of our society," he said.

From the outset the chairman struck a note of contrition which he sustained throughout the marathon meeting, thus doing much to defuse the anger of Names. He "took no pride" in announcing a record loss of more than £2 billion for the 1989 year of account, which he described as "an appalling result." One-third of the loss was accounted for by the results of only five syndicates, four of them managed by Feltrim and Gooda Walker. He understood "the sentiments of despair, anger and bewilderment" of those who had been ruined: "I accept that I, on behalf of the council, have a duty to try to explain what has happened to those people." He apologized for his delay in answering letters—he had received more than 800 in the past two weeks; he regretted that Names had first learnt about the levy from newspapers; he was sorry that it had not proved possible to help the worst hit Names. "It was certainly not for lack of effort." Despite his apologetic tone, the questioning was often blunt. Throughout David Coleridge sustained his courteous approach of *mea culpa*. Only once did his anger flash briefly when a badly hit spiral Name, Harriet Crawley, a former Conservative parliamentary candidate, questioned his good faith—"A lot of people feel bitterly that their trust has been betrayed,"—and called for an independent chairman chosen from outside the ranks of the market professionals. "I hear what you say," replied Coleridge, but pointed out that the Lloyd's Act required the chairman to be elected from within the market. This provoked shouts of "Change the act, you are compromised!" "That is an unfair slur," he retorted sharply. "We have done our best, even though we have worked all our lives in this business." The only other point at which Coleridge appeared rattled was when he was closely questioned about why the council had exempted members' and managing agencies from having to have errors and omissions insurance. He was forced to admit that underwriters were not prepared to provide cover for many Lloyd's agencies—they regarded them as too bad a risk, hardly an expression of confidence in the market.

The six-hour meeting ended with applause for what had been a notable exercise in conciliation, but it was evident that Coleridge was unlikely to remain as chairman for much longer. Privately he told friends that the battering he had received was far worse than he had anticipated. He had gained respect for his courtesy, good humour and refusal to condone what had happened, but the market was looking for a new approach. Coleridge was the last of a long line of chairmen of Lloyd's who served unpaid; from now on the market was to be organized on a more professional basis. Some months later, looking back on his chairmanship, he said that it had been a troubling period, but he drew satisfaction from having put the market onto a sounder footing: "I didn't wish to be the last chairman of Lloyd's. There were some people who were predicting that the market was in ultimate meltdown. I realize we have damaged very severely a section of our community and for that I am very unhappy. But the market is now set to go forward again."[32]

The publication of two official inquiries at the beginning of July confirmed that assessment. The Morse report endorsed the Task Force's recommendation that the governance of the market should be split between a regulatory and a market board. But it amended the proposals by saying that the council's membership should be halved to fourteen members, and that in future the chairman should be paid. The report was generally welcomed; the conflicts of interests which had dogged the old Lloyd's for so long were at last being tackled.

Sir David Walker's report on the spiral debacle, which was published at the same time, also helped the slow process of restoring confidence. As reported earlier, it concluded that there was no evidence for the allegations made by some Names that their losses were the result of conspiracy, churning or fraud. But it was scathing about the "standards of professionalism, care and diligence" achieved by some members' agents, managing agents and active underwriters. Members' agents, it noted, had taken "a very lax view of their fiduciary duties," managing agents had lacked control over their underwriters, and Lloyd's itself had failed to exercise proper supervision over the market. "Some of those practices make one's hair stand on end," commented *The Financial Times*. The report confirmed that professionals had fared better in their underwriting than external Names, partly as a result of their superior market knowledge, but also as a result of "unattractive" and "immodest" preferencing of their own interests. But overall the Walker report, though it opened the way to negligence actions, offered no encouragement to the wilder charges of fraud and corruption.

NAMES' DISCONTENTS

The suspicions of those who had been ruined were not, however, put to rest. The issue of writs and the drawing down of deposits by Lloyd's, which in some cases resulted in banks threatening to foreclose on homes pledged as collateral for bank guarantees, had focused the anger of the worst-hit Names. Their discontent exploded at an extraordinary general meeting called by two of the market's persistent critics. Claud Gurney, an accountant who had been badly hit by spiral losses, and Richard Astor, a militant young barrister, were free spirits. Neither had much support among the Names' action groups—both were regarded as erratic. But because Lloyd's constitution required only a hundred signatures to force an EGM, some of the action groups felt they had no alternative to backing the move. Four motions were proposed, calling on the council to rescind the central fund levy, to improve the operation of Centrewrite, to publish a register of interests, and to cooperate with Names' representatives. Separately they signified little, but together they amounted to a vote of no confidence in the chairman and council. The split among Names was apparent when the moderate Association of Lloyd's Members put down a contrary motion expressing confidence in the council and calling for the immediate implementation of the Task Force proposals.

The meeting, attended by 2,500 Names, lived up to its bloody promise, though a decision to allow a postal ballot on the five motions helped diffuse some of the tension. So did David Coleridge's announcement at the outset that he was stepping down from the chairmanship, and that he had nominated David Rowland to succeed him. But the anger of those who had lost everything was vociferous, and the EGM, if it served any purpose, only demonstrated how wide were the divisions within the market. "We want to rip this place apart with a can-opener," said Richard Astor helpfully on the steps of Lloyd's.[33] Inside the meeting, held on the floor of the underwriting room, the comments were no less bitter. Daniel Salbstein, who had been hit by losses on pollution and asbestos syndicates, claimed that he and other Names had looked to the council for protection, but had found only a protection racket: "The council have proved negligent, indolent and impotent. If they had a scintilla of integrity, they would resign." Jack Harris, who had joined Lloyd's in 1987, said he had yet to see a pay-day. "I have been to this building four times and if there was a turnstile at the entrance each visit would have cost me £75,000. My situation, typical of many, is a tragedy without humour. Sympathy alone does nothing for those whose lives have been ruined by this institution. It has stood by and let us be swallowed up by the sharks patrolling its murky waters." Dr. Alexander Munn said Names had lost more than £2.5 billion, but agents and brokers had escaped without paying a penny. The chairman of the Society of Names, John Rew, predicted that Lloyd's was heading for meltdown. By 1994, he said, the market could be reduced to 6,000 members and £4 billion in capacity: "We are facing a really grim future. Those who think they are sailing through, don't smile yet." All this provided a prelude to Claud Gurney's angry complaint that the council had done nothing to protect the interests of outside Names: "We have no confidence that the present members of the council are acting or will act in the best interests of Names." The meeting, he said, was an historic occasion which gave Names the chance to say goodbye to the "old order and the reign of incompetence of successive committees."

In response to this battering, David Coleridge pointed out that he had accomplished more real change in eighteen months than had happened for a long time at Lloyd's. He received influential support from Neil Shaw, chairman of the Association of Lloyd's Members, who pointed out that the dissident resolutions attacking the council were backward-looking. Lloyd's troubles, he acknowledged, had been caused by lack of governance and management controls over many years, but these problems were now being addressed.

The supporters of the old order may have been less vocal, but they knew that they had the votes of the silent majority. This optimism was borne out when the results of the postal vote were announced four weeks later. The motion expressing confidence in the council was supported by 80 percent of those who voted. The other motions were closer, but the dissident Names were well beaten, receiving just over a third of the vote. "I'm not going to make a song and dance about it, but this is a resounding vote of confidence in the council," said David Coleridge.[34] The Association of Lloyd's Members welcomed the vote as the end of an unhappy chapter. "The majority of Names want the market's business to go on," it said.

13

A New Regime

"I am often asked how Lloyd's came to fail so spectacularly.
My answer is: no management discipline or quality control from
the centre of Lloyd's to control the 1980s fever
of greed and expansion."
Robert Hiscox, deputy chairman of Lloyd's

The arrival of an interventionist chairman and an unconventional chief executive signalled a new era at Lloyd's. The appointment of David Rowland and Peter Middleton indicated that the market was heading for fundamental reform. The new chairman was so dismayed by what he found on arriving at his office on the twelfth floor that he told close colleagues: "I am not sure this market deserves to survive... I can't understand why they did not change things before." With his Geordie accent and blunt no-nonsense approach, Peter Middleton, a motorcycle-riding former monk and diplomat, struck an equally uncompromising note at his first press conference: "I look forward to managing a period of change," he said.[1]

There were other encouraging signs. Underwriters had begun to report a hardening of rates towards the end of 1992, and it appeared that resignations of Names might be barely half the 3,000 of the previous year. "The upturn has come in the nick of time," said Nigel Rogers, managing director of the Octavian Agency Group.[2] Lloyd's was also able to point with satisfaction to a study by the stockbrokers Hoare Govett, which suggested that it had stronger reserves and higher average profit margins than either British composite insurers or American property-casualty insurers. The market's capital resources, according to the study, amounted to just over £20 billion, comprising premium trust funds of £12.3 billion, members' funds of £4.6 billion, and other reserves compared with future and estimated liabilities of £13.7 billion.[3]

For all the trumpeted "good news," there was no disguising that Lloyd's was uncomfortably close to meltdown. The number of syndicates unable to close their accounts had doubled to 162. Capacity for the 1993 year was expected to be as low as £8.5 billion, a loss of nearly 50 percent in real terms compared with five years previously. The number of syndicates had declined by half, to just over 200. A third of Names were no longer trading but were unable to quit because they were trapped by open years. Worse, thousands of Names either couldn't or wouldn't pay £500 million of their 1989 losses. The appalling results of the spiral syndicates, some of whose underwriters had undoubtedly been negligent, swelled the ranks of the "won't pays" who ignored the council's rule of "pay first, sue later." To show that it meant business, Lloyd's sent formal notices to 3,500 Names, warning them that writs would be issued if they failed to make good their solvency shortfalls. Nearly 200 Names had already received summonses, prompting the formation of the militant Writs Response Group to fight their cases. On the other side of Carey Street, Names were also rushing to the courts. More than thirty action groups, representing over 15,000 Names, were engaged in litigation against their members' agents, managing agents, brokers or auditors.

Instead of waiting for the axe of bankruptcy or hardship to fall, ruined Names decided to take the initiative. Richard Platts, the retired lecturer from Queen's University, Belfast, set out the tactics of the "won't pays" at a conference held by the Society of Names at the beginning of October 1992. He predicted that Lloyd's attempt to secure a summary debt judgment under Order 14 would fail, and that the issues would have to go to full trial, which could take two to three years. "If there is a delay, Lloyd's will have a £1 billion cash flow problem; this will give us substantial bargaining power," he said. John Rew, chairman of the Society of Names, claimed the extent of Lloyd's solvency crisis had been underestimated; confidential market figures revealed that 5,000 names had lost a third of their premium limits, more than the total of their deposit. An insolvency practitioner, Gerald Hyam, told the meeting that it was outrageous that thousands of Names should be threatened with writs. "It is just not acceptable that Names are turned into cannon fodder," he said to cheers.

A determined attempt by Peter Middleton to defuse this legal confrontation was the first evidence of the new regime. After barely two months in office, and without seeking the approval of the council, Lloyd's new chief executive announced a six-month moratorium on writs. He also set up two working groups, composed of external and professional Names, to see if a way could be found through the maze of litigation. The first, advised by management consultants Mercer Consulting, was asked to look for ways of resolving the open year problem in order to provide an exit route for Names who wished to leave the market. The second, advised by consultants LEK and solicitors Simmons and Simmons, was charged with inquiring into the level of errors and omissions insurance, the target of the negligence suits being brought by Names. Peter Middleton described the moves as a bid "to lower the temperature" so that the legal disputes could be resolved out of court. The initiative was welcomed by the chairman of the Lloyd's Names Associations' Working Party (LNAWP), Christopher Stockwell. For the first time in many months, a dialogue had opened between the ruined Names and the council, though no-one imagined that a path through the legal thickets would be easy to find.

At a meeting with the LNAWP, dubbed the Super Group, on 18 November 1992, Peter Middleton set out his priorities. He was determined to address the concerns of investors and policy-holders, reduce the overblown cost basis of the market, and institute sensible business techniques. "What is going to happen from 1 January is a very different approach. Lloyd's may be unique but it needs changing." It would take some time, he acknowledged, to transform the culture of the corporation from that of a civil service department to a business. Referring to the mass of litigation threatening to swamp the market, he said it was important to get a global settlement involving the E&O underwriters, otherwise Names could find themselves with a legitimate claim but no funds available to meet it. Such an outcome would be "absolutely intolerable."

The impact of a new broom on Lime Street was reinforced by a series of cost-cutting measures designed to cut 600 jobs and £26 million from the corporation's £145 million budget. The economies began on the twelfth floor. The two waiters, who, resplendent in their Victorian navy blue and crimson tailcoats, had served tea to the chairman's visitors, were redeployed. So were two of the four chauffeurs who had ferried the chairman and senior executives; the Rolls-Royce had already been sold. The magnificent Adam Room, traditionally used to entertain important guests, was henceforward to be available for hire. "I am not prepared to entertain on Lloyd's behalf in so lavish a style as we have in the past," the new chairman, David Rowland, wrote to Lloyd's agencies. "The days when the Lloyd's chairman sent three people ahead of him on his travels to check the hotel beds have gone," said Robert Hiscox, one of the two new deputy chairmen.[4] In private, members of the new regime were scathing about their predecessors' *laissez-faire* practices, and contemptuous of the lax way the market had been administered. "For Coleridge to have said last year, 'I only run the coffee-shop,' is frankly incredible," said one member of the council.[5]

BUSINESS PLAN

At the beginning of 1993, Peter Middleton announced to a conference organized by the Society of Names that the market's first-ever business plan was being prepared. He would not be prepared to stay, he said, unless deep cuts in administration costs and fundamental reforms were made by agencies and brokers. The market must accept cuts or continue to slide: "The changes will be painful. Unless we implement them, we will have no basis on which to attract capital. Failure to implement them will condemn Lloyd's to mediocrity and irrelevance. It's that serious." Middleton was scathing about the way the market processed claims: "A flow-chart of the claims payments system resembles a combination of the New York subway, the London Underground and the Paris Metro with a map of the European railway network superimposed." He also questioned the need for members' agencies. "I think it would be better to centralize everything other than investment advice and recruitment of Names." The new Lloyd's management set an immediate example by reducing the number of committees advising the council from forty-eight to seventeen; the functions of the disbanded committees were taken over by the new market and regulatory boards.

Working groups were set up to formulate solutions to three issues: capacity, open years and costs. A key recommendation of the Task Force report, published the previous year, was that the market had to trade out of its problems, but how could growth be secured? Names were in short supply. Only sixty-seven had joined for the 1993 year; 2,000 had left. Active membership of the market had fallen by over a third to fewer than 20,000, and many of those who remained wanted to get out but were trapped on open years. The meltdown scenario was not as fanciful as some market insiders pretended. Chatset's latest discouraging prediction was that Names would lose at least another £2.5 billion in the next two years in addition to the £2.5 billion they had already lost, equivalent to double their deposits at Lloyd's.

The only way to escape from this cul-de-sac of decreasing capacity and increasing costs was, as the Task Force had suggested, to attract corporate capital. At the beginning of January 1993 Merrett, one of the largest agencies at Lloyd's, in trouble as a result of large-scale defections by its Names, announced the launch of a new company involving the US investment bank J.P. Morgan, and Marsh McLennan, the world's largest insurance brokers, to reinsure a percentage of Merrett risks under a quota-share arrangement. A few months later this deal unravelled as Merrett's old year problems turned out to be insuperable—it had lost the confidence of the market. It was obvious that sizeable amounts of corporate capital could not be attracted without "ring-fencing" the old year pollution and asbestos liabilities from new entrants to the market.

Two panels of external and professional Names trying to resolve the open year and litigation problems were hard at work; without a solution, it was doubtful whether new capital would have the confidence to back the market. The litigation/E&O panel made little progress; the professional advisers, solicitors Simmons & Simmons, alienated the external representatives by its practice of reporting directly to Lloyd's and keeping consultation to a minimum. The open year panel made more headway with a radical scheme to reinsure all pre-1985 policies into a new limited company. The cut-off date reflected the major change in policy wordings in 1985, with a move away from the "occurrence" policies which had caused Lloyd's so much grief in America. A restructuring in two stages was proposed. The first phase involved the setting up of a new limited liability company, regulated by the Department of Trade, with capital of more than £4 billion provided by pooling syndicate reserves. The company, known as NewCo (later retitled Equitas), would first establish reserving standards for all open year syndicates. Old year liabilities would be centralized only when a common basis had been achieved. The second phase, at the end of 1995, would see all old year policies reinsured into NewCo, with calls being made on Names whose syndicates were judged to be inadequately reserved. To minimize the impact on those facing heavy cash calls, a delayed payment scheme would be set up, albeit with an interest charge to maintain equity.

The third issue—the need to reduce costs by restructuring the operation of the market—proved contentious, because it trod on a number of insider toes. Both Peter Middleton and Peter Nutting, a leading member of the council, said that there were too many intermediaries at Lloyd's creaming off large amounts of revenue. They questioned the role of members' agents, most of whose functions, it was suggested, could be centralized with large savings to Names. These suggestions from the twelfth floor were ill received by those affected. Julian Crispin, chairman of the largest members' agency, Sedgwick, said that any attempt by Lloyd's to handle the administrative functions of members' agents "would cause a riot" among the agency's 1,500 Names. James Sinclair, managing director of Willis Faber Dumas, complained: "Over the loss cycle we are going to hit the Names with cumulative losses of some £6 billion. More confirmation will be given to Names of management inadequacies at Lloyd's, greed, deceit and appalling underwriting, plus never being able to get on top of the problem. If you remove Names' only (trusted?) link into the business i.e. members' agents and taking account their average age of fifty-seven, and retirement age say sixty, and loss of their big salary income, Names will herd out of the Market and that means the shutters will go up and that, as the text book says, will be that. Do not try it. Names and members' agents do not trust a bureaucratic Lloyd's Central who historically have shown they cannot do the job. Whilst Lloyd's have in the past often shown they can shoot themselves in the foot, this action is a bullet in the head, and for those who do not know it, you need only one bullet prior to the carcass being laid to rest."[6]

Another group unhappy with the direction of the business plan was the Lloyd's Names Associations' Working Party (LNAWP). Twice before, Names' hopes of a central rescue scheme had been dashed. The work of the two panels looking at the open year and E&O problems, however, had touched off a renewed burst of wishful thinking that this time a bail-out would be endorsed by the council. The mood was encouraged by the decision taken by the new Lloyd's hierarchy to encourage dialogue rather than confrontation. "We must serve all members regardless of whether they have resigned or are actively underwriting. Whether they are litigating or content, angry or happy, all are members of our society," wrote David Rowland in a newsletter.

The problem with such worthy sentiments was that the sums in dispute were so large that, even if the council could be persuaded that it had a duty to act, it was unlikely that it could persuade the rest of the market to fork out the £2 billion (roughly £100,000 per Name) that would be necessary. In an attempt to solve this dilemma, the LNAWP called for fresh capital to be raised by means of a bond issue which would be used to settle the litigation. Adapting an idea proposed by the E&O panel, it recommended that a central body, "Recovery," be set up to offer Names a non-refundable credit against their legal rights. It would pursue the legal actions on behalf of Names, with a view to reaching an out-of-court settlement with the E&O insurers. The advantage of such a solution was that it would deal with the vexed problem of double counting by releasing the £1 billion in reserves that the E&O underwriters had been forced to make against potential claims. As these reserves often came out of the pockets of the same Names who were suing for compensation, the sense of trying to reach a deal was obvious. The managing director of the Knightstone Group, Trevor Bradley, wrote to his Names: "A business plan which does not provide a mechanism to end litigation and separate the future from the past is akin to building an extension to a house while the house itself is on fire."[7] But Lloyd's reaction to the proposed bond issue was negative—the new regime regarded it as mortgaging the future of the market. And the council was distinctly cool towards the proposal put forward by the E&O panel that it should pursue litigation on behalf of the Names. This left the LNAWP with only threats in its armoury. In its submission to the market board, it said that many Names no longer believed they had an obligation to pay their losses, and it warned that the market would cease to trade by 1995 if the legal disputes were not ended: "We do not believe fresh capital on the necessary scale can be raised without a settlement of the litigation. It is unacceptable for the market professionals to envisage a future based on corporate capital with the present Names being ruined."

A FRESH START

When the business plan was published on 29 April 1993, it appeared to envisage just such a corporate future. It rejected the LNAWP's call for a bond issue as "impracticable and undesirable," and endorsed the introduction of limited liability corporate capital as the only way of strengthening the market's capital base. So far as the Names' litigation was concerned, the plan committed the council to pursuing a negotiated solution, acknowledging that this would "remove one of the major causes of the dissent and dissatisfaction." It also promised that "if a central contribution were the key to securing a resolution" of the legal disputes, it would approve such a step. But it emphasized that there was no magic fund, and that any central contribution would be limited: "The belief that a large bond could be raised substantially to be used to pay off claims is, in our estimate, wholly unrealistic as well as being undesirable. . . Any such loan would have to be repaid out of future profits. By mortgaging the future in this way, we would reduce the attractiveness of the market as a place where high returns on capital can be earned."[8]

Names' hopes that they were to be rescued were thus dashed for a third time in little more than a year. Nevertheless both the Association of Lloyd's Members (ALM) and the LNAWP welcomed the plan, encouraged by a private commitment from Peter Middleton that resolving the legal disputes would be given a high priority. The creation of NewCo to "ring-fence" the old year asbestos and pollution claims removed one of the major obstacles in the way of an overall settlement. Names stuck on open years were at last to be given some certainty about their future liabilities and a way, albeit at a price, of leaving the market. In the past decade, old year reserves had quintupled from £2 billion to £11 billion, impoverishing thousands of Names in the process. Yet the whole process had been conducted in a thick fog of ignorance. As one commentator noted: "Most of Names' capital had gone not on paying current losses but in building up reserves for future possible liabilities, thus making Lloyd's the best reserved insolvent insurance entity in the world."[9]

The business plan offered a number of concessions to ease the cash flow difficulties of Names, including allowing cash calls to be deferred, and giving Names the right to take a credit in advance of the 1993 results. Most important, perhaps, was the recognition that the old days of a free-wheeling, buccaneering market of independent businesses with widely varying standards of competence and ethics were over. In future, capacity, costs, performance and standards would be monitored and controlled. Reinforcing the message that the plan signalled a new era, the chairman, David Rowland, spelled out the consequences if it was not fully implemented: "Our current results are the worst in Lloyd's history. Many members have been brought to the brink of financial ruin, many more are fearful of the future. . . Should membership and market not unite behind this plan then Lloyd's may have no future."

The plan may have given hope to the market's professionals, but to the worst hit Names it offered little. The proposed introduction of corporate capital appeared to be a way of allowing Lloyd's to trade profitably into the future while quietly ditching those who had been ruined by its negligence and incompetence. These suspicions were aired on 4 May 1993 at an acrimonious meeting of the LNAWP, the so-called Super Group. Christopher Stockwell, facing pressure to call for an extraordinary general meeting, drafted a letter to Lloyd's new management team warning that legal action would continue for years, and Names would refuse to pay further calls, if there was no rescue deal. "The moral bankruptcy of the society is demonstrated by the plan's willingness to abandon *Fidentia* and the ruined Names," he wrote. "The choice for Lloyd's is not between a highly profitable future and a mortgaged future but between a mortgaged future and no future at all." Lloyd's response to this threat was a plea for peace from Peter Middleton. "Will you please, please, please, give peace a chance," he begged a meeting of 3,000 Names in the Albert Hall on 25 May 1993. But peace was the last thing that the more vocal and irate of the ruined had in mind. Outside the hall a number of bedraggled professional protesters held up a tattered banner: "Maxwell bust, BCCI bust, Lloyd's bust. Policy-holders won't be paid."

Inside the hall the atmosphere was no less bitter. As the chairman, the chief executive, and other members of the market's hierarchy filed onto the platform, they were greeted with boos interspersed with bellows of "liar" from the top of the hall. "I feel like a creditor at a spiv liquidation meeting; this is a spiv liquidation," said Anthony Groman, an accountant. "It's a long time since I bought a new suit. This one no longer fits, I've lost so much weight through worry. My family is bereft and I may have to apply for bankruptcy. I stand before you as a victim and a loser. There can be no plan for the future unless an equitable plan is made for the present. I was owed a moral duty of care. I accuse the corporation of wilful default, neglect, and mismanagement."

Another Name, Sally Noel, said the blame for what had happened should be acknowledged by those on the platform: "You are responsible for divorces, destruction and death—innocent people like myself were encouraged to put our trust in Lloyd's. Now you have the nerve to talk about the future, when Names are crippled by losses. But I warn you, this tribe will not lie down. It will stand up and fight for justice." Halfway through the four-hour meeting, there was a minute's silence, demanded by angry Names, to remember "those who had been driven to despair and even suicide by their losses." Lloyd's chairman, David Rowland, who admitted that he himself was "frightened" by the spectre of open year losses, told one protesting

Name: "I share your view that many things happened in this society in the 1980s which I deeply regret. Bitter and hard lessons have had to be learned." The market's deputy chairman, Robert Hiscox, was less tactful in an interview he gave to *Business Insurance*: "A minority of the membership is out to kill, regardless of logic," he complained. "And they seem to want to make so much noise that either they are deemed ungovernable so we buy them off or somehow they get their losses paid. But that's not on. They never seem to realize that it will be another Name who has to pay the losses."

The Albert Hall meeting confirmed that the burnt Names were not prepared to be ignored while the market collectively held its nose and dreamed of future profits. The clamour of the dispossessed threatened to frighten away not only policy-holders but also potential corporate investors. Yet quelling the cries of those who had been ruined was not easy. The problem of thousands of Names refusing to pay their losses because they were suing managing agents, members' agents, brokers, auditors and Lloyd's itself, appeared impossible to resolve without lengthy, hideously expensive court proceedings.

The scale of legal warfare was unprecedented. In an attempt to produce some order out of the growing chaos, Judge Saville called all the lawyers involved to a meeting on 21-22 June, to see if agreement could be reached on a timetable for hearing the cases. So much legal talent attended that it was estimated that the fees for this two-day event alone came to more than £2 million. The more money swallowed up by the lawyers, the less was left to pay claims. The main asset targeted was the agents' E&O insurance. But the amount of E&O insurance was finite, certainly far less than the Names' collective losses, while the strength of the individual cases, mostly alleging negligence against members' and managing agents, varied from the strong to the hopelessly speculative.

In an attempt to untangle this Gordian knot, David Rowland determined to make one further attempt to see if a settlement of the Names' grievances could be secured outside the court room. Two groups: a financial panel headed by Sir Jeremy Morse, a former deputy chairman of the Bank of England, and a legal panel headed by Sir Michael Kerr, a former Lord of Appeal, were charged with seeing if an offer could be produced which would be acceptable both to Names and to the E&O insurers. The legal panel would assess the strength of the various claims, while the financial panel would investigate the scale of the E&O resources and recommend a structure for a settlement. Peter Middleton, who announced the initiative at the Albert Hall meeting, confirmed that Lloyd's was prepared to make a financial contribution, but stressed that unlimited funds were not available: "We are not made of stone, but we are not made of money either," he said. It was a thin straw, but for the time being it was all that the litigating Names had to clutch.

Their worst fears were confirmed a month later, when the chairman, David Rowland, announced at the annual meeting, on 22 June 1993, that the market had lost a record £2.91 billion in the 1990 account, a result which, he said, was "unacceptable and must never be repeated." Nearly 2,000 Names, serenaded with music by Vivaldi, packed the Festival Hall. Their mood was not improved by the admission that, once again, Lloyd's forecast of losses had been hopelessly inaccurate. Nor was it much comfort that an estimated £600 million of the loss was accounted for by double counting, a result of stop loss and E&O policies being placed within the market. The dismal reality was that Lloyd's had racked up the biggest trading deficit in its history, equivalent to £100,000 per Name. Once again the results were damagingly skewed. Two percent of Names lost over £250,000 and nearly one in five between £100,000 to £250,000. The chairman admitted that things could not continue in this way. "It represents," he said, "in every way the low point of Lloyd's history." He acknowledged that some Names had lost so much that they were no longer interested in the market's survival. But he derided the option of "putting the lights out on Lime Street" and walking away from Lloyd's long-tail liabilities as dangerous nonsense which could cause even greater hardship: "We have learnt hard lessons, let us get on with the job."

This appeal produced a mixed response. Lionel Jacobs, a Name since 1986, who had nearly lost an eye in a mugging incident eighteen months earlier, protested bitterly that he was now being mugged by Lloyd's: "Surely the society must take responsibility for fraudulent losses?" Another thorn in the establishment's side was John Rew, chairman of the Society of Names and director of Chatset, who jeered that Lloyd's had "managed to turn disaster into an art form." Pointing out that the council had estimated that the market would lose only £400 million in the 1990 account year before returning to profit, he said: "I believe these forecasts were made with a complete disregard for the truth, with the aim of sucking more money out of Names into the premium trust funds."

This provoked David Rowland into making a startling admission: "I have nothing but contempt for the standards under which these forecasts were made." To which the new chairman of the market's regulatory board,

Brian Garraway, added: "I am appalled at the lack of control of information. It is not just bad business practice, but it is misleading to all members of the society." Such unqualified condemnation of previous commercial practices was not just an admission of the scale of past errors; it revealed the extent to which the new Lloyd's management team wished to distance itself from its predecessors.

In the bitter row which was subsequently fought out in the Society of Names newsletter, it emerged that the erroneous Lloyd's forecast had been commissioned by David Coleridge in January 1992 to counter Chatset's gloom. He had asked Paul Archard, then chairman of the Lloyd's Underwriting Agents' Association, to obtain "a best estimate" from twenty of the leading managing agents. The Lloyd's press notice giving the results of the survey noted that the estimates were based on only 40 percent of capacity, and stressed the difficulty of prediction. Coleridge and Archard were on difficult ground, though they fought back gamely against Rew: "How you could construe this as deliberately gulling investors and issuing a false prospectus we do not understand," they wrote indignantly. "We are advised that this is an open and shut case of the most serious nature and that we are entitled to proceed against you, the publishers and printers of the Society of Names for an injunction, damages and costs."

For the Names, the admission by Lloyd's that its past forecasts had not been worth the paper they were written on was little consolation. A gloomy assessment of the market's prospects in the Society of Names' monthly newsletter predicted that the scale of the old year problems was such that insolvency loomed for thousands of Names.[10] The mood of increasing desperation was exploited by two of the more vocal militants, Claud Gurney and Richard Astor, to call for a second extraordinary general meeting. Despite their heavy defeat at the previous year's EGM, when they had called for the resignation of the council, and their lack of support among the established action group chairmen, they were determined to press ahead. "Lloyd's is bankrupt both morally and financially," said Gurney. "Lloyd's is not a business, it is a market, and for too long they have allowed a minority of underwriters to sell whatever stinking fish they care to bring to their stalls." Gurney's legal advisor, Richard Astor, was also an advocate of the jugular school: "We have to go for the throats of these people until the interests of the members are protected."[11]

Lloyd's reacted to the renewed threat by changing the rules. Gurney and Astor needed only a hundred signatures to force an EGM; it was too late to stop them, but the council decided that in future 1,500 signatures, about 5 percent of the membership, would be required. The established action groups reacted to the call with a statement condemning the EGM initiative as "wrongly timed and positively damaging." The Association of Lloyd's Members went further, proposing a resolution endorsing the business plan. None of this deterred the Gurney-Astor duo who demanded that Lloyd's should acknowledge a duty of care to its Names, and insisted that corporate capital should not be introduced without the approval of two-thirds of the members. Though mild in tone, their resolutions were accompanied by a tougher statement: "Since last year we have moved from no admission of guilt to a bizarre situation in which both the chairman and the chief executive freely admit massive mismanagement including deception, misregulation, incompetence and lack of professionalism. . . We don't want sympathy—confession and contrition are not enough—we require restitution."

The EGM, after these preliminaries, was predictably heated; banners outside the building proclaimed: "Lloyd's Fiddles while Names Burn." Inside, tempers were short. "Never in the history of underwriting have so many pockets been picked by so many unscrupulous underwriters," complained one bitter Name. Claud Gurney, moving the resolutions, launched a personal attack against the Lloyd's hierarchy so vituperative in tone that he dismayed even his supporters. He began by calling for the resignation of David Rowland, noting that he was chairman of the leading broker Sedgwick and a member of the council at the time the disastrous LMX business was being underwritten in the market: "The best thing we can say about him is that he stood idly by while evil triumphed." He then turned his fire on Lloyd's deputy chairman, Stephen Merrett, whose syndicates 418 and 421 were being sued by Names for negligence. "I am prepared to believe that Mr. Merrett is not a crook. But he's clearly associated in so many people's minds with so much that is and was wrong about Lloyd's, it is downright stupid for him to be deputy chairman." These insults were heard in silence, but when Gurney attacked Brian Garraway, Lloyd's head of regulation, as someone "who can't walk without a stick and recently suffered a heart attack," he was angrily interrupted by David Rowland. "Mr. Gurney, your level of conduct goes below even your own," he shouted somewhat ungrammatically. "Mr. Garraway is someone of the highest repute. I will not have my colleagues attacked in this outrageous way. I have no time for you. Get on with your speech."

Gurney continued with his diatribe, but its effect was counter-productive. John Rew felt obliged to disassociate himself from the personal attacks, and the votes went heavily against Gurney's motions. The first, noting that Lloyd's had a duty of care to its members, was supported by less than a third of those voting, while even fewer voted for the resolution requiring two-thirds of the membership to approve the introduction of corporate capital. The third motion, put forward by the ALM, backing the business plan and the council, was approved by 77 percent. "Rowland may feel the same debt of gratitude to Claud Gurney as Margaret Thatcher felt to Arthur Scargill," noted the Society of Names' newsletter.[12] *Lloyd's List* was equally blunt: "A rejection of the EGM2 initiative means that many of the more militant Names are effectively marginalized."[13] Within three months Brian Garraway, who was much respected, died having suffered a stroke followed by a massive fatal heart attack.

14

Civil War

"We ventured into an Establishment thieves' kitchen and were
mugged. We can't afford to live and can't afford to die."
Outhwaite Name

A dialogue between Lloyd's and its critics began again, following the
publication of two schemes to ease the plight of those suffering the heaviest
losses. David Springbett, a retired broker, and Ralph Bunje, an American
accountant, produced their proposals separately, but they contained several
common features. The business plan had envisaged that NewCo would take
over all the pre-1985 liabilities in exchange for a pooling of the reserves of
all the syndicates for these years. The drawback for Names was that the
amount of additional reserves that might be called at the time of the transfer
was potentially very large—more than £5 billion, according to some estimates. Still worse, if the reserves proved inadequate, the Names would be
required to meet future calls from their own dwindling, if not totally de-
pleted, financial resources. A gloomy assessment by Randolph Fields, an
American lawyer specializing in long-tail liabilities, predicted that Lloyd's
would not be in a position to fund NewCo: "We have no doubt that if NewCo
is established with reserves of £4 billion, as presently contemplated by the
Lloyd's plan, then NewCo will ultimately prove to be insolvent."[1]

Both the Springbett and Bunje plans, by contrast, offered a greater
degree of reassurance to Names. They proposed a cap on all prior-year

liabilities, financed by contributions from the central fund and from those Names continuing to underwrite. This, the authors claimed, was the only way to resolve the litigation plaguing the market while allowing the worst hit to continue to trade. Lloyd's initially welcomed the alternative plans as "constructive," but soon had second thoughts, particularly about the Springbett version, which it labelled misleading. "His plan is worse than naive," said Lloyd's deputy chairman, Robert Hiscox. "It is deceptively attractive to Names, who have suffered enough, and makes a number of unsustainable false promises."[2] Peter Middleton was equally dismissive: "Mr. Springbett is entitled to advocate whatever he pleases, but it is misleading to describe a plan that would destroy Lloyd's as one which holds out promise for the future . . . ultimately it helps no one if superficial, unworkable solutions to our problems make promises to the membership which cannot be delivered."[3]

A warmer response came from James Sinclair, managing director of Willis Faber Dumas, one of the largest members' agents. Noting that the ultimate cost of the Lloyd's debacle was likely to exceed £10 billion, he accepted that ruined Names were likely to want something in return for their life savings: "Resigned Names are recapitalizing Lloyd's for the benefit of future capital providers, with what they see as no consideration, and that explains why there is so much unhappiness in this section of the society. They want to get recognition and value for what they have put into the Lloyd's pot."[4]

The battle between those whose priority was restitution, and Lloyd's new management team, whose main aim was to ensure the survival of the market, centred on the introduction of corporate capital. The Names were reluctant to approve changing the capital structure of the market before plans to settle their grievances had been agreed. They feared that once the principle of corporate members with limited liability was accepted, their own bargaining strength would be weakened.

With the market in turmoil, the mood of apprehension was increased by a fresh spate of gloomy news. Chatset, the independent market analyst, predicted that Lloyd's would lose £1.5 billion in the 1991 account year and incur a further heavy loss in the following year. "The future for Lloyd's is bleak," it noted, adding that the market faced "a lingering demise, going down with a whimper rather than a bang as Names are crushed."[5] The announcement by Lloyd's that it had to put up the whole of its central fund reserves—£1.2 billion—because of the failure of Names to pay their syndicate liabilities was another ominous sign. Pressures on weaker syndicates, as members' agents withdrew Names wholesale, was forcing a huge contraction of capacity. "A sea change in the outlook of the London market has taken place," wrote Randolph Fields. "A dense mood of pessimism overhangs all discussions. Media coverage is consistently dour. The professionals, lawyers and insolvency practitioners are gathering like vultures."[6]

The first blood-letting of this crisis came when Lloyd's deputy chairman, Stephen Merrett, resigned from the council on 8 September 1993, pleading pressure of work. For some months his group had been under pressure because of the poor performance of its syndicates, several of which faced litigation. A Lloyd's loss review report on syndicate 421 had been severely critical of its management, though the findings were disputed by Merrett, who described its comments as "ill-considered." Aloof and pugnacious, he was respected rather than liked; eventually the lack of support from members' agents proved fatal. A fellow underwriter once joked of Merrett: "Even his friends don't like him."[7] His conflicts of interest made his position as deputy chairman even more difficult. Not only was he a key defendant in one of the major actions brought by Names but, as a leading E&O underwriter, he had a keen interest in the settlement offer made to Names. Merrett's resignation was welcomed by the Names' groups which had voiced concern over his multiple roles. *Lloyd's List* called it "a victory for common sense."

The humbling of one of the market's most powerful underwriters was quickly followed by the disintegration of his agency. In mid-November, Travelers, the US insurance company, announced that it was pulling out of negotiations to take a controlling stake in Merrett's underwriting agency. A desperate attempt to secure backing from another large Lloyd's agency, A.J. Archer, also failed. The defection of three of his senior underwriters left Merrett with no alternative but to transfer the ownership of his syndicates to other agencies. Blame for the destruction of his group was attributed by *Lloyd's List* to a combination of personality clashes and the new power structure of the market: "Members' agents, which for twenty years have had to go cap in hand to underwriters for capacity, now wield immense power due to the market's recent losses and the resulting capacity shortage. And, in some cases, there seems to be no doubt that old scores have coloured individuals' judgment about continuing to support syndicates with consistent, and sometimes superior track records."[8] Stephen Merrett was philosophical when I talked to him in his office in Creechurch Lane as his professional life crumbled around him. "There's nothing I can do anymore, just wait," he said with a depressed shrug. He was sceptical whether the market would survive if it deserted its traditional area of expertise—high-risk underwriting: "I am concerned that insufficient attention is being given to what the demand for Lloyd's products is likely to be and to match supply to that demand. Because the Names say they want low-risk, high-profit syndicates, the agents are trying to market that without regard for future demand."[9]

Against this troubled background, Lloyd's launched a pre-emptive strike to gain approval of its plans for the introduction of corporate capital. In a letter to Names the chairman, David Rowland, called an extraordinary general meeting for 20 October, saying it was necessary to forestall any attempt by dissident Names to delay the introduction of corporate capital. The move put the action groups in a quandary. Most of their committees accepted the pressing need for a new form of capital to shore up Lloyd's trading base, but were suspicious that the council would feel emboldened, if successful, to brush aside the grievances of dissident Names. After some debate, the action groups decided to call on their members to sign a blank voting form for use at the EGM. Just how high the stakes were in this joust was demonstrated a month before the meeting, when Peter Middleton said that he and David Rowland would resign if the vote went against them. "To my mind all of the issues surrounding corporate capital reduce to a simple, fundamental choice," wrote Peter Middleton. "Does the membership of Lloyd's wish the Society to have a sound and profitable future or is their preference that we become a business school case study of an institution in irreversible decline?"[10] In the event the threat of resignation was unnecessary. Lloyd's secured the support of the Association of Lloyd's Members (ALM), which, with the Lloyd's Names Associations' Working Party (LNAWP), had commissioned an independent study on corporate capital from Mercer Management Consulting. The study concluded that its intro-duction would be in the interest of all Names. The two-hour extraordinary general meeting was thus a relatively calm affair, with the votes overwhelm-ingly in favour of the council's position. The LNAWP sought vainly to adjourn the meeting, but secured just a third of the votes; another indication that it spoke for only a minority of Names.

The approval of corporate capital touched off a race by financiers to secure backing for their schemes. To the surprise of the doom-mongers, there was a greater degree of institutional interest than had been anticipated. Earlier in the year, most city comment had been sceptical. "For those considering the new opportunities of incorporated membership of the Lloyd's market," wrote S.G. Warburg Securities, "faith in a successful resolution of the market's past and current difficulties, as envisaged by the business plan, must be a pre-requisite in any decision to invest."[11] But for once Lloyd's perennial optimism about its prospects was soundly based. Though it had lost its Names £6 billion over three years, had further heavy losses to come, and was still mired in litigation, it was regarded by blue chip City institutions as a bankable proposition. The appeal of underwriting on a limited liability basis, with a deposit set at 50 percent of underwriting capacity, meant that the new Lloyd's investment trusts were able to project returns of 15 to 20 percent.

Nearly twenty merchant banks and securities houses, including S.G. Warburg, Barclay de Zoete Wedd (BZW), Kleinwort Benson, and Guinness Mahon, joined in the race, with plans to raise more than £1.5 billion, enough to write £3 billion of capacity. Several of the blue-blooded, including Cazenove and Lazard, were to drop out early but the runners who remained, notably the London Insurance Investment Trust backed by Samuel Montagu and James Capel, and the CLM Fund backed by Sedgwick and BZW, were sufficient to boost the capacity of the market by nearly £1.6 billion. Added to existing Names' funds, that meant the market's capital base would exceed £11 billion in 1994, an increase of more than a quarter on the previous year. This was a solid vote of confidence in Lloyd's future. The deputy chairman, Robert Hiscox, who was in charge of introducing the new limited liability capital, was entitled to feel cocky: "There really is a story to be told of one of the biggest bits of financial re-engineering in the history of business," he wrote. "There is an excellent core to Lloyd's which is a world beater; we have to strip away all the rubbish and let the excellence prevail."[12] Corporate capital, more cynical observers noted, had arrived in the nick of time: "The revolving door at Lloyd's of London is spinning like a top. The members are rushing out and the money is rushing in."[13] When Lloyd's released the latest membership figures, it emerged that 6,000 Names had resigned over the past two years, and only sixty-three had joined for 1994, making the total number underwriting 18,400, the lowest since 1980.

While the Lloyd's professionals mulled over their corporate future, the hopes of the external Names were fixed on the work of the two panels seeking to resolve the litigation. The legal panel, under the chairmanship of retired Lord Justice Sir Michael Kerr, had barely six weeks to judge the merits of highly complex causes of action involving more than thirty syndicates and a hundred syndicate years. The financial panel, chaired by Sir Jeremy Morse, had the no less difficult task of determining the amount of money that was available from E&O insurers and then dividing it, together with any central contribution from Lloyd's, according to the legal panel's opinion of the strength of the cases. There were four ratings: strong, medium, weak, and hopeless. Such an evaluation, though dressed up as a serious exercise, inevitably contained a large element of fudge. Given the time constraints, the legal panel, as it admitted, could only take "a broad-brush approach." Its remit did not include claims against auditors and brokers, or cases where individual Names were bringing actions for negligence against their members' agents over selection of syndicates. So it was inevitable that, whatever the Kerr panel concluded, many of the actions would continue.

The financial panel was handicapped by having to abide by the principle that non-litigating Names on syndicates covered by the settlement were entitled to a share of whatever money could be squeezed out of the E&O insurers. The council of Lloyd's had ruled that offers would have to be made to all Names whether or not they were litigating. The justification for this—equal treatment—was as dubious as the logic of seeking to resolve litigation by offering large sums of money to those who were not, and had no intention of, litigating. The offers to non-litigants aggravated the problem that the amount of E&O cover was strictly limited and in dispute. Eventually the majority of the eight-member panel accepted the E&O insurers' estimate of cover of between £820 million and £1,085 million. But, due in part to the absence of any certainty on this crucial point, the three Names' representatives on the panel refused to sign the report.[14]

The lack of any guarantee against future deterioration was a major obstacle to acceptance by Names, particularly those on long-tail syndicates. Peter Middleton had promised that he was "going to find every possible way" to offer a cap on Names' losses, but found himself unable to fulfil this pledge. The risks of giving such a guarantee had apparently become too great for the council to accept, an ominous warning of the scale of losses ahead. The only way that a cap could be financed was by borrowing against the assets of the society, but the council was opposed to such a course. Once again S.G. Warburg, the merchant bank, was called in to advise that a bond issue was not practicable "given the present background of disastrous losses." This effectively tied the hands of the financial panel. In the end it had only £900 million at its disposal, less than half of which was contributed by the E&O insurers, who drove a hard bargain. The remaining £500 million came from the central fund. The shape of the settlement was dictated by the adjudications of the Kerr panel, that Names on spiral syndicates had strong legal claims, while those on long-tail syndicates generally had much weaker ones. A few big spiral losers received very large offers; a hundred had offers of between £500,000 and £750,000; forty were offered between £750,000 and £1 million. But most spiral Names found that they were being promised on average no more than 30 percent of their currently declared losses. The great majority of Names received offers of less than £100,000; many on long-tail syndicates were given only a fraction of their losses. Names on Syndicate 90, a long-tail marine syndicate whose case was rated as "weak" by the Kerr panel, were offered 2 percent. If future losses projected by Chatset were taken into account, the offer for the syndicate's Names amounted to less than one-fifth of one percent.

As the shape of the proposed settlement became clearer, the mood of the litigating Names grew more militant. At a meeting of the LNAWP on 23 November 1993, its chairman, Christopher Stockwell, warned that he and the two other Names' representatives on the financial panel chaired by Sir Jeremy Morse were not prepared to sign its report. He said the amount on offer was totally inadequate, and an insult to Names. The losses faced by those who were still trading were so large that the market would soon be in breach of its solvency limits and would be forced by the Department of Trade to stop trading, yet Lloyd's was blithely ignorant of what lay ahead because it had failed to run computer models of the cash impact of the settlement. Whether Stockwell fully believed in this doom-mongering was unclear, but he wanted to shake the council's view that Lloyd's future was best secured by abandoning the worst hit Names.

Though the LNAWP chairman spoke for a minority, a growing number of Names was determined to pay not a penny more to Lloyd's. The offer announced by David Rowland and Peter Middleton at a press conference on 7 December served to alienate an even larger group. Action groups queued up to denounce it as inadequate. Colin Hook, chairman of Feltrim, said it was an admirable settlement for E&O underwriters, whose liabilities had been capped, but did not provide Names with "commensurate benefits." Michael Deeny, chairman of Gooda Walker, noted that all the Names' representatives on the financial panel had refused to sign the report. The LNAWP said the deal was "an exercise with mirrors" which did nothing for Names. Peter Middleton, who appeared to realize that his laboriously constructed settlement was falling apart, described the complex exercise wearily as "a Rubik cube with a seventh side."[15]

Two aspects of the offer, aimed at pressurizing Names to accept, caused particular resentment. The first was Lloyd's plan to reduce the amount of E&O cover by channelling the £500 million central fund contribution through the E&O underwriters. This piece of financial jiggery-pokery was designed to discourage further litigation by stripping agents of what remained of their insurance cover, thus making it a waste of time for Names to continue with their legal actions. The second was the pressure brought on ruined Names to accept the offer on pain of being disbarred from "hardship" if they rejected it. "We accept it is in Lloyd's interest that the offer should be successful," one syndicate chairman protested to David Rowland. "But that cannot be a sufficient reason to force Names facing serious losses to surrender their legal rights. I hope you and the Council will feel on reflection that this is an unfair additional pressure to put on vulnerable Names and that you will allow them to decide whether or not to accept the offer without this 'emotional blackmail' which is unworthy of Lloyd's."

Lloyd's had not formally set a minimum level of acceptance above which it would declare the offer unconditional, but at a press conference Peter Middleton declared: "We need a substantial majority. We have said that we would not go unconditional under 70 percent." Right from the start it was an uphill battle. The absence of the promised cap or some other form of safeguard against future deterioration was a huge hurdle. Lloyd's case was not helped by the fact that serious errors had been made. All 21,000 offers had to be revised and new ones sent out. Some 13,500 Names had been offered too little; 9,300 had been offered too much. Most adjustments were small, but one Name had been offered £40,000 too much, another £90,000 too little. To add to its humiliation, barely a month later Lloyd's was forced to revise the offer again. Names on the Macmillan syndicates 80 and 843, Janson Green 1145 and Wellington 406 were notified of further adjustments. "I am astonished that Lloyd's are not able to get the offer correct," said the chairman of the Macmillan action group, Simon Blunt. "Even now, we have no way of knowing that the latest is correct."

The errors, a direct result of the way the offer had been rushed, were seized on by the critics as evidence that Lloyd's was incapable of producing a fair settlement. As syndicate litigating groups held special meetings to consider the offer, a wave of pent-up bitterness was voiced. "Dear Mr. Rowland," wrote one Name. "Thank you for your recent settlement offer, a document for which my wife and I have found a domestic use. We have only two objections to it, viz: the paper is too thick and shiny; there are no perforations where the pages join the spine. If you could rectify these omissions in future offers, you would not only save money on printing costs but also contribute further amenity to our hard-pressed household." A Dorset farmer favoured a more direct approach: "Reject the offer. Nail the bastards to the barn door and set the barn on fire." On 12 January, a rumbustious meeting of Names on Syndicate 418, a long-tail non-marine syndicate, applauded Lord Wrenbury, a member of its action group's steering committee, when he said: "What most of us want is for this whole sorry affair to go away and never hear the name of Lloyd's again." A speaker from the floor said: "No one but a lunatic would accept this settlement. It's like signing a blank cheque and giving it to someone you don't trust." The chairman, Ken Lavery, a Canadian broker, told his Names: "All of us are sick and tired of the situation but we feel we cannot recommend acceptance."

Confirmation that the peace settlement was heading for the rocks came at mass meetings of the Gooda Walker and Feltrim action groups, which represented 4,500 Names. They had been promised more than half of the £900 million offered—without their acceptance, the settlement had no chance. But both steering committees recommended rejection, and the mood of the two meetings was overwhelmingly hostile. The Gooda Walker Names voted to reject by five to one, the Feltrim Names by eleven to one. One Gooda member summed up the offer: "It has as many strings as a parachute but not the same life-saving qualities." A Feltrim member was equally sceptical: "I find it objectionable that the offer should be described as a settlement. At best it ought to be described as a partial credit." The absence of a cap, together with a widespread view that the offer, once rejected, was likely, despite denials, to be improved, was decisive. "It's Lloyd's job to say this is the final offer," said Michael Deeny, chairman of the Gooda Walker action group. "That's what people say to each other every year at the Galway Horse Fair."

The E&O insurers made one last attempt to rescue the offer by writing to the 22,000 Names involved, warning that the limited amount of E&O cover meant that they would get less from court action than they would by acceptance. But many Names appeared to be more interested in vengeance than in restitution. A cool calculation of financial interest had less appeal than prosecuting those who had ruined them. The decisive vote against the settlement by Feltrim and Gooda Walker Names set the seal. When the results were announced on 14 February 1994, it emerged that the offer had been accepted by only half the Names, representing just over a third of the offer's value, well short of Lloyd's 70 percent minimum target for acceptance.

Peter Middleton sought to play down the impact of the settlement's collapse on Lloyd's business prospects. Warning that the Names were the real losers, he said: "If they think they'll do better in the courts, that's fine by me."[16] Despite his brave words, the failure of the peace bid, on which he had worked so hard, was a serious setback. A decade of litigation costing hundreds of millions of pounds now loomed. For some Names the prospect of years of financial worry was unendurable. Three days after the offer's rejection, Admiral Sir Richard Fitch was found dead in his car near his home at Middleton-on-Sea, West Sussex. A pipe from the exhaust led to the car. "He was a member of Lloyd's and that says it all," said a member of his family. "Names are moving from one vale of tears to another," noted Tom Benyon of the Society of Names. "This is going to be a lawyer's feast," predicted Brian Smith, underwriter of one of the market's most consistently profitable syndicates. It was a forecast with which no-one could quarrel.

SAUVE QUI PEUT

The settlement's rejection led to a distinct hardening of attitudes. Some companies immediately sought to distance themselves from the litigation which threatened to swamp the market with multi-billion-pound claims. Two brokers, Jardine and Hogg, put their subsidiary members' agencies, Christand and K.C. Webb, into voluntary liquidation. "This does not adversely affect Names' rights," said Hogg's chairman, Anthony Jackson. "They still have access to E&O cover." Another Lloyd's group, London Wall Holdings, also liquidated its members' and managing agencies.[17]

The tough safety-first approach was not confined to brokers and managing agents. Many of the 17,000 Names involved in litigation, threatened with financial disaster, believed that there was little point in paying any more of their losses until their legal actions alleging negligence had been resolved. They also felt that if others were taking precautionary steps, they should do so too. Marie-Louise Burrows, the leader of the Lime Street Action Group, said that those she represented would not go down without a fight: "They overlooked the fact that Names who came in the 1980s were the *nouveau riche*. They worked for their money and they'll hang on to it until the bailiffs call."[18]

Faced by a payment strike, Lloyd's had no choice but to take action. So began what one dissident dubbed "the biggest debt-collection exercise in history." At the beginning of March 1994 Graeme King, senior manager of

Lloyd's financial recovery department, wrote to 3,000 defaulting Names to warn them that Lloyd's "can and would take legal action to secure Names' indebtedness to policy-holders." Up to this point, the council had taken a dilatory approach to chasing Names. Nearly 200 writs had been issued a year earlier but few had been pursued. Uncertain how to proceed, Lloyd's chose to look on the bright side. The letter to Names pointed out that the vast majority had, often with considerable personal and family sacrifice, fully met their obligations to policy-holders. "Very, very few Names are distancing their assets," said Mr. King. "What amazes me is the honesty and integrity of middle England. That cannot be honoured enough."

The more militant of the Names did not see it in that light. "There are people who could pay, but are determined not to, because they have been swindled," said Michael Deeny, chairman of the Gooda Walker action group. John Rew, chairman of the Sturge action group, claimed that the money being called from those who had ceased to trade was not needed, and was merely being called to bolster reserves: "Names who have ceased trading should not pay a penny piece more to Lloyd's and should resist draw downs [of their deposits]." To those who were still trading, Rew's message was equally blunt. They should refuse to mutualize the losses of those who couldn't or wouldn't pay.

Lloyd's faced serious obstacles before it could get its hands on the hundreds of millions of pounds it was owed. For a start, it appeared to be unable to distinguish the won't pays from the can't pays. The main instrument for sorting out the mess, the hardship committee, chaired by Mary Archer, was overwhelmed by more than 2,500 applications, some from Names who were simply playing for time. After more than two years, only a score of hardship agreements had actually been concluded.

One reason for the slow progress was the density of the legal thickets. The Writs Response Group, which represented the most determined non-payers, had, with the help of leading counsel, assembled what it called its master defence. Armed with this, it claimed its members could keep Lloyd's at bay for years while the issues were fought through the courts right up to the European Court of Justice in the Hague. These tactics appeared to be having some success. Two test cases were still tied up in the High Court after more than eighteen months of procedural wrangling. An initial hearing resulted in Names losing on a number of procedural issues. But in November 1994 the Court of Appeal upheld the Names' contention that Lloyd's central fund was in breach of European competition law, and ordered the issue to be tried by the Commercial Court. Delay was a crucial weapon, particularly for Names intent on distancing their assets from the maw of unlimited liability. Under the terms of the 1986 Insolvency Act, any transfer could be reversed by the courts if it was made less than five years before a bankruptcy order was made.

For some Names this tense cat-and-mouse game proved intolerable. On 25 August 1994 a coroner's inquest at Liskeard, Cornwall was told that Mr. Robert Vere Eliot, an uncle of the Earl of St Germans and a Conservative county councillor for sixteen years, had taken a massive overdose of paracetamol tablets. A consultant psychiatrist, who had treated Mr. Eliot in the weeks before his suicide, told the inquest that he was depressed because of his Lloyd's losses. "What's it all about Alfie?" wrote another despairing debtor. "Hiscox was right: we were sheep for shearing, lambs to the slaughter. We ventured into an Establishment thieves' kitchen and were mugged. We can't afford to live and can't afford to die. Thanks, Lloyd's!"[19]

ACTION GROUPS

Accusations of negligence and worse spread, but public sympathy for the Names remained strictly limited. Nearly all the action groups suffered from a propensity to split into smaller and even more militant factions. The failure of the settlement led to divisions within the so-called Super Group, the Lloyd's Names' Associations Working Party (LNAWP) on which all action groups were represented. Christopher Stockwell, LNAWP's chairman, came under increasing fire for his frequently expressed views that the market was finished, and that Names' interests would be best served if it collapsed completely. That view proved offensive to many, and it was certainly counter-productive if there were to be continuing negotiations with Lloyd's. But Stockwell, a stubborn, talented entrepreneur, refused to listen to advice. The row came to a head in June 1994 in a messy coup. The bigger action groups led by Michael Deeny of Gooda Walker split off, leaving Stockwell and a rump of smaller groups to soldier on.

Similar divisions plagued the Writs Response Group, the main body representing 2,500 Names resisting attempts by Lloyd's to draw down deposits or to issue bankruptcy orders. Soon after its master defence was completed in June 1993, it divided into three parts. The main group decided its strongest card was to continue its defence, based on an appeal to the European Court, but other Names, gathered under the banner of the Names

Defence Association (NDA), decided to plead fraud. The NDA soon split again. The amount of vituperation generated by these internecine disputes was out of all proportion to any real divisions of interest that existed. But it underlined the taste for political infighting of those whose only common interest was that they had lost a lot of money. As the Society of Names commented: "Lloyd's are lucky. They employ only one legal team to fight Names."

By the summer of 1994, Lloyd's was forced to admit that it could no longer hope to manage the debt crisis on its own. The market's chief executive, Peter Middleton, estimated that 15,000 Names owed as much as £2 billion. Even before the 1991 year's losses had been called, two-thirds of the £900 million Lloyd's central fund had had to be set aside to meet unpaid prior-year calls and solvency deficiencies. A firm of commercial debt-collectors was therefore called in. The hardship committee, chaired by Mary Archer, was scrapped and replaced by a financial recovery department with the brief of handling negotiations with the debtors. Philip Holden, a partner with Dibb Lupton Broomhead, promised that he would adopt a reasonable approach: "We are keen to avoid litigation but if people do not cooperate, we will pursue them. There is no point banging out thousands of writs because that does not address the problem. And there will be no knocking on doors at the dead of night—yet."

The immediate response of the Names and their legal advisers was defiance. One loss-making Name, asked what he was doing at the press conference announcing the new hard-line tactics, replied: "If I am going to be slaughtered, I want to check that the abattoir is up to EC standards."[20] James Finlay, chairman of the Names Defence Association, said the use of debt-collectors would accomplish nothing: "It is a callous and shameless act to terrify thousands of scared and innocent victims." Michael Freeman, a solicitor to Names seeking to prove fraud against Lloyd's, said: "They can talk about bankruptcy as much as they like but they can't do anything without a judgment."[21]

The morale of the debtors soared when Mr. Justice Phillips ruled at the beginning of October 1994 in favour of the 3,096 Gooda Walker Names, an award which they claimed was worth more than £500 million. The judgment was scathing about the recklessness with which the three Gooda Walker underwriters had placed their Names in jeopardy, and it rejected outright the argument that LMX business was well-known to be high risk: "I have no doubt," said the judge, "that there are many plaintiffs who would understandably have felt outraged had they heard the plea being advanced on behalf of their members' agents, that Names had no cause for complaint because the type of business they had chosen to write was well-known to be dynamite."[22]

The damages, likely to be the biggest ever awarded by a British court, though subject to appeal, strengthened the determination of Names on other loss-making syndicates to withhold payment to Lloyd's until their cases had been heard. Members of the Gooda Walker syndicates knew they were likely to recover only a fraction of the damages awarded by the court, as many members' agents would seek refuge in liquidation. As the Society of Names newsletter commented: "Many are reasonably asking: as Lloyd's apparently presided over a shambles in the 1980's and failed in their regulatory duties to monitor the very agents that treated them so lamentably, how can they have the brass neck to ask them to pay a single penny more?"[23]

DOUBLE COUNT

Defaulting Names were only one of the market's problems. The announce-ment of a loss of £2.05 billion for the 1991 account marked the fourth consecutive year of loss. The result would have been £500 million worse if the council had not exceptionally agreed to make an allowance for double counting. This arose from losses being counted twice as a result of Lloyd's incestuous habit of insuring and reinsuring stop loss and E&O risks within the market. Even allowing for double counting, the cumulative losses since 1988 amounted to more than £7 billion, equivalent to more than £200,000 per Name. It was too much for the equanimity of many of the losers. At the annual meeting held in the Festival Hall on 23 May 1994, the chairman and council were once again bitterly attacked for their failure to regulate the market. "When are you going to accept that Lloyd's is full of overpaid, incompetent and greedy men who make double-glazing and time-share salesmen look like amateurs?" asked one irate Name.

The most troubling aspect of the 1991 result was that over half the loss, £1.14 billion, was required to bolster reserves. If old year liabilities contin-ued at this rate, there could be little hope of profit in the years ahead. Even in an exceptional year, Lloyd's was hard-pressed to make a return of more than 10 percent, and with annual capacity less than £10 billion the prospect of adequate returns was dim. The uncertainty, caused by the acceleration of pollution and asbestos claims, had already led to an increase in syndicates unable to close their accounts, from 162 in 1991 to 478 in 1993. The capacity of syndicates' open years now exceeded the market's annual capacity. Given the escalation in old year losses and the administrative expense of run-offs, Lloyd's future looked ever more uncertain.

Lloyd's List, the market's daily paper, acknowledged that hopes of a return to profit in 1993 might vanish once losses of earlier years had been assessed and deferred calls had been taken into account.[24] Chatset, the independent market analyst, reinforced this glum message by predicting a fifth consecutive loss—£1 billion—for the 1992 year, and only a small profit of £300 million in 1993. Charles Sturge, Chatset's co-editor, claimed that old year losses were on such a scale that Lloyd's would not survive unless it abandoned its guarantee to pay all valid claims. "So long as the central fund is in place," he pointed out, "a single crook or fool can commit the entire credit of Lloyd's to his crooked or foolish contracts once he has ruined his own Names."

This echoed an earlier warning from Robert Kiln, the much respected former chairman of the Kiln Agency, that the market was set on an unsustainable course: "It is my belief that Lloyd's cannot go on trading with members having both unlimited liability for their own trading and having in addition unlimited liability for the trading of other members who either cannot, or will not, pay or reserve their commitments. That being so, we will have to introduce limited liability for this mutuality and this has now become critical."[25] Lloyd's responded bleakly that if valid claims remained unpaid, the market would be barred by regulators around the world from trading. For those Names who were continuing to underwrite, the issue of having to pay other Names' losses was highly sensitive. At some point, it appeared, the central fund would have to be replenished if the market were to continue to pay policy-holders. Only 15,000 Names were expected to continue to trade on into 1995. According to some market estimates, the shortfall of losses which the central fund would eventually have to meet might reach as high as £3 billion, equivalent to £200,000 per Name.

This gloomy arithmetic led to renewed questions about whether Lloyd's would be able to pass the annual solvency test required by the Department of Trade, without which it would be unable to continue to trade. Christopher Stockwell claimed that Lloyd's was for all intents and purposes already insolvent. Lloyd's consistently described such claims as nonsense, but there was no denying that its finances were under strain. The annual report, published on 25 April 1994, showed that £661 million had had to be set aside to meet unpaid liabilities owed by Names, double the previous year's amount and thirty times as much as four years earlier. That left only £300 million in the central fund, which appeared to be insufficient to meet what were almost certain to be even larger unpaid debts from the 1991 year's £2 billion loss.

The basis on which the market's solvency was determined was discussed at a meeting with Names at the Department of Trade on 22 March 1994. Richard Hobbs, under-secretary at the department and the senior official responsible for regulating Lloyd's, indicated that solvency was a flexible concept. The test for the market as a whole, that net assets must exceed 16 percent of premiums and 23 percent of claims, was a meaningless formality because it excluded potential future losses known as IBNR (incurred but not reported claims). The second test, that every Name must be solvent, in other words the central fund plus the corporation's own assets must exceed the total deficits of insolvent Names, was more difficult. In 1993 Lloyd's had managed to meet this only by pledging the assets of its buildings to supplement the central fund. Solvency, however, was a double-edged weapon. The DTI under-secretary quoted recent Congressional evidence given by a Tillinghast insurance actuary, Amy Bouska. She had pointed out that regulators were in an impossible situation. If they were too lax and there was a collapse, they would be blamed for failing to act. If, on the other hand, they strictly enforced solvency margins, they could precipitate a collapse. The widespread view that few insurance companies in either the UK or the US would be solvent if they ceased to trade, made the task of regulation no easier. Undoubtedly the government would do everything it could to ensure that Lloyd's was able to continue. The alternative was too much of a nightmare to contemplate.

There was no silencing the drumbeat of bad news. At the beginning of 1995, Chatset forecast that Lloyd's was under-reserved by at least $10 billion. A report by insurance consultants R.M. Fields estimated Lloyd's old year liabilities at £26 billion, five times its reserves. "I'm extremely pessimistic NewCo will be authorized by the regulators because of the utter mismatch between assets and liabilities," said Randolph Fields, the author of the report.[26] Lloyd's survival might be on a knife-edge, but support for the view that it was in a stronger position than many American insurance companies came in a study published by the US insurance analysts A.M. Best. The survey was, on the face of it, hardly reassuring. It estimated that asbestos and pollution claims would cost $132 billion, four times as much as had until now been paid out in claims and reserves. This was more than the total capital of the forty-seven insurance groups on whom the liabilities were concentrated. As John Snyder, the report's author, a senior vice-president of Best, noted: "It is hard to overstate the potential extent of the environmental and asbestos liability problem for the insurance industry." Lloyd's share of this "black hole" was not calculated, but the study's fine print supported the London market's claim that it was better reserved than many of its American rivals. Small comfort perhaps, but it suggested that Lloyd's was not alone in its trauma and that the campaign for liability reform would have strong allies.[27]

15

The Fat Lady Sings

"One of these days the folks of Louisiana are going to get good
government. And they ain't going to like it."
Governor Huey Long

Lloyd's likes to launch its new buildings with a splash. On 18 November
1986, the market's eighth home was opened by Queen Elizabeth with the
assistance of 3,000 magnums of Veuve Cliquot champagne and the City of
London Sinfonia. Almost anyone who mattered in the City was among the
5,000 invited guests. One person, however, was missing. Ian Hay Davison,
Lloyd's first chief executive, had not been forgiven for his comment on
resigning, that he had been dismayed to find more than just the odd rotten
apple in the market; the rot had spread to the barrel.

Such thoughts were banished from the celebrations for the market's
new £165 million headquarters, a glittering, ultra-modern tower, a far cry
from Edward Lloyd's coffee house in Tower Street. The startling design of
glass and steel, with a tangle of shining service pipes and lifts strung along
its sides, proclaimed unabashed confidence in the future. Lloyd's brief to the
architect, Richard Rogers, had been that the new building must be able to
cope with the market tripling in numbers and capacity over the next half-
century. The solution, a multi-layered trading floor linked by yellow-
wheeled escalators, topped by a soaring glass dome, was not to everyone's
taste. "From coffee house to an inverted coffee pot," sneered the critics. But

its sheer vitality makes it one of the most dramatic modern buildings in London.

The history of the market is one of a series of forced removals; the growth of the business and pressure for accommodation was always underestimated. This time it was to be different. Within five years of the opening of its twenty-first-century spaceship, Lloyd's lost more money than any other British financial institution in modern times. As the greatest ever transference of wealth from middle England to middle America accelerated, it became clear that the new building was a colossal white elephant. The numbers of syndicates halved from the peak of more than 400; managing and members' agencies were decimated; a core of only thirty to fifty mega-agencies was expected to survive. The sharp contraction left much empty office space; the deserted upper galleries were a depressing reminder that this was a business in dire trouble. Lloyd's chief executive, Peter Middleton, took to musing, only half in jest, that the building would be ideal for a tourist theme park. Another leading market professional speculated: "Well, if we do go bust I suppose this place would make a lovely greenhouse."

The collapse of Lloyd's has been very public. For a proud institution, the sharp reversal of its fortunes has been humiliating. Given the inbred nature of the market, and the arrogant belief of some of its practitioners that they could ignore the basic principles of insurance, it was perhaps inevitable that a complacency born of 300 years of largely successful trading would sooner or later be shattered. Insurance is about not the acceptance but the management of risk so that, in the words of the Elizabethan statute, "the losse lightethe rather easilie upon many, than heavilie upon fewe." The practice of sections of the market of funnelling risk into fewer and fewer hands was the precise opposite, and was bound to lead to disaster. The scale of the Lloyd's catastrophe is nevertheless exceptional. To chalk up losses of more than £8 billion in five years (1988-1992) and pauperize, if not bankrupt, as many as two in five of those who provided the market's capital, is an achievement unmatched since the South Sea Bubble.

The factors leading to this extraordinary collapse are complex, but undoubtedly a root cause was Lloyd's failure to manage its capacity at a time when the insurance cycle worldwide was turning savagely downwards. Between 1983 and 1988, the market's capital base almost doubled in size, an average annual growth rate of 15 percent, while premiums grew by only 3 percent. The number of Names meanwhile grew by 50 percent to 32,433. By 1987, as a result of this unsustainable over-supply, syndicates were desperately looking for business, and cutting their rates to the bone. The process was accelerated by the credit explosion of the 1980s, which enhanced property and share prices to such an extent that capacity surged. Insurance has always been a cyclical business, depending on the flow of capital. When times are good, money flows in and rates decline until losses become so painful that the excess capacity is burnt off and the cycle begins again. But there has never been anything quite like the 1980s. "The boom at Lloyd's," noted one editorial comment, "was proportionately as great in terms of reckless over-capacity as in any of the world's financial markets. The tragedies are those of gullible people sucked into a bubble."[1]

Fuelling this rapid expansion, the post-Cromer membership reforms led to a large influx of Names with inadequate capital resources, who should not have been allowed anywhere near such a high-risk market. The Names cannot deny their share of responsibility for the disaster that was to overtake them. Many of them, no doubt, were foolish, some were greedy, others naive enough to place their trust in the market's reputation for good faith. Often they were persuaded to join by commission-seeking touts who were being paid undisclosed fees by members' agents determined to expand their capacity. Lloyd's connived at such practices, and allowed its entrance regulations to be undermined. Names are not allowed to use the value of their principal residence either for their deposit or as evidence of their net wealth. This sensible precaution was sidestepped, with the council's blessing, by the use of bank guarantees. A Name with few assets apart from a house worth £150,000 was able to use this to obtain a bank guarantee to support his underwriting. The consequence of encouraging thousands of individuals with only moderate means to gamble their home away has been a disaster for the Names, for the banks, and for Lloyd's.

This mistake is now widely admitted. Sir Peter Miller, who was chairman from 1984 to 1988, said: "I think we should have been asking in crude terms—if you join Lloyd's, can you write a cheque for £100,000 and not disturb your lifestyle. We failed to raise deposits sharply enough. We should have asked more questions." His successor, Murray Lawrence, chairman from 1988 to 1991, agrees: "We lost sight of the values of the underlying assets. Names became less and less liquid. Successive committees going back to the 1970s should have been speedier to cope with inflation."[2]

EXCESS CAPACITY

The flood of new Names, and the additional capacity they brought, helped to fuel the excesses of the LMX spiral. A number of underwriters, mainly from the marine market, faced by a decline in traditional business, decided to use their surplus capacity to muscle in to excess of loss reinsurance. Despite their lack of expertise in this high-risk, specialist area, they sought to compete by offering extremely low rates, which opened up an opportunity seized on by shrewder rivals in the market. The availability of exceptionally cheap reinsurance led to basic principles being flouted. Primary insurers and reinsurers were able to accept dubious risks, confident that however bad the claims record turned out to be, they could lay off the risk and still make a handsome profit. The result was doubly catastrophic, as the Lloyd's business plan noted: "During the late 1980s, many underwriters exploited the availability of inter-syndicate reinsurance to lock in profits regardless of their own gross underwriting result. This was an effective short-term underwriting tactic but led to severe damage over the long term. As much of this reinsurance was provided by Lloyd's syndicates, this practice funnelled losses into a few syndicates; second, it undermined standards of underwriting across the market, as underwriters no longer had to exercise prudence in pricing the incoming risk correctly and so were exposed when the reinsurance market contracted."

One reason why the excesses of the LMX spiral were not tackled before they ruined thousands of Names was conflicts of interest. The fortunes of members' and managing agents and their Names should be closely aligned, but this crucial relationship was wrecked by the get-rich-quick mentality of the 1970s and 1980s. Agents, remunerated by profit commissions and fees paid by individual Names, stood to gain greatly from expansion. The temptation for agents and underwriters to expand capacity regardless of risk was increased by the desire to capitalize their businesses and sell out for large sums while the going was good, a trend criticized by the Cromer report. An early proponent of this technique was Peter Cameron-Webb, who sold out to Minet for £2 million in the late 1970s. But there were many other less flagrant operators who made large fortunes before departing, leaving their Names in an expensive hole. Colin Murray, a former deputy chairman, is in no doubt about what has gone wrong: "I believe the single factor that has taken underwriters' minds away from the interests of their Names has been the ability of agents to fatten themselves up for sale . . . this pre-occupation with personal enrichment has led to a large scale lack of concern for the vital interests of Names." Murray is scornful of the view that it was simply a failure of regulation that led to the LMX disaster. "The idea that the council can regulate the market in such a way as to avoid disasters is totally fallacious," he says. "The council can, and should, impose higher standards of competence on the market. It cannot, and should not, try to dictate to the market just how certain classes of business should be underwritten."[3]

Conflicts of interest have also exacerbated the most serious threat that Lloyd's faces—the problem of old year losses. The Lloyd's system of trading, a three-year accounting period, at the end of which a syndicate's financial position is finalized by means of an internal reinsurance premium paid to the successor year, depends on trust. During the late 1970s and early 1980s, many long-tail syndicates paid out illusory profits and reaped equally bogus profit commissions as a result of inadequate reserving; other syndicates closed years of account which should have been left open because the long-tail claims position was so uncertain.

When the stench of losses finally became too high, thousands of newly recruited Names found that they were trapped on syndicates which had inherited billions of pounds worth of pollution and asbestos claims dating back half a century. The Names believe they were gulled into joining such under-reserved syndicates in order to dilute the losses; that is why they have taken to the courts. Whether or not their legal actions succeed, the basis on which Lloyd's operated profitably for three centuries has been destroyed. Names will never again trust a system by which an underwriter, practically unchecked and with very little guidance, determines the reinsurance to close (RITC). In theory, auditors should ensure that this massive transfer of liability from one group of Names to another is fair, and that the internal reinsurance premium is soundly based. But the auditors now claim, in response to writs issued against them, that the RITC is a matter of professional judgment.

The conflict of interest between an underwriter wishing to put the best gloss on his results and a Name who needs to know what hazards lie ahead is too direct to be ignored. "The prime interest of the underwriter and the directors of the managing agents is self-interest—the continuation of the syndicate, and the declaration of profit in the year being closed," noted one market observer. "So they cannot be called impartial, yet they are the very people by whose skill and judgment the RITC premium is assessed, in situations where a prudent RITC would result in a loss for the closed account."[4]

The independent market analyst, Chatset, is contemptuous about underwriters' ability to assess a fair RITC: "The fact remains that for the past fifty years the reserving for liability business has been woefully inadequate. Lloyd's does set minimum requirements for reserving by year but history has proved these to be a joke and they probably still are." Even those underwriters—the majority—who try to be scrupulously fair, acknowledge that the RITC is badly flawed. As Robert Kiln, the distinguished underwriter, pointed out earlier, most RITCs are sheer guesswork: "It is quite absurd to pretend that any realistic figure, let alone a true and fair figure, can be put on the premiums for an RITC at the end of thirty-six months on most accounts." Kiln's further charge is even more serious: "Many Names who joined Lloyd's in the 1980s have suffered unfair and enormous losses due to the gross inadequacy of the reinsurance to close made over the past forty years and which was well known about in the early 1980s."[5]

STRUCTURAL FLAW

The discrediting of its traditional system of trading leaves Lloyd's with a difficult structural problem. Unless confidence in the reinsurance to close can be restored, the system of "annual ventures," in which a syndicate's affairs are finalized at the end of three years, is finished. But restoring confidence will require either a more rigorous system of audit or an independent RITC, conducted on a hands-off basis. A no less serious structural difficulty is the mismatch between the increasing volatility of Lloyd's capital base and the long-tail business it has traditionally underwritten. An annual venture of individual investors whose results are declared after three years is not a sensible way to cover risks which may not materialize for thirty years. The advent of corporate capital may mask these problems, but it does not solve them. Perhaps there is no solution; if so, the market will not survive into the twenty-first century.

The old Lloyd's which flourished for three centuries on the basis of individual Names risking everything on unlimited liability is, in fact, already dead. The tax reforms of the 1980s, and the halving of the top rate of income tax, fundamentally changed the risk-reward ratio. When the highest-level direct tax was at 98 percent, the risk of underwriting losses was borne largely by the Inland Revenue, leaving even Names on unsuccessful syndicates with the prospects of capital appreciation. Undoubtedly this had a malign effect on underwriting standards, for which the market is now paying. The destruction of Lloyd's as a tax shelter has coincided with a realization that the risks of underwriting with unlimited liability are folly for all but the very rich. And even for the seriously rich, the hazard of unlimited liability makes little sense.

The risks have been aggravated by the fact that members' and managing agents are no longer obliged to have E&O insurance. A decade ago, Lloyd's required cover of at least 25 percent of allocated premium income up to a maximum of £50 million. In the mid-1980s this was reduced to 12 percent for managing agents and 8 percent for members' agents. In 1990 the E&O requirement was abolished altogether, on the grounds that the cover was no longer available at a reasonable cost. No one in their right mind would dream of employing an architect, a solicitor, a doctor or an accountant without such professional indemnity insurance. Yet Lloyd's expects its Names to trade with unlimited liability in a far more exposed relationship, without protection. Many ruined Names are finding to their cost that, though their affairs have been grossly mishandled, they have no hope of recovering their losses through court action.

After the devastating losses of the past five years and the bankrupting of much of its capital base, no one, even within Lloyd's, believes that the old market, in which professionals were trusted to run the business on behalf of amateurs, can be brought back to life. "We've blown it," says the chairman of a leading members' agent, who admits he wouldn't dream of putting his children into the market.[6] If that is the view of the professionals, it is hardly surprising that the amateurs are rushing for the exits.

The new Lloyd's that is emerging is one in which big corporate players with limited liability will call the shots. A fifth of the market's capacity is already being provided by corporate capital, and that proportion is certain to grow rapidly in the years ahead. The council has proposed that the voting structure should be reformed to reflect the new balance of power. The days of bespoke portfolios of syndicates held by individual Names are on the way out. Most Names continuing to trade are now writing through a Members' Agent Pooling Arrangement (MAPA), Lloyd's equivalent of a unit trust, in which each Name has a limited line on perhaps as many as fifty syndicates. As the old Names succumb to insolvency or die, they will have to be replaced by new sources of capital if the market is to survive.

The MAPA route is one way forward, but it is doubtful whether two different sources of capital—Names with unlimited liability and corporate funds with limited liability—can continue to co-exist. A corporate investor risks only the deposit of 50 percent that he has put up to support his underwriting. If the losses are greater than the deposit, the liabilities will be borne by others in the market. Names are unlikely to be willing to tolerate this double jeopardy. As the deputy chairman, Robert Hiscox, points out: "It will be uncomfortable for Lloyd's to live with two types of shareholder." He is strongly opposed to the concept of unlimited liability: "It causes too much grief. Every thirty years or so we have blown Names out of the water. I just don't want anybody in future to have to sell their home to meet losses."[7]

The death of Lloyd's may be slow, but the old market is beyond recall. The question is whether the new Lloyd's will flourish or be dragged down by its past. The separation of asbestos and pollution liabilities into Equitas, in an attempt to ring-fence the new Lloyd's from the problems of old years, is not dissimilar to the actions of any business overwhelmed by debt. "Lloyd's 1688-1993 is dead. Long live Lloyd's, under entirely new manage-ment." Whether that cry will be sufficient to restore confidence in the market and enable it to survive is uncertain. Much will depend on whether Equitas is able to withstand the enormous long-tail liabilities it will inherit when syndicates hand over their old year claims at the end of 1995. The existing syndicate reserves of £4 billion are almost certainly far from sufficient. Chatset's estimate, at the end of 1994, that the run-off of all open years will cost a further £10 billion is staggeringly large, but may not be far off the mark if Congress fails to reform the Superfund legislation. NewCo's project director, Heidi Hutter, acknowledged the scale of the problems facing Lloyd's when she told the Insurance Institute of London at the beginning of 1994: "If the Chatset estimate is correct, then it represents a sizeable obstacle to NewCo's formation."

Those on under-reserved syndicates face large calls as the price of their exit from their long-tail nightmare. There is a limit, however, to how much can be wrung out of impoverished Names. Lloyd's is thus faced by a difficult decision; it will need to set reserves for Equitas (NewCo) at a level which will not bankrupt thousands more Names, yet be sufficient to carry credibil-ity with the Department of Trade and American policy-holders. The success of this exercise, launched on a wing and a prayer, is almost wholly dependent on legal and political developments in the United States. Should Equitas' capital run out, Lloyd's will not make good the deficit, despite the damage to its cherished reputation for always paying valid claims. Significantly, a commitment in the first draft of the corporate capital prospectus, that the central fund would be used to support Equitas, was omitted in the published version.[8] The deputy chairman, Robert Hiscox, made Lloyd's position even more explicit in a response to a question at a Names' conference. Asked what would happen if Equitas ran out of funds, he replied: "The council would have to meet to make a decision whether to top it up." But he added: "We can only levy if it's for the benefit of the society. I would submit it would be very difficult to levy old Names for the benefit of future Names." A more tactful response was given by Stephen Merrett to the same question: "If the Americans can't get the Superfund legislation right, there will be a significant number of US insurers who will be overwhelmed. The US Government would then intervene. If that happened we would be in a position to match that defensive posture."[9]

The prospect of a default is one ominous cloud hanging over the market's future. If Equitas goes down for the count, the new Lloyd's will not escape. American policy-holders who remain unpaid would try to seize the billions of dollars held on behalf of Names in Lloyd's American trust funds. They would also seek the backing of the British courts, adding to the vicious spiral of legal actions that has already so damaged the market's reputation. In theory, if Equitas did go into liquidation, each individual Name would still be responsible for his share of the losses. The new Lloyd's may believe that it is immune from the problems of the past, but it is likely to find that the ring-fence provides at best only partial protection.

Another spectre that haunts the market is the roughly 10,000 Names who have been ruined by the problems of the past. The failure to produce an acceptable settlement to the litigation has left them angered and embittered. Lloyd's has set its face against raising a loan which would enable it to fund a larger settlement. But what incentive is there for badly hit Names to continue to pay their losses and recapitalize the market in order to allow others to trade forward at their expense? If their disinclination to shell out more money accelerates, Lloyd's may be forced to raise a further levy from those who continue to underwrite. The scale of the loss in the 1992 account year is not yet known, but anything approaching the losses of the previous two years will compound the market's solvency problems. As more and more Names either can't or won't pay, the burden of their deficits will fall on the diminishing number who remain.

Meltdown is still some way off, but confidence in the market has taken a terrible battering. If Lloyd's is to have a future, some way must be found to end the litigation and alleviate the financial hardship of those who have been ruined. As the Cromer report pointed out more than a generation ago:

"If a *sauve qui peut* attitude were to be pursued on the argument that Names knew the risks they were running when they became members of Lloyd's . . . the market would, in our opinion, in time disintegrate as capital was withdrawn. . . We feel that it would be a mistake to disregard the degree of bitterness felt by some outside Names called recently to draw heavily on their personal capital to meet underwriting losses whilst seemingly the earning power of underwriting agents and brokers was less affected by such losses."

Lloyd's refusal to heed this warning makes a resolution of its crisis very difficult, despite yet another attempt this year to settle the litigation. Money could be found to resolve the debacle if there was sufficient will. Paying yesterday's claims out of tomorrow's premiums is not unknown in insurance companies faced by a cash squeeze. Lloyd's value as a continuing business could be unlocked and used as an asset against which to borrow. Businesses of comparable size, such as the Munich Re, Generali, Tokio, Zurich, and Swiss Re, are valued at up to £20 billion on stock exchanges around the world. The introduction of corporate capital will accelerate the move towards valuing syndicate participation at Lloyd's. If part of that enhanced value were applied to ending the litigation and bridging the current cash crisis, the market's future might look very different. The notion that nothing can be done, and that the burnt Names must be left to sue until they are dead or bankrupt, is short-sighted. If only a few of the action groups win in court, many members' and managing agencies will be forced into liquidation. Can the market indulge itself in another decade of blood-letting? Lloyd's would do well to remember James Baldwin's observation that there is no one more dangerous than the man with nothing left to lose. With an increasing number of Names in that position, it could well be that the choice is "not between a highly profitable future and a mortgaged future but between a mortgaged future and no future at all."[10]

Anyone who seeks to predict the future of Lloyd's is faced by the difficulty familiar to portrait painters—the sitter refuses to keep still. The biggest financial smash this century is a possibility that cannot be ruled out. Yet the market has professional skills, a world famous brand name, and an institutional resilience which should not be underestimated. The charge sheet is long, the obstacles ahead daunting, the recent history shaming, but the last act has still to be played. As the opera-loving Mafioso facing criminal indictment once growled to a pack of pursuing reporters: "The show ain't over until the fat lady sings."

Source Notes

INTRODUCTION: UTMOST GOOD FAITH?

1. Lloyd's Disciplinary Tribunal Finding. 1986—Sir Peter Green.
2. *Regulatory Arrangements at Lloyd's*. Report of the committee chaired by Sir Patrick Neill QC. January 1987.
3. Willis Faber Dumas memorandum. 1 February 1989.
4. *The Financial Times*. 23 April 1993.

1: THE LUTINE BELL TOLLS

1. *The Times*. 6 May 1993.
2. *The Times*. 8 June 1991.
3. Robert Hiscox says he saw only a tear and that the quote from *The Financial Times* was "journalistic licence".
4. Lloyd's general meeting. November 1984.
5. *An improved solution for Lloyd's*. David Springbett. 28 June 1993.
6. *Spectator*. 3 October 1992.
7. *Regulatory Arrangements at Lloyd's*. Report of the committee chaired by Sir Patrick Neill QC. January 1987.
8. Interviews with the author. June-August 1993.
9. *Independent*. 4 June 1993.
10. *Daily Telegraph*. 18 February 1993.
11. ALM Newsletter. February 1992.

2: COFFEE HOUSE TO CATASTROPHE

I have drawn principally on *A History of Lloyd's* by Charles Wright and Ernest Fayle (Macmillan, 1927), and *Lloyd's of London: A Study in Individualism* by D.E.W. Gibb (Macmillan, 1957) for much of the material in this chapter. Other sources include *Lloyd's of London: A Portrait* by Hugh Cockerell (Woodhead-Faulkener, 1984); *Lloyd's of London: A Reputation at Risk* by Godfrey Hodgson (Penguin, 1986), and *Hazard Unlimited* by Antony Brown (Lloyd's of London Press, 1987).

3: THE MARKET

1. Merrett Group annual report to Names. June 1993.
2. Interview with John Rew and photocopy of Hiscox letter. January 1993.

3. *Lloyd's, a Route Forward.* Report of the Task Force. January 1992.
4. Ibid.
5. The Cromer report. Lloyd's working party. December 1969.
6. *Lloyd's 1993 Members" Agents Profiles.* ALM & Financial Intelligence & Research Ltd.
7. *Self-Regulation at Lloyd's.* Report of the Fisher working party. May 1980.
8. *Regulatory Arrangements at Lloyd's.* Report of the committee chaired by Sir Patrick Neill QC. January 1987.

4: HURRICANE BETSY

1. Statistics Relating to Lloyd's. Lloyd's planning department. 1993.
2. Membership statistics. Lloyd's membership department. 1993.
3. *Panorama.* BBC TV. January 1993.
4. Interview with the author. September 1993.
5. Report of the *Savonita* inquiry. December 1978.
6. Interviews with the author. November 1993.
7. *Lloyd's of London: A Reputation at Risk.* Godfrey Hodgson (Penguin, 1986).
8. *Self-Regulation at Lloyd's.* Report of the Fisher working party. May 1980.

5: THE ROULETTE WHEEL SPINS FASTER

This chapter is based on Department of Trade reports of inquiries into Alexander Howden, Minet Holdings, and Unimar, and on disciplinary hearings held by Lloyd's in relation to its former chairman, Sir Peter Green. Other sources include interviews with leading underwriters and Lloyd's first chief executive, Ian Hay Davison, and also contemporary newspaper reports of police inquiries and court hearings.

1. *A View of the Room.* Ian Hay Davison (Weidenfeld & Nicolson, 1987).
2. *The Financial Times.* 18 August 1989.
3. DTI Report: Inquiry into Alexander Howden 1990.
4. Ibid.
5. *Daily Telegraph.* 18 August 1989.
6. Interview with the author. June 1992.
7. DTI Report of an inquiry into Minet Holdings and WMD underwriting agencies. 1990.
8. *Daily Express.* 30 December 1985.
9. Interview with the author.
10. General meeting of members of Lloyd's. 22 June 1983.
11. DTI inquiry into Unimar. 1986.
12. Report of Lloyd's disciplinary proceedings in the matter of Sir Peter Green. July 1986.
13. *The Financial Times.* 12 December 1985.
14. Interview with the author. 8 September 1992.
15. Report of Lloyd's disciplinary proceedings in the matter of Sir Peter Green. July 1986.
16. *Independent.* 8 May 1987.
17. *Lloyd's of London.* Fulcrum Productions. Channel 4 TV. 22 December 1991.
18. *For Whom the Bell Tolls*, Jonathan Mantle (Sinclair Stevenson, 1992).

19. Interview with the author. 18 February 1992.
20. *Regulatory Arrangements at Lloyd's*. Report of the committee chaired by Sir Patrick Neill. January 1987.
21. *Lloyd's of London*. Fulcrum Productions. Channel 4 TV. 22 December 1991.

6: ASBESTOS: THE FATAL LEGACY

The account of the American legal developments relating to asbestos relies on Paul Brodeur's book *Outrageous Misconduct: The Asbestos Industry on Trial* (Pantheon Books, New York, 1985), and *Asbestos: Medical and Legal Aspects* by Barry Castleman (Prentice Hall, 1990). A position paper, *Asbestos, a Social Problem*, published by Commercial Union in 1981, provides an insurance perspective on asbestosis. Paul MacAvoy's *The Economic Consequences of Asbestos-Related Disease* summarizes much statistical research. Other sources include underwriters" reports, medical papers, and studies carried out for the Lloyd's Names Asbestos Working Party.

1. *Insurance, Reinsurance and Underwriting Names" Liability for Asbestos-Related Diseases*. Malcolm Weller. Medicine Science and the Law 1990. Learned Journal.
2. *Occupational Respiratory Diseases*. Irving Selikoff. Public Health and Preventative Medicine 11th edition. 1980.
3. *Asbestos, a Social Problem*. (Commercial Union Insurance, 1981).
4. *Outrageous Misconduct*. Paul Brodeur (Pantheon Books, 1985).
5. Ibid.
6. Deposition in Johns-Manville Corp v. the United States of America. US Claims Court, 25 April 1984, quoted in *Asbestos Medical and Legal Aspects* by Barry Castleman (op.cit).
7. *Asbestos: Medical and Legal Aspects*. Barry Castleman (op.cit).
8. *Face the Facts*. BBC Radio 4. 7 October 1993.
9. Interview with the author. 5 March 1992.
10. *Asbestos, a Social Problem* (op.cit).
11. *Lloyd's, Why Blame the Victim?* Davies Arnold Cooper. February 1992.
12. Interview with the author. 15 October 1991.
13. *Lloyd's of London*. Fulcrum Productions. Channel 4 TV. December 1991.
14. *Insurance, Reinsurance and Underwriting Names" Liability for Asbestos-Related Diseases* (op.cit).
15. ALM newsletter. June 1992.
16. *The Litigation Explosion*. Walter K. Olsen (Dutton, 1991).
17. Speech to International Association of Defence Counsel in London. 13 July 1993.
18. Letter to the author. 4 December 1993.
19. Interview with the author, July 1993. See also *Time*, 3 May 1993; *Harpers and Queen*, August 1992.
20. Interview with the author, July 1993. See also *Harpers and Queen*, August 1992.
21. Letter to minister of trade. 12 July 1991.
22. *The Financing of Liability Payments*. Paul MacAvoy, Rand Corporation. 1992.

7: THE OUTHWAITE AFFAIR

The principal sources of this chapter are the papers assembled by John Donner, and John Moore's account of The Outhwaite Affair. Other sources are the Freshfields investigation into the Outhwaite losses, and reports of the Lloyd's Asbestos Working Party.

1.   *The Outhwaite Affair*. John Moore (Evandale Publishing, August 1990).
2.   Statement by Roger Bradley. 14 January 1991.
3.   Roger Bradley's account of a visit to New York by underwriters in 1979.
4.   Report to Lloyd's. 28 December 1979.
5.   Circular letters to market. 5 August 1980 and 10 February 1981.
6.   Report of the Freshfields inquiry. 19 May 1988.
7.   Interview with the author. June 1992.
8.   Letter to Murray Lawrence. 16 August 1989.
9.   Lloyd's note of meeting. 20 December 1989.
10. Letter from Neville Russell to Lloyd's audit department. 24 February 1982.
11. Report of the Freshfields inquiry (op.cit.).
12. Statement by Stephen Mitchell. July 1989.
13. Letter of 19 December 1989.
14. Lloyd's press release. 5 April 1990.
15. *Economist*. 15 February 1992.
16. Interview with the author. 8 May 1992.
17. Syndicate report to Names. July 1992.
18. Letter to the author. 29 December 1993.
19. Interview with the author. 8 September 1992.

8: POLLUTION: AN AMERICAN NIGHTMARE

1.   Respondent's joint brief. Shell Oil Company v. Accident and Casualty Insurance. California Court of Appeal. March 1991.
2.   Ibid.
3.   Ibid.
4.   Summit Associates Inv. v. Liberty Mutual Fire Insurance Company. 1991.
5.   *Guardian*. 7 August 1978.
6.   *Cleaning up Hazardous Waste—Is there a better way?* Insurance Information Institute Press, 1993.
7.   *The Environmental Pollution Threat*. James Capel, April 1993.
8.   *Cleaning up Hazardous Waste* (op. cit.).
9.   Amy S. Bouska's evidence to Congressional Committee on Policy Research and Insurance, based on a study by actuaries, Tillinghast, Nelson and Warren, September 1990.
10. *San Francisco Chronicle: "Toxic Cleanup a Bonanza for the Legal Profession."* 29 May 1991.
11. Hazardous Waste Remediation Project of the University of Tennessee.
12. Interview with the author. 13 October 1993.
13. *Understanding Superfund: A progress report*. Rand Corporation, 1992.

14. *US Environmental Pollution Remediation in the 1990s: The costs go onwards and upwards.* Speech by Gary Westerberg to the Insurance Institute of London. 21 March 1991.

15. *Toxic Shock.* CFO insurance magazine. April 1992.

16. John Shea, Aetna Life. World Insurance Congress, 1992.

17. Speech to the World Affairs Council. Los Angeles, 1991.

18. Superior Court of New Jersey Appellate Division A694- 89T1.

19. Supreme Court of Illinois. Docket 71753. November 1991. *The Financial Times.* 23 December 1992.

20. *Post* (magazine). 11 February 1993.

21. *The Impact of Coverage Claims for Clean-up Costs of Hazardous Wastes on the London Insurance Market.* Barry Bunshoft, senior partner of Hancock, Rothert Bunshoft.

22. *Reinsurance, Toxic Avengers.* Kieran Beer. September 1991.

23. *Lloyd's List.* 17 April 1993.

24. John Myers, managing director of the international reinsurance division of Willis Faber Dumas, quoted in *Business Insurance.* 4 January 1993.

25. Merrett Group's annual Names meeting. June 1988.

9: SPIRAL TO DISASTER

This chapter relies heavily on Sir David Walker's inquiry into the LMX spiral debacle. Other sources include the official loss review reports into the Gooda Walker, Feltrim, Devonshire, Rose Thomson Young, and other spiral syndicates.

1. Stacy Shapiro, international editor of *Business Insurance*, quoted this example in a lecture to Names. June 1992.

2. Report of an inquiry into Lloyd's syndicate participations and the LMX spiral, by Sir David Walker. July 1992.

3. Stacy Shapiro, international editor of *Business Insurance.*

4. *The Financial Times.* 6 March 1992.

5. Interview with the author. 15 January 1993.

6. Interview with the author. 15 December 1992.

7. *The Financial Times.* 6 March 1992.

8. Marie-Louise Burrows, chairman of the Lime Street Action Group. Interview with the author. July 1993.

9. *Lloyd's of London.* CBC TV. February 1993.

10. *The Sunday Times.* 28 July 1991.

11. *Independent on Sunday.* 11 August 1991.

12. Interview with the author. August 1991.

13. *Lloyd's of London.* Channel 4 TV. December 1992.

14. Interview with the author. 18 October 1992.

15. Computer analysis by Society of Names researcher. October 1992.

16. Interview with author. 18 October 1992.

17. Interviews with the author. August 1993.

18. *The Financial Times.* 2 July 1992.

19. Interview with the author. 4 January 1993.

20. Interview with the author. 12 January 1993.

21. *The Financial Times.* 17 June 1993.

22. Interview with the author. 4 July 1993.
23. Interview with the author. 2 January 1993.
24. Lloyd's Loss Review report. October 1992.
25. *Independent on Sunday*. 15 July 1992.

10: OPEN YEARS

1.   R.J. Kiln paper submitted to Lloyd's. February 1993.
2.   Society of Names newsletter. December 1992.
3.   *Chatset Guide to Syndicate Run-offs*. 1992.
4.   *Digest of Lloyd's News*. December 1992.
5.   *Chatset Guide to Syndicate Run-offs*. 1992.
6.   Interview with the author. 5 July 1993.
7.   Letter to the author. 24 October 1992.
8.   *Operation Springclean*. David Springbett. September 1992.
9.   Report of the Open Year Panel. March 1993.
10. *Planning for profit: a business plan for Lloyd's of London*. April 1993.
11. Amy S. Bouska's evidence to the Congressional Committee on Policy Research and
     Insurance, September 1990, based on a study by the actuarial company Tillinghast,
     Nelson and Warren.

11: SUE FIRST, PAY LATER

1.   Letter to the *Independent*. 2 October 1990.
2.   Lime Street Action Group submission to the Morse Panel. 30 September 1993.
3.   Boobyer v. David Holman & Co Ltd. 16 April 1992.
4.   *Lloyd's List*, 3 June 1993. ALM Newsletter, September 1993. *The Times*, November 1993.
5.   *Journal of Commerce*. 30 September 1991.
6.   Commercial Court. 5 July 1993.
7.   Writs Response Group meeting in London. 15 October 1993.
8.   *A guide to Corporate Membership*. Lloyd's of London, September 1993.
9.   *Lloyd's of London: A Reputation at Risk*. Godfrey Hodgson (Penguin, 1986).
10. Report of the Chester Committee of Inquiry. 1981.
11. *Oakeley Vaughan: The History*. Oakeley Vaughan Names Association. April 1992.
12. Syndicate 421 loss review, 1991/6.
13. Statement by Roger Bradley. 14 January 1991.

12: THE GATHERING STORM

This chapter relies on personal interviews with the leading players in the market supplemented by the day-to-day coverage of the professional watchers of Lloyd's, among them: Richard Lapper of *The Financial Times*, Michael Becket of the *Daily Telegraph*, John Moore of the *Independent*, Sarah Bagnall and Jonathan Prynn of *The Times* and Robert Tyerman of the *Sunday Telegraph*. Also *Lloyd's List*, *Chatset*, *Digest of Lloyd's News*, and many other trade publications and newspapers.

1.   Conversation with the author. 21 August 1991.
2.   *ALM News*. September 1992.

3. Lloyd's news conference. 15 April 1992.
4. *Hansard.* Standing Committee B: Finance Bill. 18 June 1991.
5. Lloyd's news conference. 6 September 1991.
6. *Guardian.* 1 July 1991.
7. *Post* (magazine). August 1991.
8. Ibid.
9. *The Times.* 8 June 1991.
10. *The Financial Times.* 30 March 1992.
11. *The Times.* 8 June 1991.
12. *Lloyd's List.* 1 December 1992.
13. Ibid.
14. *Lloyd's: a route forward.* Task Force report. January 1992.
15. *Digest of Lloyd's News.* February 1992.
16. *The Financial Times.* 30 March 1992.
17. *The Financial Times.* 29 February 1992.
18. *Independent.* 29 February 1992.
19. *The Financial Times.* 29 February 1992.
20. Ibid.
21. *The Sunday Times.* 23 February 1992.
22. *Digest of Lloyd's News.* April 1992.
23. *Digest of Lloyd's News.* May 1992.
24. *Lloyd's List.* 24 June 1992.
25. *Spectator.* 28 May 1992.
26. Conversation with the author. 3 April 1992.
27. *Lloyd's List.* 4 May 1992.
28. ALM Annual Report. June 1992.
29. *The Financial Times.* 19 June 1992.
30. *Lloyd's List.* 19 June 1992.
31. *The Times.* 4 June 1992.
32. *Lloyd's List.* December 1992.
33. *Evening Standard.* 27 July 1992.
34. *The Financial Times.* 31 April 1992.

13: A NEW REGIME

This chapter, like the previous one, relies on personal interviews and the day-to-day coverage by the professional watchers of Lloyd's working for national papers. Information is also drawn from many other trade publications and newspapers.

1. Lloyd's press conference. September 1992.
2. *The Times.* 17 August 1992.
3. Hoare Govett Investment Research study. May 1992.
4. *The Financial Times.* 21 January 1993.
5. Conversation with the author. 13 December 1993.
6. Letter to Graham Laing—Lloyd's Internal Review. 1 February 1993.
7. Knightstone Group newsletter. April 1993.
8. *Planning for profit: a business plan for Lloyd's of London.* April 1993.
9. Richard Spooner, chairman of Gresham 321 syndicate report. July 1993.

10. SON newsletter. June 1993.
11. *The Times*. 4 June 1993. *Independent*. 15 June 1993.
12. SON newsletter. September 1993.
13. *Lloyd's List*. 10 August 1993.

14: CIVIL WAR

1. *An Assessment*. Lloyd's business plan. August 1993.
2. *The Financial Times* letters page. 3 August 1993.
3. ALM newsletter. August 1993.
4. Willis Faber letter to Names. August 1993.
5. *The Financial Times*. 14 September 1993.
6. *An Assessment*. Lloyd's business plan. August 1993.
7. *Independent*. 8 September 1993.
8. *Digest of Lloyd's News*. December 1993.
9. Interview with the author. 18 November 1993.
10. Letter to Val Powell of the ALM. 4 October 1993.
11. *Lloyd's: The Business Plan Appraised*. 21 May 1993.
12. Letter to the author. 29 December 1993.
13. Christopher Fildes, *Daily Telegraph*. 23 October 1993.
14. Lloyd's settlement offer. 7 December 1993.
15. *The Financial Times*. 8 December 1993.
16. *The Financial Times*. 15 January 1994.
17. *Digest of Lloyd's News*. March 1994.
18. *Daily Telegraph*. 15 February 1994.
19. Letter to *Inside Eye*. June 1994.
20. *Financial Times*. 5 August 1994.
21. *Independent on Sunday*. 14 August 1994.
22. Analysis of judgment. Wilde Sapte. 4 October 1994.
23. *SON*. October 1994.
24. *Lloyd's List*. 18 May 1994.
25. R. J. Kiln paper submitted to Lloyd's. February 1993.
26. *Lloyd's List*. 26 April 1994.
27. Private paper by Richard Spooner. 26 April 1994.

15: THE FAT LADY SINGS

1. *The Financial Times*. 23 January 1993.
2. Interviews with the author. October 1993.
3. Letter to the author. 3 December 1993.
4. *ALM News*. April 1992.
5. R.J. Kiln paper submitted to Lloyd's. February 1993.
6. Conversation with the author. 28 November 1993.
7. *The Economist*. 27 November 1993. *The Financial Times*. 2 December 1993.
8. *A guide to Corporate Membership*. Lloyd's. September 1993.
9. Interview with the author. 18 November 1993.
10. Letter from Christopher Stockwell to Peter Middleton. May 1993.

Appendix

UNDERWRITING MEMBERSHIP 1771–1993

Year	Active Members	Year	Active Members	Year	Active Members
1771	79	1918	702	1956	4,177
1779	179	1919	814	1957	4286
1814	2,150	1920	997	1958	4,499
1819	1,691	1921	1,098	1959	4,669
1822	1,595	1922	1,108	1960	4,808
1825	1,634	1923	1,123	1961	4,938
1832	1,320	1924	1,228	1962	5,126
1837	1,223	1925	1,260	1963	5,312
1842	1,008	1926	1,265	1964	5,545
1843	953	1927	1,285	1965	5,826
1844	940	1928	1,324	1966	6,060
1853	835	1929	1,387	1967	6,080
1854	1,667	1930	1,412	1968	6,059
1857	1,057	1931	1,441	1969	6,042
1861	664	1932	1,437	1970	6,001
1865	722	1933	1,452	1971	6,020
1869	586	1934	1,521	1972	6,299
1872	698	1935	1,600	1973	7,140
1876	610	1936	1,674	1974	7,589
1880	650	1937	1,789	1975	7,710
1891	792	1938	1,882	1976	8,565
1892	784	1939	1,933	1977	10,662
1896	619	1940	1,923	1978	14,134
1899	714	1941	1,886	1979	17,279
1904	631	1942	1,874	1980	18,552
1905	666	1943	1,852	1981	19,137
1906	687	1944	1,867	1982	20,145
1907	710	1945	1,960	1983	21,601
1908	709	1946	2,079	1984	23,436
1909	688	1947	2,272	1985	26,019
1910	667	1948	2,422	1986	28,242
1911	646	1949	2,590	1987	30,936
1912	619	1950	2,743	1988	32,433
1913	621	1951	2,913	1989	31,329
1914	624	1952	3,157	1990	28,770
1915	626	1953	3,399	1991	26,539
1916	642	1954	3,618	1992	22,259
1917	663	1955	3,917	1993	19,537

Reproduced from *Statistics Relating to Lloyd's 1993* published by Lloyd's of London Press.

NUMBERS OF SYNDICATES BY MARKET 1979-93

Year	Marine	Non-Marine	Motor	Aviation	Life	TOTAL
1979	151	160	41	52		404
1980	163	175	45	54		437
1981	162	166	46	53		427
1982	164	171	46	50		431
1983	154	161	45	49		409
1984	145	164	44	46		399
1985	138	152	43	43	8	384
1986	131	150	41	40	8	370
1987	128	150	38	40	9	365
1988	132	159	36	41	8	376
1989	134	178	37	44	8	401
1990	129	184	36	44	8	401
1991	106	167	31	41	9	354
1992	74	140	28	28	9	279
1993	62	104	26	26	9	228

Reproduced from *Statistics Relating to Lloyd's1993* published by Lloyd's of London Press.

LLOYD'S TOTAL CAPACITY 1967-93

Brackets indicate minus figures

Year of account	Total gross capacity £m	Annual growth	Real Total gross capacity 1990 (£m)	Real annual growth	Capacity utilization
1967	503		3,961		
1968	592	17.6%	4,447	12.3%	
1969	741	25.3%	5,293	19.0%	
1970	761	2.6%	5,104	(3.6%)	
1971	839	10.3%	5,144	0.8%	
1972	891	6.2%	5,089	(1.1%)	
1973	1,045	17.4%	5,472	7.5%	
1974	1,162	11.2%	5,235	(4.3%)	
1975	1,365	17.4%	4,964	(5.2%)	
1976	1,828	33.9%	5,696	14.8%	
1977	1,882	2.9%	5,058	(11.2%)	
1978	2,417	28.4%	6,011	18.8%	
1979	3,049	26.1%	6,682	11.2%	
1980	3,415	12.0%	6,343	(5.1%)	
1981	3,562	4.3%	5,913	(6.8%)	
1982	4,111	15.4%	6,284	6.3%	
1983	4,381	6.6%	6,404	1.9%	
1984	5,090	16.2%	7,089	10.7%	87.2%
1985	6,682	31.3%	8,769	23.7%	92.2%
1986	8,511	27.4%	10,808	23.3%	71.9%
1987	10,290	20.9%	12,546	16.1%	61.0%
1988	11,018	7.1%	12,797	2.0%	64.7%
1989	10,956	(0.6%)	11,806	(7.7%)	69.0%
1990	11,070	1.0%	11,070	(6.2%)	79.2%
1991	11,382	2.8%	10,395	(6.1%)	
1992	10,046	(11.7%)	8,660	(16.7%)	
1993	8,878	(11.6%)	7,380	(14.8%)	

Reproduced from *Statistics Relating to Lloyd's 1993* published by Lloyd's of London Press.

LLOYD'S GLOBAL ACCOUNTS 1964-1990

Brackets indicate minus figures.

Year	£m Actual Pre-Tax Profit	£m Pre-Tax Profits 1990 Prices
1964	(1.0)	(8.8)
1965	(34.5)	(288.5)
1966	(16.4)	(132.2)
1967	2.2	17.13
1968	38.5	289.0
1969	55.1	393.0
1970	63.0	421.0
1971	71.4	437.5
1972	89.1	508.4
1973	113.1	591.48
1974	97.1	437.9
1975	142.0	516.2
1976	126.1	393.2
1977	141.4	380.4
1978	198.6	493.9
1979	229.0	501.7
1980	352.7	654.8
1981	248.3	411.9
1982	161.7	247.0
1983	119.6	174.8
1984	278.2	387.4
1985	195.6	256.7
1986	649.5	824.5
1987	509.1	620.5
1988	(509.7)	(592.0)
1989	(2,063.2)	(2,223.3)
1990	(2,915.0)	(2,915.0)

Reproduced from *Statistics Relating to Lloyd's 1993* published by Lloyd's of London Press.

Select Bibliography

A History of Lloyd's, Charles Wright and Ernest Fayle (Macmillan, 1927).

Lloyd's of London: A Study in Individualism, D.E.W. Gibb (Macmillan, 1957).

Hazard Unlimited, Antony Brown (Lloyd's of London Press, 1987).

Lloyd's of London: A Portrait, Hugh Cockerell (Woodhead-Faulkener, 1984).

Lloyd's of London: A Reputation at Risk, Godfrey Hodgson (Penguin, 1986).

A View of the Room, Ian Hay Davison (Weidenfeld and Nicolson, 1987).

Gallileo's Revenge, Peter W. Huber (HarperCollins, 1991).

The Litigation Explosion, Walter K. Olson (Dutton, 1991).

Outrageous Misconduct, Paul Brodeur (Pantheon, 1985).

Reinsurance in Practice, Third Edition, Robert Kiln (Witherby and Co. Ltd, 1990).

Asbestos: Medical and Legal Aspects, Third Edition, Barry Castleman (Prentice Hall).

Nightmare on Lime Street, Cathy Gunn (Smith Gryphon, 1992).

For Whom the Bell Tolls, Jonathan Mantle (Sinclair Stevenson, 1992).

Index